Moving Abroad

Moving Abroad

by Kristin M. Wilson

Moving Abroad For Dummies®

Published by: **John Wiley & Sons, Inc.**, 111 River Street, Hoboken, NJ 07030-5774, www.wiley.com

Copyright ©2025 by John Wiley & Sons, Inc., Hoboken, New Jersey

Published simultaneously in Canada

No part of this publication may be reproduced, stored in a retrieval system or transmitted in any form or by any means, electronic, mechanical, photocopying, recording, scanning or otherwise, except as permitted under Sections 107 or 108 of the 1976 United States Copyright Act, without the prior written permission of the Publisher. Requests to the Publisher for permission should be addressed to the Permissions Department, John Wiley & Sons, Inc., 111 River Street, Hoboken, NJ 07030, (201) 748-6011, fax (201) 748-6008, or online at http://www.wiley.com/go/permissions.

Trademarks: Wiley, For Dummies, the Dummies Man logo, Dummies.com, Making Everything Easier, and related trade dress are trademarks or registered trademarks of John Wiley & Sons, Inc. and may not be used without written permission. All other trademarks are the property of their respective owners. John Wiley & Sons, Inc. is not associated with any product or vendor mentioned in this book.

LIMIT OF LIABILITY/DISCLAIMER OF WARRANTY: THE PUBLISHER AND THE AUTHOR MAKE NO REPRESENTATIONS OR WARRANTIES WITH RESPECT TO THE ACCURACY OR COMPLETENESS OF THE CONTENTS OF THIS WORK AND SPECIFICALLY DISCLAIM ALL WARRANTIES, INCLUDING WITHOUT LIMITATION WARRANTIES OF FITNESS FOR A PARTICULAR PURPOSE. NO WARRANTY MAY BE CREATED OR EXTENDED BY SALES OR PROMOTIONAL MATERIALS. THE ADVICE AND STRATEGIES CONTAINED HEREIN MAY NOT BE SUITABLE FOR EVERY SITUATION. THIS WORK IS SOLD WITH THE UNDERSTANDING THAT THE PUBLISHER IS NOT ENGAGED IN RENDERING LEGAL, ACCOUNTING, OR OTHER PROFESSIONAL SERVICES. IF PROFESSIONAL ASSISTANCE IS REQUIRED, THE SERVICES OF A COMPETENT PROFESSIONAL PERSON SHOULD BE SOUGHT. NEITHER THE PUBLISHER NOR THE AUTHOR SHALL BE LIABLE FOR DAMAGES ARISING HEREFROM. THE FACT THAT AN ORGANIZATION OR WEBSITE IS REFERRED TO IN THIS WORK AS A CITATION AND/OR A POTENTIAL SOURCE OF FURTHER INFORMATION DOES NOT MEAN THAT THE AUTHOR OR THE PUBLISHER ENDORSES THE INFORMATION THE ORGANIZATION OR WEBSITE MAY PROVIDE OR RECOMMENDATIONS IT MAY MAKE. FURTHER, READERS SHOULD BE AWARE THAT INTERNET WEBSITES LISTED IN THIS WORK MAY HAVE CHANGED OR DISAPPEARED BETWEEN WHEN THIS WORK WAS WRITTEN AND WHEN IT IS READ.

For general information on our other products and services, please contact our Customer Care Department within the U.S. at 877-762-2974, outside the U.S. at 317-572-3993, or fax 317-572-4002. For technical support, please visit https://hub.wiley.com/community/support/dummies.

Wiley publishes in a variety of print and electronic formats and by print-on-demand. Some material included with standard print versions of this book may not be included in e-books or in print-on-demand. If this book refers to media such as a CD or DVD that is not included in the version you purchased, you may download this material at http://booksupport.wiley.com. For more information about Wiley products, visit www.wiley.com.

Library of Congress Control Number: 2025935527

ISBN: 978-1-394-32599-3 (pbk); 978-1-394-32600-6 (epub); 978-1-394-32602-0 (ebk)

SKY10104396_042525

Contents at a Glance

Introduction 1

Part 1: Beginning Your Living Abroad Journey 5
CHAPTER 1: Previewing the Living-Overseas Lifestyle 7
CHAPTER 2: Exploring the Different Paths to Moving Abroad 17
CHAPTER 3: Calculating Your Budget and Cost of Living 31
CHAPTER 4: Choosing a Destination 43

Part 2: Mastering Your Move — Relocation Logistics 67
CHAPTER 5: Planning Your Relocation Logistics 69
CHAPTER 6: Finding Your New Home Away from Home 89
CHAPTER 7: Getting Ready to Hit the Road 107

Part 3: Leaping Into Your New Life Abroad 131
CHAPTER 8: Landing in Your Adopted Country 133
CHAPTER 9: Going Farther Afield: Additional Considerations 155

Part 4: Living Your Life to the Fullest 175
CHAPTER 10: Embracing Culture Shock Like a Pro 177
CHAPTER 11: Finding Your Community 193
CHAPTER 12: Living Your Best Life 211
CHAPTER 13: Long-Term Lifestyle Considerations 223

Part 5: The Part of Tens 241
CHAPTER 14: Ten Places to Retire Abroad 243
CHAPTER 15: 10 Places to Live as a Digital Nomad 253
CHAPTER 16: Ten Places to Live for Under $1,500 per Month 261
CHAPTER 17: Ten Moving-Overseas Mistakes to Avoid 269

Index 277

Table of Contents

INTRODUCTION 1
    About This Book. 1
    Beyond the Book 1
    Foolish Assumptions. 2
    Icons Used in This Book 3
    Where to Go from Here 3

PART 1: BEGINNING YOUR LIVING ABROAD JOURNEY 5

CHAPTER 1: Previewing the Living-Overseas Lifestyle 7
    Defining What Living Overseas Means. 7
    Reaping the Benefits of Living Abroad 8
        Lowering your cost of living. 8
        Leveling up your quality of life. 9
        Reducing your taxes 9
        Enjoying new experiences 10
        Broadening your worldview. 10
        Expanding your community. 10
        Acquiring new skills. 10
        Enjoying better healthcare. 11
        Uncovering new job opportunities 11
    Acknowledging the Drawbacks of Living Abroad 12
        Coping with culture shock 12
        Living far from family and friends. 13
        Keeping yourself safe 13
    Deciding Whether Living Abroad Is Right for You. 13
    Setting Your Goal of Moving Abroad 14
    Overcoming the Fear of Failure. 15

CHAPTER 2: Exploring the Different Paths to Moving Abroad 17
    Assessing Your Budget and Lifestyle Goals 18
        Defining your lifestyle. 18
        Calculating your budget 19
        Putting it down on paper 19
    Knowing the Different Paths to Living Abroad 20
        Moving through your job 20
        Finding a job overseas 20
        Investing in a business or real estate 22
        Qualifying for citizenship by descent 22

Retiring abroad..23
Reuniting with family (or starting a new one)..............24
Studying abroad and exchange programs.....................24
Volunteering and government work............................26
Enjoying a working holiday...27
Working abroad remotely..28
Selecting a Path to Going Abroad...29

CHAPTER 3: Calculating Your Budget and Cost of Living......... 31

Determining Your Current Cost of Living and Income...............32
Creating a budget..32
Assessing your income...34
Accounting for a pension or passive income sources.....34
Forecasting Your Cost of Living Abroad...............................35
Researching cost of living online.................................35
Buying a book...36
Asking a local...37
Estimating Your Moving Fees and Shipping Your Stuff Overseas....37
Deciding what you want to ship..................................37
Itemizing your belongings..38
Getting shipping quotes...38
Figuring Out How Much You Need to Save.............................39
Setting an Ideal Timeline to Move.......................................41

CHAPTER 4: Choosing a Destination............................. 43

Identifying What You Want in a Destination..........................44
Visualizing Your Ideal Lifestyle...45
Previewing the Top Living-Abroad Destinations....................47
Choosing Your Destination...48
Considering the climate and geography........................49
Confirming your cost of living.....................................50
Choosing a new culture..51
Finding better healthcare...51
Learning a new language..52
Living your best lifestyle..53
Discovering the best location.....................................53
Choosing your time zone..54
Thinking about community...54
Keeping the lights (and Wi-Fi) on................................55
Acknowledging a country's political system..................55
Practicing your religion (or not)..................................56
Seeking equality and avoiding racism..........................56
Staying safe..57
Paying the tax man..58

Visa and Residency Options..59
    Business visa...59
    Digital nomad visa...59
    Education or student visa....................................59
    Entrepreneur or startup visa.................................60
    Retirement or non-lucrative visa.............................60
    Tourist visa..60
    Residence permit...61
    Work permit..61
Golden Visa or Second Passport....................................61
Making Your Country Selection.....................................63
Planning an Exploratory Trip......................................63
Choosing More Than One Place......................................64

PART 2: MASTERING YOUR MOVE — RELOCATION LOGISTICS...........67

CHAPTER 5: Planning Your Relocation Logistics.................69
Preparing Your Banking and Finances for Living Internationally.....69
    Following a financial prep checklist.........................70
    Sending, spending, and receiving money with finance apps.....71
    Opening a bank account in your new home country..............73
    Getting a travel credit card.................................75
Talking About Taxes...76
Organizing Your Paperwork...77
Deciding What to Do with Your Stuff...............................79
Moving with Kids..81
    Finding new schools..81
    Keeping them healthy and safe................................82
    Adapting to life in a different country......................82
Moving with Pets..83
Evaluating Whether You Want Relocation Support....................85
    Before-the-move tasks..86
    During-the-move tasks..87
    After-the-move tasks...87
Selecting a Relocation Expert.....................................87

CHAPTER 6: Finding Your New Home Away from Home...............89
Clarifying Your Property Needs....................................89
Checking Out the Different Types of Accommodations................90
    Renting short-term vs long-term..............................91
    Narrowing down a location....................................92
    Searching for property strategically.........................92

    Buying Property Abroad...97
        Choosing where to buy..98
        Getting help from professionals..............................99
        Paying cash or financing....................................100
        Buying leasehold property...................................100
        Negotiating real estate abroad..............................101
    Solving Renting Problems..104

CHAPTER 7: Getting Ready to Hit the Road.........................107
    Applying for Insurance..107
        Emergency travel medical insurance..........................107
        Local or international health insurance.....................108
        Emergency evacuation and repatriation insurance.............110
        Getting insurance over 65...................................111
        Exploring other types of insurance..........................112
    Booking Your Flight...113
        Weighing value versus convenience...........................113
        Working with your airline...................................114
        Staying organized...114
        Booking flights online......................................115
        Going roundtrip...116
    Packing Like a Pro..116
        Making your list and checking it twice......................117
        Sorting through your excess baggage.........................122
        Carrying it all on the plane................................122
    Checking Your Paperwork...123
    Shipping Your Stuff Internationally.............................125
        Looking into international movers...........................125
        Coordinating an international shipment......................126
        Downsizing..126
    Saying Your Goodbyes..127

PART 3: LEAPING INTO YOUR NEW LIFE ABROAD........................131

CHAPTER 8: Landing in Your Adopted Country.......................133
    Navigating Your First Day in a New Country......................133
        Getting through the airport and immigration.................134
        Activating your cellphone...................................135
        Accessing your cash...136
        Arriving at your destination................................137
        Checking into your new home.................................139
    Getting Settled During Your First Month Abroad..................140
        Exploring your new surroundings.............................141
        Learning the lay of the land................................142

        Becoming a navigation whiz 143
        Identifying important places and contacts 143
        Setting up your utilities and Internet 144
        Making your house a home 146
        Hiring domestic help..147
        Registering with your embassy 148
        Meeting your new neighbors.................................148
        Sourcing food and water 148
        Settling into a routine 149
    Receiving Your Paycheck or Pension 150
        Wiring money internationally 152
        Opening a local bank account 152

CHAPTER 9: Going Farther Afield: Additional Considerations 155

    Adjusting to the Infrastructure 155
        Outsmarting power and water outages.......................156
        Keeping fast Wi-Fi 157
        Getting from here to there...................................157
    To Own or Not to Own a Car: That Is the Question 158
        Bringing your car 158
        Buying a car 160
    Driving Abroad..161
        Figuring out what you need to drive abroad...................161
        Getting a local driver's license 162
    Enrolling in Schools or Daycare....................................163
        Public versus private education 163
        Navigating the enrollment process...........................164
        Homeschooling abroad 165
        Finding daycare abroad 166
    Booking Your First Healthcare Appointment Abroad.................167
        Finding a doctor..168
        Preparing for your appointment..............................168
        Going to the dentist 169
        Finding a telehealth doctor 169
        Getting emergency care 169
        Making health insurance claims 170
    Receiving Your Mail Overseas 171
        Know your local mailing address 172
        Get a courier...172
        Set up a virtual mailbox 173

PART 4: LIVING YOUR LIFE TO THE FULLEST 175

CHAPTER 10: Embracing Culture Shock Like a Pro 177
Understanding Culture Shock 178
Riding the Curve of Cultural Adjustment 178
Tracking Your Own Cultural Adaptation Curve 181
    Preparing for take-off 181
    Initial shocks and the honeymoon phase 182
    Frustrations and adaptations 182
    Finding your rhythm 182
    Transformation and integration 183
Coping with Change 183
Learning the Language................................. 184
    Practicing with locals............................... 185
    Tips for language learning 186
Overcoming Loneliness 187
Managing Your Expectations............................ 188
Solving Problems When Things Go Wrong 191

CHAPTER 11: Finding Your Community 193
Meeting the Locals 193
    Putting work (or school) into making friends 194
    Moving to a small town............................. 194
    Moving to a friendly country 195
    Learning the lingo 195
    Setting up your social life.......................... 196
    Putting down roots and branching out 196
    Offering a helping hand 197
Making Friends Across Cultures 197
    Choosing a foreigner-friendly destination............... 197
    Finding your people 198
    Making the most of technology...................... 199
Meeting a Mate or Life Partner 199
    Swiping left and right 200
    Dating across cultures 201
    Going to the matchmaker 203
    Relating in your current relationship 203
Volunteering Opportunities............................. 204
Taking Your Career Networking to a New Level 206
    Attending conferences and events.................... 206
    Contacting chambers of commerce 206
    Getting active online 207
    Joining a coworking space 207
Staying in Touch with People at Home.................... 207
    Communicating in multiple ways 208
    Visiting in person.................................. 209
Making the Most of Your Life Abroad..................... 210

CHAPTER 12: Living Your Best Life ... 211
- Planning Things to Do in Your New Country ... 211
  - Celebrating local traditions ... 212
  - Picking up a new hobby ... 213
  - Adding fun things to your bucket list ... 214
- Making Time for Rest and Relaxation ... 216
- Staying the Course During Tough Times ... 217
  - Addressing homesickness ... 217
  - Avoiding travel burnout ... 218
- Sharing Your Experience with Others ... 220
  - Blogging ... 221
  - Podcasting ... 221
  - Public speaking ... 221
  - Sharing via social media ... 222
  - Starting a YouTube channel ... 222

CHAPTER 13: Long-Term Lifestyle Considerations ... 223
- Paying Taxes at Home and Abroad ... 223
  - Knowing your tax domicile ... 224
  - Getting familiar with global tax systems ... 224
  - Paying Uncle Sam ... 226
  - Paying zero taxes ... 227
- Investment Opportunities Abroad ... 229
- Extending Your Stay Abroad ... 230
  - For short stays ... 230
  - While working (or studying) abroad ... 231
  - Being a true resident ... 231
  - Going for citizenship ... 231
- Renouncing Your Citizenship ... 232
- Staying Out of Trouble ... 233
- Designing Your Expat Exit Strategy ... 234
- Thinking about Going Home ... 235
  - Changing gears (and countries) ... 236
  - Saying your goodbyes ... 236
  - Returning home and reverse culture shock ... 237
- End-of-Life Planning for Expats ... 239

PART 5: THE PART OF TENS ... 241

CHAPTER 14: Ten Places to Retire Abroad ... 243
- Costa Rica ... 243
- Ecuador ... 244
- France ... 245
- Malta ... 246
- Mexico ... 247
- Panama ... 248

Philippines 249
Portugal. 250
Spain 251
Thailand 252

CHAPTER 15: 10 Places to Live as a Digital Nomad 253
Bali, Indonesia 254
Bansko, Bulgaria 254
Buenos Aires, Argentina 255
Cape Town, South Africa 255
Chiang Mai, Thailand 256
Madeira, Portugal 256
Medellín, Colombia 257
Pipa, Brazil 258
Riviera Maya, Mexico 258
Zagreb, Croatia 259
Traveling Nomadic Tribes 260

CHAPTER 16: Ten Places to Live for Under $1,500 per Month 261
Albania 261
Colombia 262
Cambodia 263
Georgia 264
Malaysia 264
Peru 265
Paraguay 266
Romania 266
Turkey 267
Vietnam 268

CHAPTER 17: Ten Moving-Overseas Mistakes to Avoid 269
Skipping an Exploratory Trip 269
Investing in Real Estate (at First) 270
Neglecting Visa and Residency Research 271
Failing to Integrate with the Culture 271
Isolating Yourself 272
Being Too Trusting 272
Expecting a Place to Change for You 273
Underestimating the Cost of Living 273
Getting Too Many Opinions 274
Going It Alone 274
Waiting Too Long to Move 275
Staying Stuck When Things Aren't Working 276

INDEX 277

Introduction

By picking up this book, you've taken a significant step on your journey toward living abroad. Whether moving overseas is something you've recently considered or something you've pondered for years, this book can help you make your dream a reality.

Living abroad provides an exciting and enriching experience, but you may find figuring out how to get there overwhelming. From calculating your budget and deciding where to move, to applying for visas and finding the right housing, you have to deal with many moving parts in any relocation plan.

This book distills 25 years of my experience as a world traveler, living abroad and helping thousands of others do the same. It's your guide for what to do when — before, during, and after your move (while avoiding common mistakes).

About This Book

I wrote this book as a practical guide to moving abroad for work, study, retirement, or simply a change of scenery. It's packed with essential info that helps you master the logistics of your move and thrive in your new home and culture.

This book is designed to help you make sense of the many steps that go into planning an international move — putting everything in the right order so that you can spend time getting things done, rather than wondering what to do. It's the roadmap I wish existed when I moved abroad for the first (and fifth) time. My goal in writing this book is to save you time, effort, and money (and your sanity) while making the process as stress-free as possible.

Beyond the Book

In addition to the tips, resources, and step-by-step guidance in this book, you can find free bonuses available online.

Navigate to www.travelingwithkristin.com/moving-abroad for extra content, including moving abroad checklists and packing lists, budgeting templates, a property search form, an exploratory trip planner, visa resources, and departure and arrival itineraries.

Foolish Assumptions

I may not know you personally, but if you picked up this book, I assume that you:

- **Want a change in your life:** Whether you're seeking a new community, a better climate, a safer environment, or a lifestyle that offers the potential to experience new places and adventures.
- **Have gathered some (or tons) of info about moving abroad:** But you feel overwhelmed with everything out there. Perhaps you suffered a case of analysis paralysis (more than once) while combing through the infinite well of information on Google, YouTube, Facebook, forums, and Reddit.
- **Want to know more about how you can potentially save money by moving abroad:** You've heard that you can lower your cost of living while increasing your quality of life, and you want to find out if you actually can.
- **You have or haven't traveled internationally before:** This book is for you whether you're an aspiring, new, or experienced traveler. No passport is required — at least, not yet!

In addition, one or more of the following categories might describe you:

- Interested in exploring work or study opportunities in foreign countries. You may also be moving abroad on an international assignment for your employer, government, or volunteer organization.
- A remote worker, online freelancer, or digital nomad who can live anywhere with an Internet connection. You want to take advantage of your location freedom and flexibility.
- An entrepreneur, business owner, or investor who wants to set up shop abroad.
- Want to see the world, immerse yourself in foreign cultures, and experience life in a new community. If you have children, you want to offer them the same opportunity.

- » Want to achieve a personal goal, such as learning a foreign language, lowering your cost of living, acquiring permanent residency elsewhere, or obtaining a second passport or citizenship as a Plan B for your future.
- » Retired (or retiring soon), and you want to enjoy your golden years somewhere that fits your lifestyle and budget. You want access to affordable healthcare, an ideal climate, and a rich atmosphere that offers plenty of sightseeing, culture, and things to do.

Icons Used in This Book

Throughout this book, three types of icons appear to highlight important information.

The Tip icon provides practical advice that can make your relocation process smoother by saving you time, money, and hassles.

Pay extra attention when you see the Remember icon. It underscores key information that you may want to bookmark for future reference.

Don't miss the Warning icon, which helps you steer clear of trouble. It points out potential pitfalls and risks to your health, finances, and safety.

Throughout this book, you can also find sidebars, which offer extra info related to the topics in each chapter, as well as stories and advice from global citizens who've gone before you. Don't feel obligated to read these sidebars, but feel free to dive in whenever something piques your interest!

Where to Go from Here

How you use this book is up to you. It serves you whether you want to read it cover-to-cover or hop around different parts, chapters, and sections. For example:

- » **If you're moving abroad for the first time:** Read this book from front to back as a guide for setting your goals, overcoming your fears, and planning your relocation from start to finish.

- » **If you're stuck on where to start, where to move, and which residency option to choose:** Begin with Part 1 of this book, which helps you clarify your goals, budget, and options for your move.

- » **If you have a destination in mind:** To jump into the nuts and bolts of your relocation plan, skip to Part 2. Chapter 5 covers taxes, paperwork, and moving with kids or pets. Chapter 6 helps you buy or rent housing abroad, and Chapter 7 covers healthcare, insurance, packing, and travel logistics.

- » **If you're moving soon:** Check out Part 3. The chapters here guide you through your first days, weeks, and months abroad — from navigating public transport and receiving mail to enrolling your kids in school.

- » **If you're already living abroad:** Part 4 of this book can help you adapt to a new language, culture, and lifestyle, while finding your community and planning your long-term expat exit plan.

And don't miss the Part of Tens at the end of this book, which gives you ideas for affordable destinations, the best places to live or retire, and the top moving-abroad mistakes to avoid.

In addition to the content in its pages, this book comes with a free, access-anywhere online Cheat Sheet that offers additional moving abroad advice at a glance. To access this Cheat Sheet, go to www.dummies.com and search for "Moving Abroad For Dummies."

1
Beginning Your Living Abroad Journey

IN THIS PART . . .

Explore the potential of an overseas lifestyle.

Visualize your life as an expat or immigrant.

Know the pros and cons of living abroad.

Identify your reasons for moving to a foreign country.

Calculate your budget and decide where to move.

> **IN THIS CHAPTER**
> » Understanding what it means to live abroad
> » Overcoming fear and setbacks
> » Weighing the pros and cons of changing countries
> » Determining whether an international move aligns with your goals

Chapter 1
Previewing the Living-Overseas Lifestyle

Living abroad is a life-changing experience that offers endless possibilities. It's an opportunity to design your life down to the details, choose your location, and become part of a new culture and community. Whether you see yourself adopting a relaxed coastal lifestyle, landing a job in a foreign city, or retiring in a quiet European village, the future you imagine is possible. But how do you know if moving abroad is the right choice for you?

This chapter explores what it means to expatriate from your home country and the benefits and drawbacks of doing so. I fill you in on the different types of overseas lifestyles and how to overcome the fear of making such a big life change. This chapter can help you decide whether you want to commit to your goal of moving abroad or whether it's not for you.

Defining What Living Overseas Means

"Wherever you are, there you are." — Confucius

An early step in deciding whether to move abroad is considering if a temporary or permanent move is right for you. Moving abroad can be a chapter in your life, after which you return to your home country. Or it can mean emigrating somewhere with the intent to acquire permanent residency or citizenship. In either case, you have an opportunity to adapt to a different culture and language while you're there.

Some people leave their home countries out of necessity, such as in the case of economic hardship, political turmoil, or security concerns. Others move for career and educational opportunities or to unite with family members. If you have the luxury of choosing to live in another country for lifestyle reasons, you're in luck and in for an adventure.

You can find many paths to living an overseas lifestyle: work abroad, study abroad, retire abroad, or travel slowly as a digital nomad. You can apply for temporary residency, permanent residency, citizenship, or simply pass through places as a perpetual tourist who has a passport from your home country. See Chapter 2 to find out the different means of living in other countries.

Whatever you choose, millions of people live a lifestyle that you dream about — and you can do it, too!

Reaping the Benefits of Living Abroad

From pursuing a life in your perfect climate to expanding your worldview through cultural immersion, choosing a new country to call home can come with many benefits. Your motivation for moving likely comes from a combination of factors. The following sections explore the most popular reasons for people to move abroad.

Lowering your cost of living

One of the driving factors behind why folks decide to move to another country is to lower their overall living expenses. The average cost of living in the top 50 U.S. cities in 2024 is more than $4,000 per month (about $50,000 per year).

If you're from a high-income, developed country, you can often save money in all areas of your life by living abroad.

At the time I write this, many U.S. citizens pay upwards of $700 per month on a car payment and spend $20 to $30 on lunch at a restaurant. But prices are more affordable in many countries. In Bali, Indonesia, you can rent a moped for $6 per day (about $180 per month) and enjoy a heaping plate of *nasi goreng* (fried rice) for $2.

When considering housing prices, the average rental price in Chicago, Illinois in 2024 was $1,848 monthly. In Medellín, Colombia, however, you can find a 1-bedroom apartment for $500 per month or a room to rent from $200 to $300 per month.

If you want to live comfortably on a modest pension or save money while bootstrapping your new business, moving to a more affordable place helps. If this prospect sounds exciting to you, make sure to read Chapter 3. It tells you how to calculate your approximate cost of living in another country.

The cost and quality of healthcare are other reasons people move abroad. The average U.S. retiree spends $165,000 on healthcare in retirement, but that's not the case everywhere. As a legal resident or citizen of another country, you can access its public healthcare system. Learn more about healthcare and insurance in Chapters 7 and 9.

Leveling up your quality of life

What does quality of life mean to you? Whether you envision shopping for fresh produce at a Tuscan market, waking up to the sound of howler monkeys in Costa Rica, or walking on the beaches of Mexico each day, you can find the lifestyle that you dream of available somewhere.

For me, quality of life means living somewhere I can get around in without needing a car; having access to fresh, organic food; and being in a community where I feel welcome.

For you, it could mean finding quality, affordable healthcare; living in a more peaceful environment; or living in a warm climate year-round.

Reducing your taxes

Moving to a new country can save you a lot of money in taxes, depending on where you're from (and where you're going). You can potentially change your tax rate by changing your tax residence, also known as a *tax domicile*. You may also qualify for income tax credits, extra write-offs, and other perks. Many countries have tax treaties to help prevent double taxation. Others offer retirement visas where foreigners can live without being taxed on their pensions. Find more about taxes in Chapters 4 and 5.

Enjoying new experiences

Traveling presents the opportunity to see and do new things. And when you live long-term in a foreign country, you have more time to explore near and far.

Growing up in Florida, I was 15 years old when I saw snow for the first time. Another 15 years later, I found myself drifting through fresh powder on the Japanese ski slopes of Niseko, Japan.

What are you looking forward to that you can experience only in a different country? Whether you dream of trekking Machu Picchu or the Himalayas, living abroad can put you closer to reaching your goals.

Broadening your worldview

Living as an outsider in a new place can feel awkward and uncomfortable at first. Soon, however, you start to see the world in a different way. Studies show that travel increases compassion and empathy, and living abroad can open your mind in ways you've never experienced before. You figure out how to step outside your comfort zone, overcome challenges, and develop a stronger sense of independence and self-reliance.

Expanding your community

Whether you want to make new friends, fall in love, or find a new business partner, moving to a new country provides plenty of opportunities to meet new people. Chapter 11 provides ways to get to know local people, connect with fellow expats, and expand your network.

Acquiring new skills

You can expect to pick up a slew of new life skills if you move to a new nation. A few examples include:

» **Communication:** You can learn a new language, get better at reading body language, and decipher foreign food labels at the grocery store.

» **Cultural awareness:** You become more accepting and knowledgeable of customs and cultural norms and gain a new perspective on life.

» **Financial planning:** You gain experience budgeting for your move, haggling at local markets, negotiating the terms of your rental property, and planning your taxes across borders.

- **Life skills:** You figure out how to navigate public transport links, pay bills from a foreign bank account, and convert currencies and time zones in seconds.
- **Personal development:** You develop soft skills such as patience, resilience, adaptability, and a flexible mindset.
- **Relationships:** You get the opportunity to strengthen relationships at home and build a new support network.

Enjoying better healthcare

Depending on where you're from, your country may have a fabulous universal healthcare system. Or perhaps getting good care is expensive or hard to find. When you move abroad, however, you can opt into a better healthcare system that has more affordable care and insurance options. Chapter 7 gives you the lowdown on healthcare overseas.

Uncovering new job opportunities

You can find many exciting options to work overseas. You can apply for a working holiday visa in some countries (if you're below age 30-35), you can work remotely as a digital nomad, or you can apply for a job abroad and obtain a work permit. See Chapter 2 for ways that you can work abroad and Chapter 11 for volunteer opportunities.

TIP

For guidance on finding jobs overseas, check out the book *Global Career: How to Work Anywhere and Travel Forever*, by Michael Swigunski, New Nomad Publishing (2018).

> ### WHY WE MOVED ABROAD
>
> I asked *Traveling with Kristin* podcast listeners and YouTube subscribers why they moved abroad and how the experience changed their lives. Here are some of their responses:
>
> Claudia, Canada: "I moved abroad because I was newly married, and we felt ready to conquer the world and chart our own life path. I have no regrets at all. I've become even more open minded, independent, resilient, empathetic, and took charge of my health. Plus, I'm fluent in another language. I'm living my life — not the one some people thought I should live."

(continued)

(continued)

> Dave, Portugal: "My wife and I moved abroad because we wanted a new life experience. We traveled the world and, on our journey, fell in love with Portugal. We love the cultural vibe, peace, safety, and overall lifestyle."
>
> John, Italy: "[Living abroad] made me wealthy, gave me a global point of view, and an appreciation for other people. In the 51 years since I graduated from college, I've spent over 70 percent of my time overseas, on all the continents. In short, it's given me everything."
>
> Mohammed, Digital Nomad: "Living abroad has profoundly reshaped my life in ways I never anticipated. It expanded my worldview, made me more adaptable, and instilled a sense of confidence in navigating uncertainty. Professionally, it opened doors to international opportunities that I wouldn't have accessed otherwise. It's not always easy, but the sense of accomplishment and the memories made along the way have been invaluable. It's a journey I'd recommend to anyone looking for growth, adventure, and a deeper understanding of what it means to be part of a global community."
>
> Ujjwal, USA: "I met my then-girlfriend and now wife while working and living in the United States. She stayed with me in Nepal after marrying according to our Hindu traditions and became pregnant with our baby. After thinking about our children's future, we decided to move back to America where we felt our daughter would have a compelling future."

Acknowledging the Drawbacks of Living Abroad

Living abroad isn't all sunshine and roses. Like with any major decision, you have challenges to face and downsides to consider.

Coping with culture shock

Everyone who moves abroad experiences some degree of culture shock, although everyone experiences it differently. Only time will tell how hard it hits you and how long it lasts. Fortunately, you can reduce the adverse effects of culture shock and overcome it faster; Chapter 10 gives you tips for how to weather these feelings of loneliness and discomfort.

Living far from family and friends

But for many folks, being thousands of miles away from loved ones can cause emotional turmoil. For others, it provides peace of mind (no judgment). Surprisingly, many expats report having better relations with their family members after they move abroad. I talk more about staying in touch with your friends and family in Chapter 11.

Keeping yourself safe

Moving abroad can occasionally expose you to new threats, especially if you're on a work assignment in a high-risk area or if a conflict breaks out. Chapter 13 gives you ways to stay as safe as possible.

Deciding Whether Living Abroad Is Right for You

In my 20 years of experience helping people move abroad, I've observed that the desire to live in another country tends to stick with you. Whether it's an idea that you're just beginning to explore or a long-held dream that you've been putting off for months, years, or even decades (yep — it happens more often than you think), the book you hold in your hands gives you the tools to make it a reality.

You can benefit from living abroad if:

» You're intrigued by the idea of living outside your home country.

» You want to experience life in a different culture.

» You're open to new experiences.

» You have strong personal reasons or motivations to move.

» You want a change in your life.

» You have a job or income stream that allows you to live in another country.

» You simply want to!

If one or more of the above reasons resonate with you, you can take the next step of clarifying your reasons for moving abroad, which you can do in the next section.

Setting Your Goal of Moving Abroad

There's no one-size-fits-all path to moving abroad. Your journey will be unique to you. Before you jump into planning your relocation, however, reflect on your deeper motivations for making this life change, which can keep you focused when the going gets tough.

Ask yourself the following questions. Journal about them or discuss them with a trusted family member, friend, or therapist:

» **Why do you want to move abroad?** Your answer is the right one — dare to dream here!

» **What excites you most about living in a different culture?** Do you look forward to meeting new people, trying new foods, learning a second language, or something else?

» **What practical reasons do you have for moving to a new country?** Perhaps you aim to lower your cost of living, receive better healthcare, or reconnect with family members overseas.

» **What does success look like for you?** Your desired outcome might be retiring in Thailand on a $1,500-per-month pension, finding a high-paying job in Hong Kong, teaching English in Spain, moving your family to Costa Rica, or getting a digital nomad visa in Portugal.

» **What obstacles might you face along the way?** Anticipate anything that can slow or derail your progress, such as budget constraints, an uncooperative employer, family responsibilities, or limiting beliefs.

» **How can you overcome setbacks?** Developing soft skills, such as a patient, determined, and resilient mindset, can help you persist through struggles. You can also get support from other expats and relocation professionals, which Chapter 5 helps you with.

Action Step: Write your moving abroad mission statement:

I want to move abroad because: _____
_____.

When something gets in my way, I will: _____
_____.

Overcoming the Fear of Failure

Moving abroad is a psychological challenge as much as a logistical one. Fear of failure and fear of the unknown are two factors that keep people from pursuing their dreams of living overseas. If you feel hesitant, don't worry; it means you're human. Uncertainty is part of the process. Begin this journey with an open mind and an acceptance that you don't have to have everything figured out yet.

Each step you take in planning your move brings you closer to your goal. (When in doubt, look at the Table of Contents in this book and jump to the topic you need help with.)

Reframing fear as growth

Humans evolved to feel fear as a survival mechanism. In the past, fear protected us from (often physical) threats, such as a saber-toothed tiger lurking around the corner. But in modern society, feeling apprehensive is often a sign that you're doing something difficult or straying outside of your comfort zone. It can be a good thing, leading to personal growth and a sense of accomplishment.

Every big life decision comes with risks, rewards, and uncertainty. You've faced the unknown before, and you can do it again. The key to success is identifying possible pitfalls and ways to overcome them.

Transforming your fear into action

How are you feeling right now? Describe any emotions that come up and subtle fears that might hold you back from pursuing your goal of living abroad. For each fear, counter it with a possible solution.

For example, perhaps you're afraid that you'll spend a year or more preparing to move then hate it once you arrive. Sometimes, you just need more time to adapt, which Chapter 10 can guide you on. But what's the worst-case scenario if you move abroad and change your mind? Maybe it's a sign to shift to a different country. Or maybe it means that you spent some money and time, had an experience, learned a few things, and returned home to find a new job and a place to live.

Journal about your fears regarding the move, what to do if things don't go as planned, and how you can handle possible outcomes.

You can gain clarity about your decision by future pacing or envisioning the impact of your choices in the future. Ten years from now, will you wish you'd moved abroad? Ten years from now, what will your life be like if you stayed where you are?

WHAT'S IN A NAME? EXPAT OR IMMIGRANT

When you move abroad, how should you self-identify? Many people call those who voluntarily move to other countries long-term as *expats*.

No consensus exists on what it means to be an expat, exactly. The term comes from the word *expatriate,* meaning to leave one's country. But for how long, exactly? No one knows. You can call yourself an expat in the same way that you can declare yourself a chocoholic. Whether your annual chocolate consumption per annum makes you one depends on opinion.

In my view, an *expat* is someone who leaves their country temporarily, either on a work assignment or voluntarily, for a few months or years.

Suppose you move to another country permanently to become a permanent resident or citizen. In that case, some would say that puts you in the immigrant category. (An *immigrant* is someone who moves permanently from the country of their birth.)

If you reside abroad long-term without a home base, you could consider yourself a tourist, expat, digital nomad, slow traveler, or roving retiree. Or any term that you can think up! Some folks like to call themselves *flexpats,* which loosely means to live abroad sometimes.

As I write in *Digital Nomads For Dummies* (John Wiley & Sons, Inc.), a label is simply a label. You can identify with one or not.

Do what you feel. Whether you see yourself as a visitor, expat, citizen, immigrant, the choice is up to you.

> **IN THIS CHAPTER**
>
> » Considering your budget and goals
>
> » Knowing about the ways to move abroad
>
> » Understanding visa and residency requirements
>
> » Starting on a path to live abroad

Chapter 2
Exploring the Different Paths to Moving Abroad

How do you go about moving to another country? It's not as easy as just hopping on a plane and setting off on your new adventure. In fact, if you walk to an airport check-in desk with a one-way ticket to Morocco and declare that you're moving there, the attendant may just turn you away. Or, at least, they'll ask you for proof of return travel (more on that in Chapter 7).

In reality, you can't move to a new country if you don't have permission to live there. You can visit, however, as a tourist, volunteer, or business traveler. And you can stay for as long as your short-term visa allows — typically anywhere from 30 to 180 days.

But if you want to experience residing in another country for a long period of time — to work, to study, retire, or just to immerse yourself more deeply in the culture, you need to plan ahead and ensure that you have all the documentation so that you can do so legally.

In this chapter, I lay out the different ways to officially live in a foreign country, how to prepare financially, and how to choose the best path for you.

Assessing Your Budget and Lifestyle Goals

Before packing your bags and setting sail for a new life abroad, you need to figure out how you plan to support yourself when you arrive at your destination. Without at least *some* money, you can't get very far when moving abroad (both literally and figuratively). After helping more than 1,000 people move to new countries, I noticed they all had one thing in common — a substantial amount of savings or a recurring income stream.

When you plan your move overseas, consider how you'll support yourself. The most common ways to fund your move include:

>> **A local job in your destination country:** If you plan to work while abroad, find out how you can work in the country that you choose.

WARNING

Under most short-term visitor visa rules, you can't work in a foreign country without express permission from that country's government. Secure the proper authorization, such as a work permit, prior to arrival.

>> **Passive income or pension:** Income from investments, a passive income business, or pension accounts helps you qualify for an investor, retirement, or other non-lucrative visa in a country.

>> **Personal savings:** Proof of financial solvency helps you to qualify for various types of short-stay visas or temporary residence permits.

>> **Remote income:** Earning income from a remote source gives you the opportunity to apply for digital nomad visas, which you can read more about in this chapter.

So, if your plan involves going somewhere and figuring out how to make money after you get there, take a pause. See where you are now financially and what you can afford to do. Determine if you must add a new revenue stream to your bank account or get permission to work in another country before booking your plane ticket.

TIP

If you want to move to a country without having a job, yet, apply for a job seeker visa or permit, which grant you 6 to 12 months to find a job after arrival. Austria, Denmark, Germany, and Portugal offer such a visa.

Defining your lifestyle

What will you do when you live abroad? Contemplate what your role will be while residing in a different country. Will you study abroad or work for a foreign company? Will you work remotely while traveling or living as a digital nomad? Will you invest in a country in exchange for a golden visa (which you can read about later in this chapter)? Will you enjoy your retirement and live on savings? Write your answer below:

While living abroad, I will: _____

Calculating your budget

Your current income source and amount may change when you move abroad. If you plan to move after you retire, your income may change from a paycheck to a pension or Social Security. If you're in school, your funding could come from a scholarship, grant, student loan, or summer job. If you're working, perhaps your employer is funding your move; or maybe you're changing careers to something more flexible that allows you to live overseas.

Putting it down on paper

Whatever your situation, take a moment to write the following information down for quick reference when determining how you will fund your move. The following is a worksheet that can help you get started planning your budget.

My current location (Home country): _____

My current monthly income: $_____

My current average cost of living: $_____

My current savings for the move: $_____

My desired destination (Foreign country): _____

When living abroad, my income will come from: _____

My future estimated monthly income: $_____

My ideal cost of living abroad: $_____ (per month/year)

You don't need to be a math whiz to get a solid overview of your financial situation. The information above can help you figure out which path to living abroad works best for you and how long your savings might last you. Chapter 3 helps you calculate your budget and estimated cost of living abroad in more financial detail.

TIP

Start thinking the creature comforts you currently enjoy and ways you can simplify your lifestyle to save money for your move.

CHAPTER 2 **Exploring the Different Paths to Moving Abroad**   19

Knowing the Different Paths to Living Abroad

Your age, income level, employment status, career expertise, and family ties can affect where you can move, how long you can stay, and how you can qualify to live there. Each relocation path has certain requirements, benefits, restrictions, and costs. Choosing the right option can help streamline your transition to living overseas.

Moving through your job

A popular way to move abroad involves getting a job overseas or landing an international assignment with your employer. If you work for a multinational corporation, ask your employer if the company has any international placements available. Getting paid to move abroad is a good deal. Employers often offer relocation assistance and financial support through a housing stipend, bonus, cost-of-living adjustment, shipping credit, private schooling for your kids, and other perks. According to American Relocation Connections (ARC), a global relocation company, corporate relocation packages in 2024 could range from $2,000-$100,000.

To qualify for a global corporate assignment where a company pays you to move overseas, you typically need a lot of experience or longevity in your role or hold a C-level job title (you have to be one of the chiefs — chief executive officer, chief financial officer, and so on). However, it never hurts to ask.

TIP

If you don't have a high-powered corporate job, consider inquiring about a part-time role or taking an overseas sabbatical.

Finding a job overseas

If you don't have the option to transfer within your company internationally, you can change employers or apply for jobs in your desired destination country. You can job opportunities abroad in many ways:

>> **Direct outreach:** Many remote and international companies have careers pages on their websites or a method to apply directly online. If you dream of working for a particular company abroad, contact them. That's how one of my YouTube subscribers got a job with Booking.com in Amsterdam.

>> **Entrepreneurship and remote work:** If you work for yourself as a freelancer or online business owner, you may have the flexibility to work from anywhere. Numerous countries now offer digital nomad visas for people who earn an

online income from outside the country that they're applying to stay in. You can also consider getting a freelancer, entrepreneur, startup, or small business visa.

TIP

To find remove work opportunities, search job boards, such as FlexJobs (www.flexjobs.com), Remotive (www.remotive.com), and We Work Remotely (www.weworkremotely.com).

Consider these options for finding a job abroad:

- **Hospitality and contract work:** Apply for a job with a hotel, cruise line, events company, or as an au pair. Inquire if the country you're interested in offers an au pair or working holiday visa. I know people who lived in London as au pairs, held tourism jobs in Australia, and worked on tree-planting operations in Canada.

- **Internal job transfer:** Ask your manager or Human Resources department about transferring to a different company location. One of my relocation clients scored a job transfer from New York to Ireland. Another has the option of working in Australia or New Zealand.

- **International job boards:** Websites such as GoAbroad.com, Google (www.google.com), and Indeed (www.indeed.com) list international and remote job openings.

- **Language teaching programs:** You can find work online or abroad by teaching English as a second language. Find courses and certification options through the website TEFL.org.

- **Networking:** Connecting with peers in your industry, online or in person, can produce opportunities. Join Facebook groups and Reddit threads in your area of expertise, follow people of interest on X and LinkedIn, and attend virtual job fairs. One of my contacts found a job with an international touring musician this way.

TIP

My book *Digital Nomads For Dummies* (John Wiley & Sons, Inc.) has multiple chapters on how to find or create a remote job of your own.

- **Recruiters and head-hunters:** For experienced workers, recruiting agencies such as Adecco (www.adecco.com) and Robert Half (www.roberthalf.com) have thousands of open positions worldwide with locations in various countries. You can also connect with recruiters through LinkedIn (www.linkedin.com).

» **Volunteer and work exchange programs:** Organizations such as Worldwide Opportunities on Organic Farms (WWOOF; www.wwoof.net) offer short- and long-term work opportunities in tourism, agriculture, and service industries. The website Workaway (www.workaway.info) has more than 50,000 opportunities for cultural exchange or working holidays. Through United Nations Volunteers (www.unv.org), you can apply to volunteer abroad if you're 18 years of age or older. Check out the section "Volunteering and government work," later in this chapter, for details about volunteer opportunities.

Investing in a business or real estate

Money might not buy happiness, but it can buy the ability to live in another country. Investing money in a property, business, the stock market, or a government donation can earn you a golden visa, also known as residence by investment (RBI) or citizenship by investment (CBI). With RBI, you can live in a country temporarily or permanently. With CBI, you become a citizen of a country with voting rights and a passport.

Greece, Malta, Portugal, Spain, and the United States each have an RBI program, while Dominica, Turkey, and Vanuatu offer popular CBI options.

The processing time for residency or citizenship by investment varies depending on the country and category in which you invest. In some cases, a government can process an application in as little as 30 to 60 days, but you may have to wait as long as 6 months. Buying this type of residency or citizenship costs from six to seven figures.

TIP

A benefit to investment-based residency programs is that you may be able to hold residency in a country without living there full-time. There may be a low or no annual minimum stay requirement.

Check out Chapter 4 for more information on applying for golden visas and CBI.

Qualifying for citizenship by descent

If you're lucky to have a close relative born in a different country, you might qualify for citizenship by descent (CBD), which allows you to become a citizen of another country through familial lines. To qualify, you must have a parent, grandparent, or (in some cases) a great-grandparent born in the country to which you want citizenship. If you're from the United States, your mom was born in the United Kingdom, and your grandfather was born in Italy, you could theoretically obtain citizenship in three countries and get three passports.

Having citizenship in another country gives you all the rights of any other citizen who was naturalized or born there — you can vote, join the healthcare system, enroll in school, and pay taxes (congratulations!). Most notably, you can also live there and potentially get access to travel to more countries visa-free than with your current passport.

To determine whether you qualify for CBD, research your family tree and see whether you're a descendant of anyone from a different country. If you aren't sure, inquire with your relatives. Then, reach out to the closest consulate near you to find out the process for reinstating your citizenship. Certain lawyers and agencies you can find online may also offer advisory services. Find out more details about obtaining citizenship abroad in Chapters 4 and 13.

Retiring abroad

Many countries offer a retirement visa or residency option if you plan to retire overseas. With this type of permit, you need passive income to qualify — usually from a pension, Social Security, or other recurring investment income. Some countries allow you to continue to work part time — or full time — while on such a visa (Colombia, Peru, or Ecuador, for example), while others, such as Spain and Italy, strictly enforce the non-lucrative aspect of the visa. That means those countries discourage or outright prohibit earning extra income from side hustles. (Check with your new country's immigration department or a lawyer for current rules.)

Retirement visas have many benefits, from tax credits, to duty-free allowances on imported belongings, to free healthcare.

Panama offers a *pensionado* (retired person) visa for applicants who are at least 18 years old. This visa is valid indefinitely if you meet the income requirement of $1,000 per month from a pension or similar source. In addition, you can also gain residency in Panama by investing in real estate.

The Philippines has a program called the Special Resident Retiree's Visa (SRRV) that you can qualify for from 50 years of age. The income requirement for the "Classic" option is $800 per month for single applicants or a combined $1,000 per month for couples, plus a $10,000 deposit. If you don't have a pension, the minimum deposit is $20,000.

For ten popular places to retire abroad, see Chapter 14.

CHAPTER 2 Exploring the Different Paths to Moving Abroad 23

Reuniting with family (or starting a new one)

Almost every country has a provision for a spouse or family reunification visa. If you get married or have a baby abroad, you may be able to qualify for residency status, depending on the country's laws. Brazil, Costa Rica, and Mexico are three countries where you can become eligible for residency if you marry or have kids and your child born there can become a citizen. In other places, it's more complicated.

WARNING

Take caution when relying solely on marriage or children as your primary means of moving to a new country. Many governments have strict regulations in place to prevent fraudulent marriages and family reunions. "Birth tourism" — the practice of traveling to a country to give birth — is also discouraged.

If you have close relatives overseas, you may be able to get permission to visit them on an extended basis or move close to them. Most countries offer a family reunification visa for parents with children or dependent relatives and elders under certain conditions.

Studying abroad and exchange programs

Studying abroad lets you try out an overseas lifestyle for a few months, a year, or longer. My first experience living abroad was as a Rotary Scholar in Costa Rica when I was 20. Following that enriching experience, I continued living abroad by studying international business at Griffith University in Australia for a semester.

Whether you're young or old, studying abroad may be an option for you.

If you're currently enrolled in high school or college, check with your school to find out about available options. They may have existing exchange programs set up with foreign institutions that you can choose from. If your school doesn't have a program in place, consider contacting the school where you want to study abroad and inquire about what they offer. You can also ask your school's administrators if you can design your curriculum abroad and get credit for it (that's what I did to be able to study in Australia).

You can also study abroad if you're an experienced scholar or professor. You can take a sabbatical to work on a book, paper, or research project. You can also apply for a grant to conduct research studies in a different country.

Adults who want to study abroad for fun also have options. You can opt for a language immersion program, attend a writer's retreat, or take cooking classes.

If you're a home chef, consider enrolling in one of the global Le Cordon Bleu campuses. You can also study spirituality, religion, or any topic you're interested in that qualifies you for a study permit. If you want to live in Italy, for example, you can apply for a one-year study permit to learn Italian.

Resources for finding study abroad, educational travel, and language immersion programs include:

- **CIEE** (Council on International Educational Exchange; www.ciee.org): A non-profit organization offering a comprehensive selection of study abroad, internship, and cultural exchange programs for students and recent grads.

- **GoAbroad.com:** Founded in 1997, GoAbroad.com offers thousands of study abroad options, including programs for volunteering, teaching, adventure travel, and learning a language or job skills. The organization also has gap year, high school, and college degree programs.

- **Go Overseas** (www.gooverseas.com): A website and community of more than 100,000 members offering study abroad program reviews, photos, and articles about traveling overseas. Go Overseas provides volunteer study and work abroad programs for adults and seniors.

- **Semester at Sea** (www.semesteratsea.org): A unique, floating college that takes students to ten-plus countries while they study for college credit.

- **ISA by WorldStrides** (www.studiesabroad.com): Offering study abroad, internship, and intercultural learning programs worldwide since 1987.

- **Voluntourism:** Contribute to local causes — from animal welfare, to environmental conservation, to human rights — through organizations such as the Earthwatch Institute (www.earthwatch.org), Habitat for Humanity (www.habitat.org), and the Peace Corps (www.peacecorps.gov). You can find more details about volunteering abroad in the following section.

TIP

Multiple universities, such as Harvard, Stanford, Yale, Cambridge, and Oxford, offer opportunities to learn and travel without pursuing a degree through executive education and non-degree offerings. INSEAD (www.insead.edu): Known as "the business school for the world," INSEAD (*Institut Européen d'Administration des Affaires*) has campuses in France and Singapore, and also offers online courses, with open programs in management, leadership, finance, and corporate governance.

If you feel that studying abroad long-term is a good fit for you, you can opt to enroll as a full-time international student. To apply to a school abroad, decide which subject or field you want to study, research schools in your destination of choice, and contact the international admissions office for up-to-date

CHAPTER 2 **Exploring the Different Paths to Moving Abroad**   25 requirements. You can find out about study permits directly with your program coordinator, embassy abroad, or the immigration department or department of foreign affairs in your destination country.

REMEMBER

Tuition fees for international students can be higher than you might expect. Inquire about scholarship and financial aid options at the school where you're applying. Tuition fees can range from $10,000 to $50,000 per year.

Volunteering and government work

Want to help change the world (and possibly yourself) through living abroad? Consider volunteering or pursuing a job through your country's government or a non-governmental organization (NGO):

- » **Conservation programs:** If you're passionate about animal and wildlife conservation, look for opportunities such as the volunteer programs offered by A Broader View (www.abroaderview.org). For example, you can work at a dog shelter in Argentina, an elephant sanctuary in India, or a veterinarian's office in Costa Rica. The website International Volunteer HQ (www.volunteerhq.org) also offers options.

- » **Doctors Without Borders** (www.doctorswithoutborders.org): For qualified professionals, positions at Doctors Without Borders last 9 to 12 months. The organization offers medical and non-medical roles, and they don't have an application age limit. However, remember that some assignments may be located in challenging areas that have extreme weather or living conditions, as well as intense physical requirements.

- » **Government programs:** Some countries offer gap year programs to their citizens. The U.K. provides volunteer opportunities for people aged 18 to 25 through its International Citizen Service program (www.gov.uk/government/collections/international-citizens-service-ics-programme), while Australia has its Australian Volunteers Program (www.dfat.gov.au/people-to-people/australian-volunteers-program). Contact your Department of Foreign Services or search online to find opportunities specific to your country and age group.

- » **Oyster Worldwide** (www.oysterworldwide.com): This U.K.-based organization helps people of all ages experience safe, ethical work and volunteer programs lasting from two weeks to one year.

- » **Peace Corps** (www.peacecorps.gov): As a Peace Corps volunteer, you can live and work in one of 60 countries while receiving a living allowance and cultural adaptation support. Projects last 3 to 12 months in environmental, education, health, and agriculture categories.

While you can request a Peace Corps destination where you'd like to serve, preferences aren't guaranteed.

- **Volunteer in your industry:** If you have work experience, you have specialized skills that can help people anywhere in the world. Create opportunities by contacting companies or organizations in your field and offering to work or volunteer for them abroad.

- **Worldwide Opportunities on Organic Farms** (WWOOF; www.wwoof.net): An educational and cultural exchange program that links volunteers with organic farmers. You can find more than 12,000 opportunities in 130-plus countries, from flower farms in Italy and fruit and nut growing in Switzerland, to animal welfare on the Greek island of Attica.

Mission work with a church or religious organization is also an option to live abroad.

Enjoying a working holiday

Working holiday visas (WHVs) allow people to live, work, and travel in a country for a set period, typically one to two years.

WHVs vary by country, but these programs are designed for people aged 18 to 35 who want to gain work experience in a temporary position.

Australia's working holiday visa is one of the most popular and well-known of its kind. If you qualify for it, you can live in Australia for up to one year and renew for two or three years.

Under such a visa, you can work in a variety of pre-approved job categories, including roles such as

- **Agriculture:** Farming, fruit picking, tree planting
- **Childcare:** Nanny or au pair
- **Hospitality and tourism:** Cafés, restaurants, and ski resorts
- **Retail and seasonal jobs:** Clothing stores, ice cream parlors, and special events

In contrast to volunteer opportunities, you can earn an income from your WHV job.

Working abroad remotely

Since 2020, many countries have launched a type of digital nomad visa designed for online freelancers, business owners, and remote workers. You can often qualify if you're a remote employee, independent contractor, or entrepreneur. Coaches, consultants, creatives, and most online professionals who earn an income remotely may qualify for this visa type.

The basic requirements for a digital nomad visa include

- » Stable monthly income of $1,000 to $5,000, with supporting documentation, such as pay slips, bank statements, or service receipts.
- » You may also need to present professional credentials, such as a higher education degree or professional certification, work or client contracts, or proof of licensing and expertise.
- » An application form, which you can fill out online or at an embassy or consulate.
- » Proof of residence or housing, such as a housing contract or Airbnb reservation.
- » Proof of travel or health insurance.
- » Valid passport.

To qualify for a digital nomad visa, your income must come from a source outside of the country to which you want to travel. This rule helps protect local jobs from foreign workers. If you plan to work in person where you're applying for a digital nomad visa, you may need a work permit instead, which I discuss earlier in this chapter. Or a freelancer, entrepreneur, startup, or small business visa, which I provide examples of below.

The first country to announce a digital nomad visa was the Caribbean nation of Barbados, with its Barbados Welcome Stamp. This stamp allows people who earn at least $2,000 per month for up to one year to live and work online in Barbados.

Estonia, a country in Northern Europe, followed shortly after that with the Estonian digital nomad visa, application for which costs €70 to €90 ($74-95). To qualify, you must prove at least €4,500 ($4,735) in monthly income from clients outside of Estonia. The visa is valid for a stay of 12 months.

Some countries, such as Cyprus (an island nation in the Mediterranean), limit the number of digital nomad visas they generate to 500 permits per year. Remember that some countries may also require that you get your application documents notarized and apostilled to certify them for international use.

Processing times vary greatly, from 7 to 14 days for the African island country of Seychelles' Workcation visa, to a few months in European countries such as Portugal, Hungary, and Romania.

You can get remote work visas faster and easier than a traditional work permit. These visas often have smaller application fees than residence permits do. For example, it takes around $250 and three to four weeks to get a digital nomad visa in Malaysia, a nation in Southeast Asia, compared to an investment of $250,000 and a few months or more to get a golden visa there. Malaysia's digital nomad visa allows you to stay there for up to 12 months, compared to 90 days as a tourist who has only a passport.

A digital nomad visa permits you to legally work remotely in the country, whereas a tourist visa does not.

The downside of most digital nomad visas is that they don't necessarily give you a path to permanent residency or citizenship. After your visa's up, you have to move on or apply to stay under a different visa category. An exception to this rule is the digital nomad visa for the European country Italy, which you can renew each year for five years, after which you can apply for permanent residency.

If you would like to move to a country that doesn't offer a digital nomad or remote work visa, see if it offers a freelancer, entrepreneur, small business, or startup visa. Such visas can serve as an alternative to remote work visas. Examples include the German freelance visa, the Czech Republic self-employed worker visa, and the Taiwan Gold Card, a combined visa, residence permit, and work permit for skilled professionals.

Digital nomads and remote workers may have to pay taxes in their new countries. In Albania, in Southeastern Europe, digital nomads who stay over 183 days per year may be subject to a 15 percent flat tax on income. The European countries of Estonia, Hungary, Spain, and Portugal have similar provisions. For a portal of countries that offer digital nomad visas, including requirements and application times, visit CitizenRemote.com.

Selecting a Path to Going Abroad

Now that you know how to live abroad, which country will you choose? Think about which path suits you best: studying or retiring abroad, working online as a digital nomad, investing in a golden visa, starting a small business, or something else.

After you choose a route to living overseas, dive deeper into the visa and residency options available in the country or countries that you're interested in by contacting the closest consulate, searching government immigration sites, or soliciting help from a residency attorney or other advisor. Get help with choosing a destination in Chapter 4 and hiring relocation professionals in Chapter 5.

EXPAT JOURNEYS: HOW THEY DID IT

The number of ways to move abroad is as varied as the people who've done it. Whether you want to pursue a new career opportunity, retire, or start a family, you have multiple paths to do so. Here are a few examples of how people managed to move abroad or travel long-term:

- **Abir, Switzerland:** I got a student visa to be able to move to Switzerland. There are lots of of rules but they're super clear and efficient. I love the competence that came with dealing with the Swiss — it's definitely unlike any other country I've dealt with.

- **Brenden, China and Europe:** I moved to China for my career and got married in Denmark. Eventually my wife and I moved to Paris to start a family. (We now have a one-year-old daughter who was born in Paris!)

- **Chase, Spain:** I was working remotely and used the non-lucrative visa in Spain to provide proof of funds and a reason to be there. These days, a digital nomad visa is more suitable for remote workers, however.

- **Erin, Mexico:** I had a remote job when I made the move. I started with applying for residency from the U.S. Later, I hired an immigration attorney to help me in Mexico before I arrived. I had an appointment at the immigration office two days after I landed to finish everything.

- **Joe, Costa Rica:** I took the route of going from a full-time W2 employee to being self-employed and starting my own company. I work as a contractor or digital nomad on my terms. After the requisite amount of time, I applied for the Costa Rica investor visa. I hired an immigration lawyer, and the process took two years — *pura vida* speed!

- **Karen, Albania and France:** I retired early at 54, got a residency permit in Albania, and then a long-stay visitor visa for France.

- **Richard, UK:** I found a job before going, so I didn't have the extra worry of having to wonder how long our money would last. Having a job offer also made the visa process easier. I applied for a skills-based visa scheme.

> **IN THIS CHAPTER**
>
> » Figuring out your financial foundation
>
> » Knowing where you can afford to move
>
> » Setting a savings goal

Chapter 3
Calculating Your Budget and Cost of Living

Whether you're moving down the street or to Timbuktu, you need money to make it happen.

Moving costs can add up quickly when you go overseas. You want to budget carefully for startup expenses such as flights, housing, shipping, exchange rates, and import taxes. Although you may save money long-term because of a lower cost of living in your destination, you may also face the opposite situation (where your expenses increase), so you have to account for that.

Fortunately, you can make a move abroad happen, including on the cheap. This chapter helps you calculate and estimate your expenses in detail, minimizing any surprise costs. As a result, your move may end up costing less than you expect!

Determining Your Current Cost of Living and Income

How much do you spend in a month? If you track your expenses on an app, spreadsheet, or plain old paper, you may already know your exact cash flow. But if you don't know for sure, jot down your main recurring living expenses.

Here's a basic equation:

Monthly Income − Monthly Cost of Living = Monthly Surplus (or Deficit)

For example, say that your current monthly income living at home is $5,000 and your monthly cost of living is $3,100:

$5,000 − $3,100 = $1,900

So, you have a surplus of $1,900 a month.

If your income covers your expenses and you have a little bit extra, you can start putting money away toward your future move. If your expenses exceed your income, aim to pay off debt and save money before you go.

TIP

You can lower your costs by moving to a more affordable country. See Chapter 4 for details on choosing a destination.

Creating a budget

Having a realistic idea of your expenses can help make your move (and life) easier. Here are some common lifestyle costs to consider:

- » **Rent or mortgage:** Most people pay approximately 30 percent of their salary.
- » **Utilities:** Including electricity, water, cable, and Internet.
- » **Food:** Buying groceries and dining out.
- » **Cell phone:** See Chapters 7 and 8 for cell phone and data options at home and abroad.
- » **Health, fitness, and wellness:** Medical expenses, gym memberships, therapy, and self-care.
- » **Insurance** (home, health, life, other): See Chapter 7 for health and other insurance information.

- **Monthly subscriptions:** Streaming services, memberships, cloud storage, and other monthly fees.
- **Tuition fees:** Calculate tuition and related fees if you or your children will be attending school abroad.
- **Car/transportation:** Estimate your cost for a car or public transportation to get around. Find out about owning a car and using transport options in Chapters 8 and 9.
- **Entertainment:** For example, movies, concerts, events, hobbies, nightlife, and travel.
- **Business expenses:** If you own a business or work for yourself, you may pay corporate filing fees, taxes, and operating expenses, such as website hosting, payroll, and software subscriptions.
- **Taxes:** You can owe taxes in your home country, host country, or both. See Chapters 4, 5, and 13 for information about paying taxes at home and abroad.
- **Debt:** You need to make payments if you have any outstanding debts.
- **Savings:** Try to put a little away every month in a savings account so that you build a safety net of 3 to 6 months of living expenses.
- **Other:** Life happens. Save an extra buffer for emergencies and unplanned expenses, such as medical and legal expenses or big-ticket items, like furniture.

In addition to recurring monthly expenses, it's also important to account for one-time moving costs, such as:

- Airfare and baggage fees
- Customs and import duties (if applicable)
- Emergency fund
- Home setup costs (furniture, linens, household goods, and utilities deposits and installation fees)
- Pet transport (if applicable)
- Purchasing a vehicle
- Rent and security deposit
- Shipping costs
- Storage fees
- Temporary housing
- Utilities installation
- Visa, residency, legal, and administrative fees

TIP

For a detailed moving-abroad budget template, visit www.travelingwithkristin.com/travel-budget.

Assessing your income

Adding up your income tells you how much money you currently have coming in. Consider these categories when you assess:

» **Salary/business income:** If you're working for a company, include your salary, benefits, commissions, and bonuses. If you have your own business, calculate your average monthly earnings.

» **Scholarship income:** If you're a student with financial aid, you may receive tuition, housing, and a living stipend.

» **Pension or Social Security:** You may get a pension after retirement, and if you're in the U.S., you probably also receive Social Security benefits.

» **Savings account:** Your savings account is a form of income that you can use to fund your move abroad. You can also include savings from cutting expenses (eliminating your mortgage and/or car payment, reducing insurance costs, and cancelling monthly subscriptions and utilities).

» **Investment and interest income:** If you earn interest or dividends on investments, include it.

» **Inheritance or gifts:** Maybe your grandmother left you a little money when she passed away, or maybe your uncle won the lottery and wants to share.

» **Miscellaneous income:** Do you have money coming in from freelancing gigs, side hustles, or tax refunds?

» **Selling your stuff:** Make a list of everything that you want to sell before you move, from your vehicle to designer handbags to that fine china that's still in the box. You can find out the going rate for similar items on sites such as craigslist (www.craigslist.org), eBay (www.ebay.com), Facebook Marketplace (www.facebook.com/marketplace), or your local classifieds site. (For more on selling your stuff, see Chapter 5.)

Accounting for a pension or passive income sources

When estimating your cost of living abroad, take into account all forms of income you'll still have, such as passive income. Dividends, interest, investment income, and other forms of cash flow can help support your lifestyle overseas.

In many countries, as a U.S. citizen eligible for Social Security benefits, you can collect that money into a local bank account. For instance, Costa Rica, Italy, Panama, Portugal, Spain, Thailand, and the Philippines allow you to receive U.S. Social Security income by direct deposit.

For more on how to collect your government pension abroad, contact your country's related government agency. For U.S. citizens, go to the Social Security Administration International Programs page (www.ssa.gov/international). For Australian citizens, you can contact the Services Australia branch of government (www.servicesaustralia.gov.au).

In many cases, depending on which country you're from, you can continue receiving your pension to a bank account in your home country (after you move abroad), which you can transfer to yourself internationally. See Chapters 5 and 8 for how to prepare your banking and finances and receive income abroad.

Forecasting Your Cost of Living Abroad

How do you figure out how much it costs to live in another country if you've never been there, let alone lived there? That used to be a tricky question to answer, but the Internet has all the info you need to paint an accurate picture of how much you'll spend overseas.

Say you estimate your income living abroad as $3,000 and your cost of living abroad at $2,000:

$3,000 - $2,000 = $1,000/month

So, if your estimates are right, you'll have a total monthly balance of $1,000.

The following sections give you three easy ways to estimate your future living costs.

Researching cost of living online

In a quick Internet search, you can get a ballpark idea of the expenses in your desired destination. Here are some of my favorite websites for figuring out your cost of living:

>> **Expatistan International Cost-of-Living Comparison tool** (www.expatistan.com/cost-of-living): Compare the cost of living between two cities or countries. It can tell you that living in Dubai, in the United Arab Emirates, is

CHAPTER 3 **Calculating Your Budget and Cost of Living** 35

40 percent cheaper than living in London, England; and Buenos Aires, Argentina is 30 percent more expensive than Bogotá, Colombia.

Try plugging in your hometown (or the closest big city) and your desired destination country or city, and see what comes up! The site also has an annual country and city ranking by cost of living for ideas of where to live.

- **Livingcost.org:** Provides a crowdsourced database of more than 9,000 cities and 197 countries, presented in lists on the main webpage. When you click a location on that page, a page opens showing you the total cost of living in that destination, with and without rent, as well as the average costs of common needs and wants, and that location's population.

- **Nomads.com:** Designed for long-term expats and nomads, this website has a feature that shows the estimated cost of living for tourists, nomads, expats, and locals in a given destination. Chock-full of data, you can find out the air quality in Lahore, Pakistan, the average Internet speeds in Sofia, Bulgaria, and how female- or LGBTQ+-friendly a location is. What about happiness? Nomads has a meter that gauges how much foreign residents enjoy living there, based on data from website-member contributors. You can join Nomads for a $99 one-time fee.

- **Numbeo Cost of Living** (www.numbeo.com/cost-of-living): Compare the cost of living between two places. With data on 11,555 cities at the time of this writing, it's the world's largest cost-of-living database. Numbeo also has handy info about safety, healthcare, transportation, and housing — much of it crowd-sourced from at least 776,000 contributors. Want to know what a carton of milk costs in Niksic, Montenegro, or how much beer runs in Berlin, Germany? What about the mortgage rate in Melbourne, Australia? Numbeo is your place.

Buying a book

You have this book in your hands, which I see as a smart move — congrats! After you know which country you're moving to (or at least have it narrowed down to a few top choices), buy a book or get one from the library that's specifically about the country that you plan to go to. With 197 countries worldwide, I can't fit the data for every place and budget into this particular book. But regardless of where you're going, you can find a book about moving there that details the local cost of living. To find such a book, search online for a book on "living abroad in [country]," check out a few reviews for the books that pop up in your search results, and buy (or borrow) one that looks like it can give you the information you want.

Asking a local

Ask a local resident for the most up-to-date info about prices abroad. If you don't know any local people personally, join a Facebook group or overseas forum about the country that you're interested in. First, search the group or website to see whether anyone's already having a discussion about the cost of living. If you can't find what you're looking for, make a post with your questions or ask someone in the group if they would be open to sharing their budget with you.

TIP

The InterNations website (www.internations.org) can help you connect with expats around the world online or in person. When you create an account or become a member, you can message people around the world or join in-person events in 420-plus cities worldwide.

Estimating Your Moving Fees and Shipping Your Stuff Overseas

Beyond calculating the cost of living in your destination (see the section "Forecasting Your Cost of Living Abroad," earlier in this chapter, for a rundown of this calculation), you need to factor in the cost of moving your stuff (if you're bringing anything with you).

Moving fees can take a large chunk of your budget if you're planning to ship your car, furniture, or other belongings. The following sections discuss a few steps that you can take to calculate the cost of moving your personal items abroad.

Deciding what you want to ship

What do you need to bring with you, and what can you sell, donate, and live without? Many items can fit in your luggage or excess baggage. In contrast, others, such as musical instruments, kitchen appliances, beds, artwork, books, and photo albums, are too big, heavy, or bulky to fit in your suitcase (let alone the overhead bin).

If you have things that you can't part with, you might want to ship a crate, palette, or container to your new home. One couple I helped move to Costa Rica shipped their high-end mattresses, kitchenware, and other items that made their new house feel like home. But not everyone opts to ship their goods to their new home. After helping a client in Dubai calculate the shipping costs of his furniture, he decided to sell or donate all of it before leaving. In many cases, shipping and paying import duties can cost more than the value of the items that you're sending.

See Chapter 7 for packing tips and Chapter 5 for advice on deciding what to do with your stuff.

If you're traveling with excess baggage, consider shipping your luggage with a company such as Luggage Forward, LugLess, Send My Bag, or ShipGo, which can also accommodate oversized items, such as sporting equipment.

It's often cheaper and easier to move with less stuff. Store, sell, or discard anything you don't need or can repurchase abroad. My friend Dave, who moved from the U.S. to Europe, confided, "We waited a long time to send our items in storage from the U.S. When they arrived to Portugal, we ended up keeping less than half of the items. I wish we had sent the items sooner and not sent so much 'stuff.'"

Itemizing your belongings

Shipping companies ask you for a list of items that you want to ship, along with their value, dimensions, and weight. Calculate these figures for each belonging and estimate the total weight, dimensions, and value before contacting shipping companies for the most accurate quotes.

Check the voltage in your destination country to determine whether it's worth shipping appliances and large electronics.

Getting shipping quotes

Search online for international moving companies in your hometown and destination. Inquire with each of them and compare the services and quotes that you receive. You can select from international shipping companies or providers that specialize in certain countries.

Questions to ask shipping providers include:

- » Do you pack my items for me?
- » Do you pick up at my address in my home country?
- » What's the estimated time from pick up to delivery?
- » How much do I have to pay in import taxes on my items?
- » What paperwork is needed, and who provides it?
- » What potential delays might happen, and how can I resolve them?
- » Do you deliver directly to my home in the new country?

>> How can I track my shipment?

>> What happens if items are lost or damaged in transit?

>> What insurance should I get, or does insurance come included with the price of shipment?

>> Do you have any extra fees that don't appear in the estimate?

If you're applying for residency abroad, you may qualify for a shipping or import credit, depending on the residency category that you qualify for. There's a catch, though. You may not have access to this credit until your residency status becomes official. So, suppose you move abroad before applying for residency. In that case, you must pay regular customs duties or wait until the government approves your application to take advantage of import credits.

Are you more of a minimalist than an over-packer? If you decide you don't want to ship anything that you own, that can keep things simple. But you need to sell, donate, recycle, store, or discard anything that you don't bring with you. Chapter 7 tells you how to go about that.

Ask shipping companies if you can save money by packing items yourself. If you're moving from the U.S. or Europe, the company, UPakWeShip (www.upakweship.com/) offers a self-service option.

Figuring Out How Much You Need to Save

How much to save for your move depends on your:

>> **Income level:** How much you earn now and expect to earn while abroad.

>> **Estimated moving costs:** See the section "Estimating Your Moving Fees and Shipping Your Stuff Overseas," earlier in this chapter.

>> **Projected cost of living in your destination:** Covered in the section "Determining Your Current Cost of Living and Income," earlier in this chapter.

>> **Risk tolerance:** Your comfort level with the uncertainty and changes that can come with an international move, such as your employment status and possible fluctuations in income and expenses.

What's your financial comfort zone? Some folks don't mind a financial cushion of 3 to 6 months, while others want at least one year of savings before making an overseas move.

TIP

Whatever amount you budget for your move, save an extra 10 to 20 percent as a buffer for unanticipated costs along the way.

Suppose your income stays the same after you change countries, but your cost of living decreases. In that case, you might feel comfortable with less of a financial runway saved up than if you were in the opposite scenario.

If you expect your income to drop when you move abroad — especially if you plan to quit your job, change to a part-time career, or retire on a small pension — you may want to have more savings stockpiled for a rainy day.

TIP

For additional help budgeting for your move and calculating your tax burden, hire an accountant or tax professional, which you can find more about in Chapter 5.

EXPATS SHARE THEIR MOVING ABROAD STORIES

I asked my clients and YouTube subscribers if moving abroad cost them or saved them money in the long term. Each person's situation is as unique as yours. Here's what they had to say (quotes have been edited for clarity):

Ujjwal, Nepal to USA: "The whole immigration process entails thousands of dollars: collecting documents and papers, airplane fares, and adjusting to the high cost of living in the U.S. It was taxing financially. I'd have been better off if I could be more resourceful."

Abir, Canada to Europe: "You can definitely save money by moving abroad, depending on your destination. If you bring a North American salary to Eastern Europe, you'll live like royalty with low taxes and living costs. If you get a high-paying job in Switzerland, you'll also make a lot, although life is more expensive there."

Karl, USA to Mexico: "I saved a lot of money by moving abroad. My only income is from my social security disability, and I raised a family on that in Mexico. In the USA, I would be on the streets."

Subharup, India to USA to Switzerland: "I wanted to try living in Europe, so I did a lot of research and Switzerland looked like the best option. I was lucky to get a job there and moved in 2023. While Switzerland appears expensive, the salaries keep pace with the cost of living. I make slightly more in CHF than in the United States and my quality of life is infinitely better. I save three times as much as I could in the U.S."

Mohammed, Digital Nomad: "Moving abroad helped me save money, especially when I relocated to countries with a lower cost of living than major Western cities. In places like

Turkey and Southeast Asia, everyday expenses — from rent to groceries and dining out — were significantly cheaper. This allowed me to redirect funds into my business and enjoy a more comfortable lifestyle. The lower cost of living also meant I could afford luxuries that would have been expensive back home, like living in nicer apartments, hiring domestic help, or traveling frequently. This shift improved my overall quality of life and made it easier to maintain a work-life balance.

Alex, USA to Latin America: "Moving abroad was a huge benefit. My cost of living from Boston dropped nearly 3x."

Chase, Spain: "Some things you might consider normal at home are considered a luxury abroad, so they come with a premium price, which can be shocking. I once paid $70 for a basic coffee maker while living in Ecuador, which would have been $15 back in the U.S. But, for the most part, I find life in foreign countries to be much less expensive than the U.S."

Living abroad can increase your living expenses, as I found out when I spent time in cities such as Tokyo, Japan, Reykjavik, Iceland and Sydney, Australia. Staying in each country cost more than my average monthly budget in Florida.

Setting an Ideal Timeline to Move

There's no right or wrong time to move, as long as your timeline works for you. When you decide when to set your target move date, consider three options to get a good range of possibilities:

» **Ideal move date (ASAP):** The soonest you'd like to move (if the stars align).

» **Acceptable move date:** A realistic target you can reach when allowing time to plan and save money.

» **Worst-case-scenario move date:** Your latest acceptable move date (in case of delays). This is your backup plan in case your first two choices don't work out.

Beyond allocating time to plan the travel, financial, and logistical aspects of your move, additional factors to take into consideration when choosing a move date include:

- **Applying for a visa, residency, or citizenship:** Some visas take weeks to process, others take months, and some you can apply for from abroad. See Chapter 4 for information on visa and residency options.

- **Caring for a loved one who can't travel:** Many of my relocation clients plan their move dates around caring for a sick or elderly friend, family member, or pet, or make alternative care arrangements.

- **Coordinating with annual school calendars:** If you want to time your move with a school holiday or prior to the start of a new school year.

- **Finding a new job or starting an online business:** Finding a job abroad or online or launching a profitable new venture can take months or years.

- **Finishing any location-dependent projects that you're working on:** Perhaps you're renovating your house or finalizing the sale of your business.

- **Getting accepted to a school or study abroad program:** Budget time to apply to schools and move for the start of the semester or school year.

- **Notifying your work of your departure (or applying for new jobs):** Determine how much advanced notice to provide.

- **Passport renewal times:** May take 4 to 6 weeks with standard processing, or less time with expedited service.

- **Planning around peak holiday and travel periods or life events:** Accommodations and airfare cost more during busy travel times, such as summer and holiday seasons. Chapter 6 helps you find housing and Chapter 7 helps you book your flight.

- **Selling or renting your car or home (or waiting for your lease to end):** Estimate from 1 to 12 months, depending on market conditions.

- **Tax and estate planning:** Consult with a tax advisor, which you can find more about in Chapters 4, 5, and 13.

- **Waiting for children to reach a certain age or move away:** My clients often plan to move after their children graduate from high school or college.

- **Waiting until you can retire:** Many people move after they reach retirement age and can receive their pensions. Some people are able to retire early through prudent financial planning and investment income.

After setting your move date, organize your relocation plan to fit within your desired timeline.

TIP

For a moving abroad checklist and timeline, download the bonuses for this book at www.travelingwithkristin.com/moving-abroad.

PART 1 **Beginning Your Living Abroad Journey**

> **IN THIS CHAPTER**
> » Figuring out where you want to live and why
> » Looking over some popular spots for expats
> » Weighing your visa and residency options
> » Making a choice (or more than one)

Chapter **4**

Choosing a Destination

Choosing where to live in the world is an exciting aspect of moving abroad. You may feel exhilaration when you think of all the places that you can go and what your life could be like when you get there. But you have a lot to consider when choosing a new home base, so you want to get it right.

This chapter helps you figure out how to make this decision wisely and proceed with confidence. You get clearer on what you want in your travels, gain resources to evaluate the characteristics of a place, and preview popular living abroad destinations.

With so many possibilities, it's easy to feel stressed or overwhelmed during this process. But don't worry, because you have the tools you need in this chapter. There are likely many countries that fit your budget and needs while providing the lifestyle, community, and experience you seek.

Identifying What You Want in a Destination

Before diving into visa applications or researching destinations, reflect for a moment (or two) about what you want in a place. Many people seek external guidance for the "best" countries to live in the world, but identifying your personal goals and values is a more effective approach.

The following questions help you clarify your wants, needs, and desires so you can choose a location that aligns with your ideal lifestyle.

- **What do you hope to gain and experience by moving abroad?** Recall your mission statement from Chapter 1.
- **How long do you want to live abroad?** Knowing your timeframe helps you identify appropriate visa or residency options.
- **Which countries come to mind first?** What places have you always wanted to go to, or you've traveled to and feel the most comfortable in?
- **What's most important to you when choosing a destination?** Identify and rank your top priorities. Are job opportunities, cost, and visa options most important? Or do you prioritize healthcare, safety, and low taxes?
- **What's your ideal cost of living and tax rate?** See Chapter 3 for help crafting your budget.
- **Which climate do you crave?** Do you see yourself in the tropics, living down under in the Southern Hemisphere, or a cool, northern climate?
- **What types of food do you like to eat?** Consider if the local cuisine fits your diet and nutrition preferences. In the Caribbean and the Netherlands, fried food is common. In Nicaragua, my diet consisted of rice, beans, chicken, and fish. It was hard to find specialty imported products and organic produce. In Eastern Europe, many traditional dishes are heavy on meat, potatoes, and dairy.
- **What type of housing do you prefer?** Do you see yourself living in a city studio, a quiet suburb, or an ocean view villa? Chapter 6 helps you find proper housing.
- **What kind of community do you seek?** Consider if you want to live somewhere with a strong expat network or in a country that speaks your language.

>> **What are your non-negotiables or "deal breakers" in a destination?** Perhaps you refuse to live in a cold climate, or you'll only go somewhere with a path to permanent residency or citizenship, or you must be near good schools for your kids. Maybe you need a place that's handicap accessible with free public healthcare and equal rights for society.

If you can't easily articulate what you want, think about what you *don't* want, and then explore the other side of that. If you're tired of living paycheck-to-paycheck, explore places with low living costs. If you hate sitting in traffic, look for destinations with good public transportation.

Find a destination worksheet along with bonuses for this book at www.travelingwithkristin.com/moving-abroad

Visualizing Your Ideal Lifestyle

When choosing an overseas destination, you could open a map, spin a globe, or ask other people where to go. You could also spend months crafting an elaborate spreadsheet that ranks countries on every factor imaginable. However, you can save a lot of time by envisioning what you want before beginning your research.

Allow me to recommend a visualization exercise. If you think I'm getting all woo-woo on you, humor me for a moment and try it. Doing this visualization gives you a starting point for your research that's slightly narrower than the whole of planet Earth. Just follow these steps:

1. **Find a comfortable place to sit.**
2. **Close your eyes, clear your mind, and breathe for a minute or two.**
3. **Every time a thought pops into your head, acknowledge it and let it go.**

    This process is just like meditation.

4. **Imagine you're already living in your dream destination. What do you see around you?**
5. **From the moment you wake up until the moment you go to sleep, walk through each hour of your day in your mind.**

Don't judge anything that floats through your brain; be curious instead.

Here are a few question prompts to get you started:

- What time do you wake up? Does your alarm go off, or do you wake up naturally?

CHAPTER 4 **Choosing a Destination** 45

- What's the temperature in your room?
- What do you see when you open your eyes?
- Who's with you?
- What type of accommodations are you in (house, tent, cottage, tiny home)?
- What does your room look like?
- What do you see when you look out the window?
- After brushing your teeth, what's next on your agenda? Do you open the back door of your van and see a view of the Mount Kilimanjaro? Do you creep down the narrow stairs of your Amsterdam flat and bike to your favorite coffee shop? Or do you walk outside to a row of palm trees swaying in the breeze?

TIP

The questions in the preceding list focus on the morning, but you can apply the same thinking to the other segments of your day. Walk through each step of your ideal day, from what you eat to where you go, what you do and see, and with whom.

6. **Repeat Steps 4 and 5 for your typical school day, workday, and weekend or holiday. If you're retired, one round of this exercise may suit you.**

7. **After completing the visualizations, take notes.**

    Jot down on your phone, computer, or journal what you saw, felt, and anything that surprised you. Save these notes to refer to when evaluating destinations. They can help you narrow down areas to focus on, places to discard, and choose housing, which you can read about in Chapter 6.

Perhaps you always assumed you would move to a tropical place, but you envisioned yourself living in the snow-capped mountains of Patagonia. Or maybe you thought about living in a Tuscan village, but you pictured yourself in Italy's bustling capital, Rome.

Here's an example visualization one of my relocation clients shared with me:

I wake up around 9 am in my comfortable bedroom suite with a spa-like feel. I open the window and look out at nature (a lake or beach). I walk outside to sit in the sun on a cute patio for my morning coffee. I may also decide to walk to a nearby café for a chai latte and a homemade pastry. While there, I chat with the barista in Spanish and enjoy a leisurely morning.

As I walk home along the cobblestone streets lined with shops, I wave and greet the local merchants that are setting up their stores for the day. I stop to buy some fresh fruits and vegetables at one of the markets.

Once I'm back at my apartment, I dedicate a few hours to work remotely with clients before grabbing my favorite sneakers for a walk around the city center. I take photographs along the way to share with my family and friends.

I finish my day with a bottle of red wine, get cozy on the couch, and plan the next day or weeks ahead. Some days will consist of outdoor activities, shopping, and sightseeing. Other days will consist of language classes, community meet-ups, and volunteering.

When you've finished your visualization, reflect on what you saw and identify places that would be a good fit. The lifestyle described above could be possible in a variety of cities in Spain or in towns in Latin America, such as San Miguel de Allende, Mexico, Boquete, Panama, or Cuenca, Ecuador.

Type your vision into an AI website, such as ChatGPT, for additional ideas about places to consider. In this scenario, ChatGPT suggested Antigua, Guatemala, Medellín, Colombia, and Bariloche, Argentina as alternatives.

Download a guided audio and PDF for this exercise by searching in any podcast app for *Traveling with Kristin* podcast Episode 141 – Your Perfect Day-in-the-Life as an Expat Abroad. Or, navigate to www.podcast.travelingwithkristin.com/141.

Previewing the Top Living-Abroad Destinations

Moving to another country can give you an opportunity to create your ideal life and transform your daily experiences. Some countries are especially attractive for various reasons, so consider them in your search.

According to InterNations (www.internations.org), the organization behind the annual Expat Insider (www.internations.org/expat-insider) country rankings list, the best places for expats to live rank high in multiple categories:

>> **Quality of Life:** Broken down into the subcategories Environment & Climate, Healthcare, Safety & Security, Leisure Options, and Travel & Transit

>> **Ease of Settling In:** Subcategories of Finding Friends, Culture & Welcome, and Local Friendliness

>> **Working Abroad:** With the subcategories of Career Prospects, Salary & Job Security, Work & Leisure, Work Culture & Satisfaction

» **Personal Finance Index:** Based on living expenses and income prospects

» **Expat Essentials Index:** Divided into the subcategories of Admin Topics, Housing, Digital Life, and Language

The Expat Insider report is the largest expat survey in the world, and InterNations has published it annually for more than ten years. In 2024, more than 12,500 people of 175 nationalities in 174 countries responded by sharing their opinions about their everyday life in their adopted home countries. Due to the scope and breadth of this study, it's a resource that you can rely on for diverse opinions about living in individual countries.

In 2024, the top 10 places expats voted for included:

1. Panama
2. Mexico
3. Indonesia
4. Spain
5. Colombia
6. Thailand
7. Brazil
8. Vietnam
9. Philippines
10. United Arab Emirates

Don't fret if your favorite country didn't make the Expat Insider top ten — this list just gives you an example of ten of the most popular countries for foreigners to choose.

TIP

On my YouTube channel, *Traveling with Kristin* (`www.youtube.com/travelingwithkristin`), you can find hundreds of videos about the best places to live or retire abroad in various categories, from the cheapest countries in the world to the best places for quality of life, as well as videos about specific countries, such as Costa Rica, France, Italy, and Spain.

Choosing Your Destination

Choosing a country is like choosing a partner. You want the match to be as compatible as possible, while realizing that differences are inevitable. No one person or place is perfect — you may have multiple "soul mates."

Use the topics in the following sections as a guide for what to assess in each place that you consider moving to. You have a good match if somewhere meets 50 to 80 percent of your wants and needs, not necessarily 100 percent.

Considering the climate and geography

When choosing where to live in the world, think about the year-round climate, as well as the seasons and geography of a place.

While I write this sentence, I'm sitting in the open-air lobby of a locally owned *pousada* (guest house) in Salvador, Brazil. It's a balmy 86 degrees Fahrenheit, but my phone tells me it "feels like 93." Without air conditioning, the lobby is sweltering (and so am I). While the beaches of northern Brazil are a tropical paradise, they're not for me (at least, not to live in full-time).

Living in Europe is more my style (except in the winter). Come December, I prefer to head south to places like Miami, Florida, or the Canary Islands, where the temperature hovers between 65 and 75 degrees throughout the winter. I guess you could call me a snowbird!

Which climate works best for you — cold winters or an endless summer? Some people thrive in the heat of Southeast Asia, while others struggle with the humidity. Contemplate where you feel most comfortable and choose destinations that align with your preferences.

TIP

In addition to average temperatures and weather patterns, note if your destination has four seasons (winter, spring, summer, fall), two seasons (rainy and dry), or a mild climate year-round.

You can find the average weather in a destination by searching online or by checking the following websites:

Wikipedia (www.wikipedia.org), World Population Review (www.worldpopulationreview.com), Nomad List (www.nomads.com) and World Economics (www.worldeconomics.com) have lists of the average weather by country. Quora (www.quora.com) and Reddit (www.reddit.com) are two resources where you can ask the community about the weather in different places or search existing posts for answers.

WARNING

Natural disasters also play a part in deciding where to go. Chile and Costa Rica are prone to earthquakes, while Thailand and the Philippines experience tsunamis. Many parts of the world are becoming more vulnerable to the effects of climate change, including hurricanes, tornadoes, flooding, and drought. Be mindful of possible risks, while remembering that finding happiness is more about what you're seeking rather than what you're escaping

CHAPTER 4 **Choosing a Destination** 49

REMEMBER

Climates vary widely throughout a country. Panama City, Panama, is hot and muggy year-round, but Boquete, in the mountains, is more temperate. Rome, Italy offers a Mediterranean climate, while Cortina d'Ampezzo, in the Dolomites, has snowy winters.

Confirming your cost of living

What's your ideal monthly budget? Calculate the average cost of living in your destination(s) of choice by using the resources mentioned in Chapter 3.

If your budget falls above or within the average range that you find, pursue moving to this country with confidence. If your income is less than the average cost of living there, you can still go there, although you may have to adjust your lifestyle.

REMEMBER

People of all income levels exist in every country. You can live anywhere in the world on a wide budget range, although your quality of life will vary. Living on $1,200 per month would put you under the federal poverty level in the U.S. But that same amount would provide for a comfortable, generous lifestyle in Bulgaria, Thailand, or the Philippines.

> ### DIFFERENT COUNTRIES AND CURRENCIES
>
> The currency you earn and spend in affects your cost of living in another country. If you live somewhere that has high inflation, such as Argentina, the purchasing power of local people goes down. In contrast, foreigners who have different currencies, such as dollars, euros, or yen, can benefit.
>
> Look up the currency and exchange rate in the country or countries that you want to move to and examine how that could affect you. When I lived in Australia in 2003, the U.S. dollar was almost two times stronger than the Australian dollar. But in 2011, the Aussie dollar hit a record high against the USD. In 2024, USD $1 was equal to AUD $1.51. It's also important to know what currency your salary is in if you plan to work in for a company abroad.
>
> To find the current exchange rate, you can use Google (www.google.com), currency conversion sites such as Xe (www.xe.com) or Wise (www.wise.com), foreign exchange marketplaces, investing platforms and brokerages, or central bank websites.

Choosing a new culture

A country's culture may influence your decision to move there. *Culture* is defined as the combination of language, beliefs, art, music, foods, laws, religion, politics, and people that make up a society.

Moving to a new country presents an opportunity to share your culture with the people you meet while adopting aspects of theirs. You could feel drawn to the relaxed lifestyle in the Caribbean, the food and wine culture of Paris, or decide to move to the Polish village your grandma is from.

Consider what attracts you to certain cultures more than others and how a different society and customs could impact your daily life:

» **Students:** If you're moving abroad to study, pay special attention to admission requirements, the school system's structure, grades, and the language in which your classes will be taught.

» **Workers:** If you're moving overseas for work, look into business regulations and tax laws. Consider enrolling in cross-cultural training for the workplace, which can help you communicate well with coworkers and understand how the organizational hierarchy works.

» **Digital Nomads:** If you're working remotely abroad, find out about Internet speeds, taxes, and if there's a local nomad community in place.

» **Retirees:** If you're planning to retire abroad or roam for leisure, you may be more interested in social and societal aspects of culture, such as knowing the acceptable length of a *siesta* and how to greet people.

Watching videos, reading books and poetry, and listening to music can give you insight into a country's culture.

Find out how similar or different your culture is to that of your destination country by using The Culture Factor Group's Country Comparison Tool (`www.theculturefactor.com/country-comparison-tool`).

For help adjusting to culture shock, see Chapter 10.

Finding better healthcare

For many people, living in a place with affordable, high-quality healthcare is a priority. Fortunately, you can often gain access to a country's healthcare system by becoming a resident or citizen. When researching visa and residency options in your destination (which you can read more about in the corresponding section below), find out about the private and public healthcare and insurance options available. Chapter 7 provides more information on healthcare and insurance abroad.

Health and wellness also start with prevention, and some countries offer conditions for a healthier lifestyle than others. Take the *blue zones*, for example: pockets of the world where a high concentration of people live to be 100 years old. Nicoya, Costa Rica; Ikarios, Greece; Sardinia, Italy; Loma Linda, California; and Okinawa, Japan all have conditions that support longevity among their citizens. An abundance of fresh, local produce, a terrain that encourages physical exercise, and strong community ties contribute to a long life expectancy.

Before choosing where to move, search online for the healthcare ranking of the countries that you're interested in. Inquire with your embassy, consulate, or residency advisor about access to healthcare. You can also contact local hospitals, doctors, and insurance companies for specific information about your needs.

Healthcare quality and access vary within a country. You typically find more modern hospitals and facilities in cities compared to the countryside and rural areas. When choosing a location, determine how far you'll be from medical care.

Learning a new language

With more than 7,000 languages spoken worldwide, where you live determines how you'll communicate. Consider whether you want to move somewhere that speaks your native tongue, or if you want to challenge yourself to learn a new language.

If you speak English and you want to move to an English-speaking country, you have options (although you may need to adapt to a new accent). You could live in the U.S., U.K., Canada, Ireland, India, New Zealand, Australia, Belize, Uganda, South Africa, or the Caribbean.

If you're from France, you can move to Quebec, Canada, or another country where French is spoken, such as Belgium, Madagascar, Morocco, Algeria, Vanuatu, or the islands of Martinique, Haiti, Réunion, and Corsica.

If you're Spanish, you can opt for a variety of countries in Central or South America, such as Mexico, Colombia, Peru, Bolivia, and Guatemala.

If Portuguese is your native language, you can communicate well in Portugal, Brazil, and Cape Verde.

If you speak Dutch, you could consider living in Belgium, Suriname, or Sint Maarten.

Chapter 10 gives you tips for learning a language fast.

Living your best lifestyle

Moving abroad is an opportunity to choose a new lifestyle. On the beaches of Puerto Vallarta, Mexico, golfing, surfing, and beachfront dining are high on the to-do list. If you live in Hong Kong, shopping, markets, and dim sum may become part of your daily life.

Review your vision from earlier in this chapter about a typical day in your future home country. Will you be awakening to freshly brewed Argentinian maté, or chai tea in Goa, India? Does a day in your life include trekking in Nepal or going for a swim in a tranquil Thai bay? Will you be working from an office in Dubai or teaching English in Japan? I chose to study abroad in Australia while furthering my surfing career. Twenty years later, I spent six months in Manchester, UK, learning music production. If you can dream it, you can do it. It's a matter of choosing a destination that supports your ideal lifestyle. Want to learn Italian? Apply for a one-year study permit in Italy.

TIP

In addition to positive attributes, try to uncover the downsides of the places that you're considering. Buenos Aires is a cosmopolitan city that has a low cost of living and plenty of art, culture, and activities to offer, but it's also known for its gridlock traffic and urban sprawl. When you uncover challenges, look for solutions, such as choosing a walkable neighborhood where you don't have to drive. Or maybe a house in the countryside would better suit you.

Discovering the best location

Location is an important factor in choosing a country to live in. First, consider the broader region and distance from your home country, especially if you plan to travel back for visits. Also determine if the time zone works for your needs, which you can read about in the following section.

Think about where you see yourself living: in a city, in the mountains, on an island or beach, on a houseboat, or somewhere else. Which type of environment will lead you to feel the happiest and most fulfilled?

After you narrow down a country and city location, you can explore the details of what it's like to live there, including the neighborhood and street that you'll call home:

TIP

>> Look up your favorite destinations on Google Maps or Google Earth, and poke around for restaurants, supermarkets, transport stops, amenities, and places of interest.

>> Watch YouTube videos and read blogs about the destinations that interest you.

>> If you have the time and resources, book an exploratory trip to visit a destination in person. (You can find a guide for planning an exploratory trip in Chapter 5 and information on how to find housing abroad in Chapter 6.)

Choosing your time zone

If you expect to work remotely and make international Zoom calls while living abroad, your new time zone is of the utmost importance.

For instance, most of my relocation clients are based in the U.S. and Canada. I could live in the Americas and work fine. However, I enjoy residing five to eight hours ahead of the North American time zones. Having my mornings free from meetings allows me to focus on writing and deep work done during the day. Then, I can take calls and answer e-mails in the afternoon.

You might prefer the opposite, however. Perhaps you like to work with your colleagues early in the morning and focus on personal projects or free time in the afternoon. One online professional I met in Japan worked through the night to keep his company's office hours in California.

Time zones are less of an issue if you're retired, of course. But time differences are something to consider when keeping in touch with friends and family. For tips on staying in touch while overseas, see Chapter 11.

Thinking about community

People make a place. Maybe part the reason you're moving somewhere is to make friends and find community.

When deciding on a destination, do a search online for local clubs and groups that you can join and things that you want to do. Two of my favorite ways to meet people while living abroad are through the expat networking website,

InterNations (www.internations.org) and the social website Meetup (www.meetup.com). Volunteering is a way to give back, feel good, and meet like-minded people. (I talk about more ways to make foreign and local friends and find volunteer options in Chapter 11.)

You can also find ideas for things to do by checking out expat Facebook groups in different destinations or through Facebook Events and events websites such as Eventbrite (www.eventbrite.com).

If living somewhere with a strong expat community is important for you, check out the InterNations Expat Insider survey at www.internations.org/expat-insider. It also gives you an idea of how hard or easy it is to adjust to the community in a new place.

Keeping the lights (and Wi-Fi) on

Whether you're working online or just concerned with the quality of life in your destination, find out how reliable the infrastructure is:

- » **Are power and water outages the norm?** If so, a backup battery, generator, and water tank can provide interim solutions.
- » **How are the roads?** I lived on dirt roads full of potholes in Costa Rica and Nicaragua and often had to cross rivers in a 4-by-4. Sometimes, the roads washed away, or my car engine got flooded.
- » **How fast is the Wi-Fi?** If you work online, you need reliable connectivity.

Check average Internet speeds per country on Speedtest (www.speedtest.net) or inquire with local Internet service providers (ISPs).

For how to cope with infrastructure challenges, see Chapter 9.

Acknowledging a country's political system

Politics may be a taboo topic at the dinner table, but you need to consider it when you choose a country to move to. For example, independent women may want to avoid living in Saudi Arabia, where laws long restricted women from driving and many women still live under official male guardianships.

LGBTQ+ couples may want to choose somewhere that same-sex marriage is legal and they can enjoy equal rights, such as in the Netherlands, Canada, Ireland, Iceland, and Spain.

If you're looking for a country that has a strong social safety net, Norway, Germany, and France are known for their social welfare systems.

Your country's political situation may also prompt you to move abroad. Every time a presidential election occurs in the U.S., interest in moving to Canada spike. According to the U.S. Treasury Department, more than 5,000 people renounced their citizenship in 2023, with political and tax reasons at the forefront.

Whether you're moving away from a political system or ideology, or going towards one that you identify with more, politics can play a critical role in your decision.

Practicing your religion (or not)

Religion (or lack thereof) can act as a driving force in choosing where to live:

- **Christianity:** If you're a devout Catholic, living among cathedrals in Italy or Spain might offer you an intriguing option. For Protestants, the U.S., U.K., and Nordic countries have large Protestant populations.
- **Buddhism:** Countries such as Thailand, Myanmar, Sri Lanka, and the island of Bali offer a welcoming environment for practicing Buddhists.
- **Hinduism:** India, Nepal, Fiji, and Mauritius all include Hinduism as a significant religion.
- **Islam:** If you're Muslim, you may want to move to Turkey, Morocco, Egypt, or the UAE, which are among the 57 Muslim countries in the world.
- **Non-religious:** If you're atheist or agnostic, living in a more secular society, such as Sweden or New Zealand, could suit you.

If you want to live somewhere that has religious diversity, you can find people practicing Islam, Christianity, Judaism, and more in places such as the United States, Canada, Cyprus, Singapore, and Bosnia and Herzegovina. In Istanbul, you can see mosques, churches, and synagogues built in the same area and sometimes next door to each other.

Seeking equality and avoiding racism

Throughout history, people have traversed the world in search of more peace, freedom, and equality. Today is no different. Whether you're an African American seeking to avoid discrimination and police brutality in the U.S., a gay couple from Libya yearning for the right to marry, war refugees fleeing violence, or a single female looking for a safe place to put down roots, changing your country of residence may help you achieve that.

The World Justice Project has an interactive ranking of countries on fundamental rights at www.worldjusticeproject.org/rule-of-law-index.

If you're curious, Denmark scored at the top of the list in 2024, followed by Norway, Finland, and Sweden. China, Egypt, Myanmar, and Iran came in at the bottom.

Staying safe

The idea of safety means different things to different people. A country's crime rate, political and economic instability, and the threat of war, disease, natural disasters, or conflict can affect your experience of living there.

For many citizens of most countries, the idea of traveling to the United States, where it's legal to own guns, is scary. At the same time, U.S. citizens might feel at ease in their own country but nervous about traveling to Mexico or the Middle East.

I spent years living in Costa Rica, which is known as the "Switzerland of Central America" — but that doesn't mean it's safe. It's normal to see armed security guards at malls and banks, bars on windows, and walls topped with broken glass or metal spikes to deter theft.

But in Scandinavian countries such as Sweden, and Denmark, people feel safe enough to leave their babies unattended in strollers outside of shops and leave laptops on tables while they use the facilities in coffee shops.

The Svalbard archipelago in Norway is one of the safest places in the world when it comes to the crime rate. But walking outside can be dangerous because of the high risk of polar bear attacks.

Bali is generally accepted as safe from a security standpoint, but the water quality isn't. Drinking the tap water often results in *Bali belly* (traveler's diarrhea). Dangerous surfing and moped accidents also happen often.

You can find out about the safety in your destination by using the following sources:

>> Check the Global Peace Index, released yearly by the Institute for Economics and Peace (www.economicsandpeace.org/global-peace-index), a ranking of countries on 23 peace indicators, such as the crime rate, organized conflict, political instability, and militarization.

>> Check for current travel, political, weather, and other warnings and advisories with your current country's state department or department of foreign affairs.

>> Research healthcare standards through websites such as the World Health Organization (WHO; www.who.int); International SOS (www.internationalsos.com), a health and security risk management company; or your health insurance provider.

Paying the tax man

Taxes may play a big role in your reasons for moving abroad. Some folks even move for the sole purpose of lowering their tax liabilities. Personal finance is a topic for another book, but it's no secret that changing your tax base can save (or cost) you a lot of money.

Before deciding where to move, find out what your tax liability will be. Some countries have zero income tax, such as the Turks and Caicos, the Cayman Islands, and the UAE. Other countries offer tax incentives for foreigners who move there. Spain's Beckham Law gives new residents a local tax break for the first five years. And in Italy, retirees pay a flat tax of 7 percent on their worldwide income, including pensions and retirement accounts.

Other countries, including Bulgaria, Georgia, Serbia, and Montenegro, have a low, flat income tax of 9 to 10 percent for all residents, both locals and foreigners.

With the emergence of digital nomad visas, countries such as Albania offer an income tax-free period of 12 months upon arrival, while Estonia, Hungary, and Iceland don't tax digital nomads who live there for less than 183 days per year.

Furthermore, many countries have territorial tax systems, which don't tax worldwide income. That means you can potentially pay zero taxes if you live in Panama, for example, but earn income abroad.

Don't take my word for it, though, because I'm not an accountant. Instead, consult a licensed professional in your country of origin or your destination country. The following companies specialize in international tax matters:

>> **Greenback Expat Tax Services** (www.greenbacktaxservices.com): Tax prep company for Americans abroad.

>> **Nomad Capitalist** (www.nomadcapitalist.com): A company that helps people legally reduce taxes and acquire residency or citizenship in various countries.

>> **Taxes for Expats** (www.taxesforexpats.com): A women-owned tax service for U.S. citizens abroad.

» **Taxhackers.io:** A global consulting service that offers to help non-U.S. digital nomads worldwide become tax-free.

For more about paying taxes at home and abroad, see Chapter 13.

Visa and Residency Options

One of the most important considerations in choosing a destination is whether you can legally live there. Make sure you qualify for a visa, residency permit, or citizenship before making plans to move somewhere.

Most countries offer at least one type of visa or residency permit in the following categories:

Business visa

One of the shortest types of visas, this one gives you permission to enter a country for short-term business purposes, such as attending a conference, meeting, or event. When I went on a business trip to Ireland, I was given permission to stay for 11 days, compared to the 90-day stay you can receive as a tourist.

Digital nomad visa

Designed for remote workers, freelancers, and online entrepreneurs, these visas let you live and work online in a country from six months up to five years. Nearly 70 countries launched or announced plans for a digital nomad visa between 2020 and 2023, so check whether the place you want to move to offers one. An easy way to find out is to search online for "[country name] + digital nomad visa."

For a database of countries offering digital nomad visas, check out CitizenRemote.com.

Education or student visa

This gives you — usually for a period of 6 to 12 months, but in some cases for consecutive years. As a bonus, some countries offer the potential to transition to a longer-term visa or residency option when you graduate.

CHAPTER 4 **Choosing a Destination** 59

Australia's Temporary Graduate visa gives you up to two additional years to enjoy the land down under after finishing school, and Singapore gives new grads up to 90 days to find a job under its short-term visit pass. You can also apply for a work permit after graduation, such as Canada's post-graduation work permit (PGWP) or South Korea's E-1 visa.

Entrepreneur or startup visa

If you want to start a local business in a foreign country, consider apply for a small business or startup visa. Requirements may include presenting a business plan, hiring employees, and demonstrating how your company will contribute to the local economy. Examples include the Dutch Startup Visa, the French Tech Visa, and the UK Innovator Founder Visa.

Retirement or non-lucrative visa

Designed for retirees or people who have passive income streams. A benefit of retirement visas is that the minimum income threshold to qualify for one can be quite low, such as $600 to $750 per month in Nicaragua or $1,000 per month in Peru.

Some retiree visas are long-term, whereas others you have to renew, usually on an annual basis. The Philippines, Panama, Belize, and Uruguay are known for having permanent retiree visas. Portugal, Mexico, Italy, and Indonesia offer renewable visas, which can become eligible for permanent residency after five years.

WARNING

Some countries, such as Italy and Malta, prohibit working while on this type of visa, while other countries (such as Colombia and Ecuador) are more lenient. If you want to work or have a side hustle in retirement, make sure to check if that's allowed under the visa that you want.

Tourist visa

Allows you to visit a country for fun or leisure. Many tourist visas let you stay in a country for 30 to 90 days, although some allow for a tourist visa to last 180 to 365 days. Citizens from a range of countries can receive an authorization to visit Canada or the U.K. for up to 180 days per calendar year. Georgia and Albania are even more flexible, allowing citizens of some countries to stay there visa-free for up to one year.

Residence permit

Gives you legal resident status in a country, either temporarily or permanently; it allows you to live, work, or study there.

You can qualify for residency in many ways, including through some of the other visas on this list. After getting a study visa, you could get a job and qualify for a work permit before ultimately applying for permanent residency or citizenship. In other cases, you can acquire a residence permit through an investment in real estate, a business, or a golden visa (discussed in the following section).

A retirement visa may also offer a path to permanent residency. Spain's non-lucrative visa grants qualified applicants a residence permit that's renewable every two years. Portugal's D-7 visa gives you two years to live in the country with an option to extend for three more years, and the UAE's golden visa offers recipients a permit to stay for five to ten years.

Work permit

If you're seeking full-time employment abroad, a work permit could be your path to living overseas. Work permits may be valid for up to five years. Consider getting a work permit if you want to stay in a country long-term and qualify for healthcare, paid leave, and other workplace benefits. A downside to work permits is that, as a foreigner, you may find them hard to get because countries want to protect local jobs. You may need to be a highly skilled worker or have a company sponsor you to qualify. In most cases, you must receive a job offer before applying for a work permit.

Golden Visa or Second Passport

A *golden visa* gives you a way to get residency or citizenship in a country through an investment. Typical investment types include real estate, opening a business, or purchasing stocks, government bonds, or other approved assets.

The allure of having a golden visa is that it's fast. The processing time for many golden visas can be from 60 days to 6 months.

Another benefit of golden visas is the opportunity to get an additional passport. If you're from a country that has a *weak* passport (meaning you can't travel to many countries visa-free), getting a second passport can really help you increase your freedom and mobility. Turkish-born Derin Emre from the YouTube channel

Yes Theory (www.youtube.com/@YesTheory) became a dual citizen of Turkey and the island nation of St. Kitts and Nevis in 2021. His Turkish passport gave him access to 114 countries visa-free as of 2025, while his second passport gave him access to 155 countries.

WARNING

Find out how strong your passport is by searching for it on the Henley Passport Index (www.henleyglobal.com/passport-index/ranking).

The cost of a golden visa ranges from 250,000 euros ($262,000) for real estate in Greece to 3 to 10 million euros ($3.1-10.5M) in Austria through a government-approved investment.

If you have a relative from a foreign country, you may qualify for citizenship by descent. Ireland, Italy, Poland, Romania, the U.K., and more countries offer the option to gain citizenship through ancestral ties, after which you can live in that country and apply for a passport.

Getting citizenship by descent in the European Union (EU) is particularly valuable because it would allow you to live and work in any other EU or European Economic Area (EEA) country.

To establish your lineage, documents to collect typically include:

» Birth certificates for yourself and your ancestor(s) in the line of descent, potentially including a parent, grandparent, or great-grandparent

» Death certificates for any deceased ancestors in the line of descent

» Marriage certificates for yourself and ancestor(s)

» Passports for yourself and living ancestors

» Citizenship or naturalization records of your ancestor who naturalized

» Your police reports or criminal record

» A health evaluation of yourself provided by a qualified physician

» Proof of your current address

You may also need to pass a language test and take an oath of loyalty to the country's government to get citizenship in that country.

Making Your Country Selection

When you choose a destination, you don't get a parade or marching band to celebrate, but you can smile knowing that you're one step closer to achieving your goal of moving abroad.

Your chosen place should make sense based on the elements you considered in this chapter — a place you can afford, where you can qualify for a visa, and that offers the culture, lifestyle, and other factors you seek. The thought of moving there should excite you while being practical. You should also *feel* good about it. Before making your final decision, check in with your intuition. Is this a place you've always been curious about, intrigued by, or inspired by? Does the idea of living there resonate with you?

There's no right or wrong answer when it comes to moving abroad. Wherever you choose to go, you'll have a life-changing experience. Even if you move somewhere for a few months or years and change your mind, you can learn a lot about yourself in the process.

Where do you want move? Write down your top three choices below:

1._____

2._____

3._____

You can list pros and cons, research destinations until you're blue in the face, and dutifully crunch the numbers on your cost of living. But sometimes, deciding where to live abroad is emotional rather than logical. You *can* choose somewhere to live that doesn't "make sense" on paper, costs more than you'd prefer, or doesn't have *everything* you're looking for. If you feel drawn to a particular place, go there! And see what life has in store for you.

Planning an Exploratory Trip

If you struggle to decide between two or more destinations, a pre-move scouting trip can help you choose where to go.

An exploratory trip allows you to feel a physical and emotional connection to a place. You get to experience the local lifestyle in-person, tour towns and neighborhoods, and talk with people in the community.

Consider the following elements during your fact-finding mission:

1. **Define your goals.** What do you want to accomplish and find out during your trip? Perhaps you want to look at real estate options, visit schools for your children, or set up meetings with residency or relocation advisors.

2. **Set your timeline.** How long can you afford to stay? A trip length of one to four weeks is ideal, but shorter trips of a few days can also be valuable.

3. **Plan your itinerary.** Determine which locations to visit and how long to spend in each place. Decide whether to rent a car, hire a driver, or use public transportation. Reserve your flights and accommodations.

4. **Experience the surroundings.** Live a day in your future life! Walk around, ride the bus or metro, go grocery shopping, run errands, and visit banks, pharmacies, and doctors' offices. Hang out in cafés, parks, and restaurants to get a sense of the vibe around town.

5. **Talk to the locals.** Connect with local citizens and residents from other countries at co-working spaces, events, or meetups. Ask questions that you have about living there. See Chapter 10 for ways to meet people abroad.

After you return from your trip, reflect on your experience. Write down your impressions: What did you love about the places you visited? What didn't you like? Were there any dealbreakers? Which questions remain? Are you ready to take the next step in your relocation plan?

REMEMBER

An exploratory trip isn't a vacation — it's a structured visit to help you get answers to your questions, preview housing options, set up key meetings, and handle logistics in advance of your move.

Choosing More Than One Place

If you dream of living overseas but can't decide on one place, you could choose more than one. Some expats employ a slow travel strategy, where they pass through multiple countries per year as perpetual tourists. Other expats choose to live one country for a year or so, with a long-stay visa or working holiday visa, then move to another place.

Some digital nomads and jet setters travel long-term on their passports using a rotating 6/6, 6/3/3, or 3/3/3/3 *strategy*. This approach involves spending three to six months in two to four places per year. Although, it's possible to change countries monthly or more often.

If you spend your time in multiple countries, you get to experience a lot of variety in climate, culture, and community throughout the year. Like a snowbird, you can choose to live an endless summer, traipsing from one tropical place to another. Or you can mix things up, spending part of the year in Europe, part of the year in Africa, and part of the year in Southeast Asia. By returning to the same places time and again, you experience the following benefits:

» Establish a familiarity with the environment, culture, people, and language.

» You don't need to find housing if you return to the same property each time.

» Know your way around, so you experience less culture shock each time you return.

A downside to this lifestyle is that renting short-term or owning, and maintaining multiple properties can be expensive. However, you can consider renting out a property when you're not there.

While I was on Nomad Cruise 12, a floating conference from Spain to Brazil in December 2023, I met a German couple who earn a livable income from managing vacation rentals. They identify properties that they can rent out for a good price, negotiate long-term leases with the owners, and get permission to sublease them. This technique allows them to stay in multiple countries while providing a livable, remote income.

WARNING

Moving around can make it hard to maintain close friendships. When you live somewhere long-term, you can focus on integrating with a society. But if you leave countries after a few weeks or months, you may find it more of a challenge to adapt to the culture and community in each place.

Changing locations can also affect your visa or residency status. Most nations require you to reside in a country for a minimum number of days per year to maintain your residency. Roaming around for a few months at a time is akin to *perpetual tourism*, where you stay in countries on temporary tourist visas, but you don't officially live anywhere.

CHAPTER 4 **Choosing a Destination** 65

TIP

You can choose more than one country to live in. You can hold dual citizenship in two different countries while maintaining residency status in another. For example, you can be an Italian and U.S. citizen who has a work permit in Ireland. Or you can be a dual citizen of Canada and New Zealand who lives in Australia and stays in Malaysia part-time with a My Second Home visa, which is valid for 5 to 20 years.

TIP

For a list of popular visa and residency programs around the world, download the bonus content for this book at www.travelingwithkristin.com/moving-abroad.

HOW EXPATS CHOSE THEIR DESTINATIONS

My YouTube subscribers shared with me how they decided on a country to move to:

- **Dave:** My wife and I traveled the world for four years and fell in love with Portugal along the way after visiting several times and hiking the north and southern coasts.

- **Claudia:** What led us to choose Canada were the economy (estimated difficulty to get a job), financial requirements to obtain a visa, adventure, language (English), and cost of living, which was much lower than our home of California at the time.

- **Mohammed:** The key factors that influenced my choice of destination were tax efficiency, business opportunities, and lifestyle. I was looking for countries with favorable tax policies for entrepreneurs and expats and regions with a growing market for my services. The final decision often came down to balancing personal goals with business needs. I researched extensively, consulted with local legal and tax professionals, and sometimes visited the countries beforehand to get a feel for the environment.

- **Joe:** After years of traveling to Costa Rica on business, I made the decision to get residency, buy a property, and live outside of the U.S. while still being close to family. Identify the location, area, and lifestyle you think can meet your objectives. Identify your top 7-10 criteria and stick to them. Do your due diligence, and don't compromise.

2
Mastering Your Move — Relocation Logistics

IN THIS PART . . .

Find out about visa and residency options.

Draft your moving-abroad plan.

Find proper housing and insurance.

Prepare to move with kids, pets, or stuff.

Pack for departure.

IN THIS CHAPTER

» Arranging your banking, finances, and paperwork

» Hiring relocation support or going the DIY route

» Managing logistics for your move

» Bringing your kids or furry friends with you

Chapter **5**

Planning Your Relocation Logistics

Moving abroad has many moving parts, from knowing what to pack to finding the perfect place to call home. The less glamorous side of your relocation plan involves collecting cash, getting your paperwork in order, and beginning to sort your stuff.

In this chapter, I share the various logistics to consider in planning your relocation and options forsupport during this process. I also provide guidance on what to think about when tackling money matters, and considerations for moving with pets and kids.

Preparing Your Banking and Finances for Living Internationally

To manage your finances for an international move, organize everything at home before you go, including calculating your budget, which Chapter 3 helps you with. You should also decide where to keep your money and ensure that all of your accounts are accessible from abroad. Taking these steps now can simplify your financial life and stay tax compliant.

After you handle the essentials at home, you can focus on setting up the financial systems that you'll need in your new destination, such as opening a local bank account or using financial apps to manage your money. Where you earn your income also determines your tax obligations, which you can find more about in the section, "Talking About Taxes" in this chapter.

Following a financial prep checklist

The checklist in this section highlights the essential steps to take care of your finances before your move, from updating your accounts to setting up tools for managing money overseas. Completing these tasks before you leave can help you stay organized, avoid financial disruptions, and maintain access to your funds, no matter where you go.

Use the following guide to get started:

TIP

- ❑ Assess whether to keep your home country bank account or change banks. Your bank should offer international online banking access, the ability to send wire transfers remotely, and low or no foreign transaction fees on your associated credit or debit card. Certain small banks and credit unions may not offer the features you need, while large banks may charge high fees.

- ❑ Add beneficiaries to your domestic and international accounts if a beneficiary designation is available.

- ❑ Cancel services and subscriptions that you no longer need. Switch all bills and statements to electronic delivery.

- ❑ Check with your accountant about any additional tax reporting requirements related to your move overseas. Find out what your local tax liability will be abroad, how to file, and whether the country you're moving to has any tax treaties with your home country. See the section "Talking About Taxes" in this chapter for further reference.

- ❑ If you're a retiree, contact your retirement or pension plan providers to ensure that you won't have any interruption in payments while you're abroad. For example, ask whether you can receive your Social Security benefits to a foreign account.

- ❑ Review your will and estate plan. Consult with a local attorney to determine if your will is recognized abroad or if you should draft a second one — especially if you plan to open a bank account or purchase property in a foreign country.

- ❏ Renew any expiring debit and credit cards. See the section "Getting a travel credit card" below.
- ❏ Save up money for your move — anywhere from 3 to 12 months of living expenses. See Chapter 3 for budgeting resources.
- ❏ Update your address and contact info with banks and institutions.

Some domestic banks and financial institutions in your home country may close your account if you move abroad permanently. Contact each one to find out about their policies and maintaining a mailing address.

- ❏ Upload copies of important documents (such as your passport, birth certificate, marriage certificate, Social Security card, and estate planning documents) to a secure cloud storage account.

To log into some accounts, you may need two-factor authentication (2FA) or the ability to receive a text message. Before leaving home, ensure that your financial institutions have your up-to-date contact information and that you have authentication apps downloaded to your phone. If you receive codes by text message, update your contact numbers accordingly. See Chapters 7 and 8 for how to stay connected while abroad.

Sending, spending, and receiving money with finance apps

When I first moved abroad in the early 2000s, smartphones didn't yet exist and online banking was rudimentary. I would open bank accounts in many countries I traveled to so I could transact locally. But with today's technology, you can access your money almost anywhere through websites, online wallets, and apps, which reduce the need to open an account at a brick-and-mortar bank abroad.

If you open an account with such finance apps, you can often save money compared to traditional banks, which are known to charge high wire fees and markups on foreign exchange rates (see Figure 5-1).

You can find the following finance apps in this list in your phone's app store or through the companies' websites. By using these apps, you can transfer money across borders, open accounts in multiple currencies, and connect with your home country account — all without entering a bank:

Each money-transfer platform offers the capability to link a bank account, credit card, or debit card to the app. They also offer personal and business account options, although features and availability can vary by country.

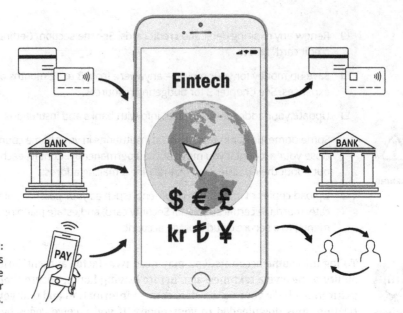

FIGURE 5-1:
How money flows through these money-transfer apps.

- » **Cash App** (www.cash.app): Available in the U.S. and U.K., this finance app allows you to save, send, and receive money, in addition to investing in stocks and Bitcoin. It offers a free debit card and a Cash App Taxes feature to help users file federal and state tax returns.

- » **PayPal** (www.paypal.com): A global platform that you can use to send and receive money and make payments and purchases. PayPal operates in website and app form.

- » **Revolut** (www.revolut.com): An all-in-one finance app available in more than 160 countries that allows users to hold and exchange money in 25-plus currencies. Revolut also offers a debit card to customers in some countries, and savings and investment options.

- » **Skrill** (www.skrill.com): An international digital wallet that allows users to link multiple bank accounts, hold funds in various currencies, and send money worldwide. Skrill also offers a debit card to users from certain countries and supports cryptocurrency transactions.

- » **Wise** (www.wise.com): An international money account and app that offers high-speed, low-fee transfers in 40-plus currencies. More than half of the money transfers on Wise are delivered in less than 20 seconds. Residents of

Australia, Brazil, Canada, the European Economic Area (EEA), Japan, New Zealand, Singapore, Switzerland, the U.K., and certain European microstates and UK territories can receive a Wise debit card for use at ATMs or with Apple Pay and Google Wallet. As of 2025, Wise cards were temporarily unavailable to customers in Malaysia, Philippines, and the U.S.

Find online banks in your area by searching online for "digital bank *country*," "online bank *country*," or "multicurrency account *country*." Examples include Bunq (www.bunq.com) in the Netherlands, Monese (www.monese.com) in the U.K., N26 (www.n26.com) in Germany, Nubank (www.nubank.com.br) in Brazil, and TymeBank (www.tymebank.co.za) in South Africa.

The requirements to open an online account with a money-transfer app or platform include the following:

» E-mail address.

» I.D. verification: Some online banks and financial technology (fintech) apps allow foreign residents who have passports to use them, while others require clients to provide a local ID or proof of permanent residency status.

» Password and security questions.

» Phone verification: Some banks and money apps allow you to register international phone numbers, while others may require a local number.

» Proof of address: Often in the form of a lease agreement or utility bill.

» Tax ID or business registration number: May be needed for personal or business accounts with online banks abroad. For example, you need a European identity document or Dutch BSN (citizen service number) to open an account with Bunq, an online banking app in the Netherlands. For other financial providers, a foreign passport may suffice.

Opening a bank account in your new home country

The best way to find out if you can open a bank account in a foreign country is to visit the bank in person. In my travels, my ability to open an account often depended on the bank branch and the executives who happened to be working that day. Requirements may vary between branches of the same bank. However, it's always a good idea to contact the bank first and ask for a list of requirements for foreign residents.

CHAPTER 5 **Planning Your Relocation Logistics** 73

TIP Relocation consultants (which I talk about in the section "Selecting a Relocation Expert," earlier in this chapter) can also often help you open a bank account or provide a list of requirements.

Standard requirements to open a bank account abroad include one or more of the following:

» **Proof of address:** A rental agreement, house deed, or utility bill in your name. Some banks require a water or electricity bill, while others accept a cable or Internet bill.

» **Proof of identity:** A valid passport or local ID. Some banks require a local visa, residency permit, or tax ID number.

» **Proof of income:** Some banks request financial statements, paycheck stubs, or a notarized letter from an accountant verifying your income and its source.

» **Reference letter:** Some banks require a reference letter from one or more customers of the same bank.

WARNING Deposits in foreign bank accounts may not be government-insured. Check with a local attorney, accountant, banker, or financial advisor to verify and read the fine print of all banking paperwork. Also inquire about monthly account fees.

In addition to opening an account with a local bank, you can consider opening an account with an international bank with global account options:

» **Barclays** (http://international.barclays.com): This UK bank provides international banking services catering to UK expats and non-UK residents in 35 qualifying countries. Clients who have £100,000 (or currency equivalent, USD $129,300) can qualify. A personal relationship manager is available to clients who have at least £250,000 ($323,400).

» **Charles Schwab** (www.schwab.com): A popular bank for U.S. customers who travel abroad often. The company reimburses ATM fees for certain account types and doesn't charge foreign transaction fees.

» **BNP Paribas** (www.group.bnpparibas): This French bank is the largest bank in Europe. It has a non-resident service designed especially for expatriates, including entrepreneurs, corporate employees, and managers who want to invest in France.

» **Citi** (www.citi.com): Offers Global Executive banking account packages for U.S. citizens to receive their pay abroad and manage accounts digitally.

» **HSBC** (www.hsbc.com): An international bank that offers expat-centric accounts in multiple currencies, such as U.S. dollars (USD), British pounds (GBP), and euros (EUR). With at least $100,000 in deposits or investments, you can qualify for a Premier account, which offers various privileges, including the ability to open an account overseas before you move abroad.

U.S. citizens abroad can have a particularly tough time opening international accounts. Banks that have U.S. customers must comply with extra paperwork due to the U.S. federal government's Foreign Account Tax Compliance Act (FATCA), which requires foreign financial institutions and other entities to report assets held by U.S. citizens.

Getting a travel credit card

Changing or upgrading your credit card before you move abroad allows you to earn rewards on travel and other expenses. Major card providers such as Visa, MasterCard, and American Express are accepted worldwide and can send you a replacement card when needed. On the downside, credit cards come with interest rates, while debit cards don't. To get the maximum value from your credit card benefits while avoiding interest, spend what you can afford and pay off your balance monthly.

When deciding which credit card to apply for, choose one that has a fee that you can afford (or no fee) and that doesn't have foreign transaction fees.

Popular travel cards include:

» **Airline cards:** Most global airlines offer credit cards, which can come with perks such as free or discounted checked baggage, priority boarding, seat selection, airport lounge access, and the ability to earn miles when you spend money. Most cards come with different levels, benefits, and annual fees, from less than $99 to $500-plus per year. Choose the one that fits your budget and needs.

» **Bank travel cards:** Many banks offer branded credit cards, such as the Bank of America Travel Rewards Card (U.S.) and the Scotiabank Passport Visa Infinite Card (Canada). If you choose a travel credit card through your bank, you can see your bank account and card balances in the same website. You may also qualify for special offers as an existing customer.

Online banks and financial apps (which I talk about in the section "Sending, spending, and receiving money with finance apps," earlier in this chapter) offer debit cards that have no foreign transaction fees and some travel benefits, such as travel insurance and premium lounge access.

CHAPTER 5 **Planning Your Relocation Logistics** 75

» **Capital One Venture cards:** Capital One (www.capitalone.com) has three tiers to its Venture cards (VentureOne, Venture, and Venture X), with annual fees ranging from $0 to $395. You can earn Capital One Miles on most purchases. If you're a frequent traveler, consider the Venture X Rewards card, which comes with a complimentary Priority Pass membership, Global Entry and TSA PreCheck application fee credit, and $300 annual travel credit.

» **Chase Sapphire cards:** Chase Bank (www.chase.com) has two tiers of travel rewards cards — the Sapphire Preferred and Sapphire Reserve cards. The Preferred card costs $95 per year with a 25 percent redemption bonus on travel booked through the site. The Reserve card costs $550 annually with a 50 percent travel redemption bonus. Chase cardholders earn Ultimate Rewards points, which can be transferred to participating airline and hotel partners.

Most cards offer first-time cardholders a welcome bonus in points or miles. I've seen bonuses of 20,000 to 175,000 points or miles when the accountholder hits the minimum spend requirement. Check with websites such as The Points Guy (www.thepointsguy.com) and Daily Drop (www.dailydrop.com) for descriptions of new card offers.

Talking About Taxes

Before moving abroad, talk with your tax and financial advisor about how leaving the country will affect your tax liabilities and investments (if at all). For instance, U.S. citizens must file an annual tax return, regardless of where they live in the world, due to the country's citizenship-based taxation policy. You have more options if you're from a country with a residency-based tax system that allows you to change your tax domicile based on where you live (not where you're from).

When it comes to taxes and finances, get multiple opinions before making any adjustments. Few domestic accountants and CPAs understand the nuances of an international lifestyle. Your current bookkeeper may not know about reporting requirements and savings, such as the Foreign Bank Account Report (FBAR) and Foreign Earned Income Exclusion (FEIE) for U.S. citizens. Whatever country you're a citizen of, get familiar with international tax credits, write-offs, and tax treaties.

To cover your bases, consult with local professionals in both your home and destination countries, as well as someone who specializes in international taxes. Depending on your visa or residency permit, your new country of residence could tax your income at a higher, lower, or similar rate as your home country does.

You can find a tax advisor by asking a legal, real estate, or relocation professional for a referral, contacting your country's embassy or consulate in your destination, inquiring in expat Facebook groups and forums, or searching online for an "expat tax advisor" in your destination country.

Ensure that the person or company you hire to help with your taxes and finances is legitimate and holds appropriate licensing and certifications according to local laws.

For more information about paying taxes abroad, see Chapter 13.

Organizing Your Paperwork

When planning to move long-term, gather any paperwork that you might need while you're abroad. Organize your digital files in folders on your computer, hard drive, or cloud storage. Create a physical file of paper documents and arrange them by category or account.

Ensure important documents, medications, valuables, and anything you can't lose are in your carry-on rather than checked bags when you fly.

Documents to consider bringing with you or saving to your file include:

» **Your passport:** You need a passport to travel internationally. Apply for a passport if you don't have one, or ensure your passport is up to date if you do. Renew your passport if necessary. For leisure travel, confirm that your passport will remain valid for at least 6 to 12 months past your departure date. In the case of moving abroad long-term, you might want to have a few years' cushion before it expires. However, don't stress; you can renew your passport by mail or at an embassy abroad, if needed.

» **Prescriptions:** Bring a list of medications to refill abroad and a prescription or doctor's note if you're traveling with multiple months of supplies.

» **Travel and health insurance info:** Never travel without emergency travel medical insurance or an international healthcare policy. Find more about insurance options in Chapter 7.

» **Visa and residency paperwork:** Some countries issue visas electronically, while others may stamp your passport or give you another form of travel authorization. Ensure that you have the proper permission to travel to your destination and bring supporting documents with you.

If you're applying for a visa or residency permit, you may also need:

- **Birth certificate:** Prepare a notarized, apostilled, or certified copy (as needed for your visa or residency category). I talk about finding out what documents you need in Chapter 4.

- **Marriage or divorce certificates:** Collect if applicable to your family situation and visa category. Check with your residency advisor to see if you should submit documents for your application in the months before your departure or after arrival.

- **Proof of income:** Prepare bank or credit card statements in case you need proof of income to rent a property or to qualify for a digital nomad visa or remote work permit.

- **School or employment records:** If you're moving abroad through a work or study permit, you may need to provide transcripts or professional certifications, as well as immunization records in certain scenarios.

TIP

Check with your embassy, government travel authority, or residency attorney to find out which original papers you need to bring. Note which papers you need to translate or certify, and what you can make copies of.

You may also want to keep some records with a trusted party in your home country, such as a lawyer or family member, or in a safe deposit box:

- **Business documentation:** If you own a business entity you plan to operate while abroad or if you work as a sole proprietor, include documents such as the business registration, operating agreements, and articles of incorporation for your company. If you plan to apply for a freelancer, digital nomad, or remote work visa, you may need to provide financial statements, client contracts, and invoices.

- **Financial information:** Financial statements, wills, and trust documents.

- **Power of Attorney (POA):** Assigning a POA to a trusted party allows them to handle matters on your behalf while you're abroad. With technology, you can accomplish many tasks remotely online, such as filing taxes and e-signing documents. But a POA can be useful for any in-person matters, such as representing you in legal matters, managing financial accounts, or carrying out real estate transactions. See Chapter 13 for information about end-of-life planning while out of your home country.

- **Tax records:** Notify your state and national tax authorities and retirement or pension providers if you change your address or move countries, so that you continue to receive important notices. Maintain copies of 3 years of tax returns for your records.

TIP If you're from the United States, explore changing your residency to a tax-friendly state before you move abroad, such as Florida, Nevada, or Texas.

Deciding What to Do with Your Stuff

For some people, moving abroad is about embracing minimalism, while other folks feel happier bringing their belongings with them. However you feel about it, you'll undoubtedly have some things to part with before going overseas.

If you rent a furnished apartment, it comes equipped with furniture, linens, dinnerware, and more, which means you don't have to bring yours with you. If you rent or buy an unfurnished property, you can find a local version of almost anything abroad. (See Chapter 6 for options to find housing abroad.)

You have four choices when it comes to organizing your stuff:

» **Sell or donate it.** Sell anything valuable, including furniture, electronics, and art. Check what similar items are selling for on sites such as Facebook Marketplace (www.facebook.com/marketplace), OfferUp (www.offerup.com), or your local classifieds site. Donate items in good condition that might not earn big bucks, such as books, clothing, and home goods. Contact local churches, charities, and Goodwill for donation options. Said Subharup, who moved to Switzerland: "Before I moved abroad, I sold or gave away all my possessions. It gave me a deep sense of peace and freedom to not own more than the necessities."

TIP Organize a garage or yard sale to attract buyers for your items.

» **Throw it away or recycle it.** Discard anything not worth selling or storing; for example, papers, toiletries, and those mysterious cables that you've collected over the years. Recycle anything that you can.

Companies such as TerraCycle (www.terracycle.com) help you responsibly discard toothbrushes, coffee capsules, batteries, and more. Patagonia's Worn Wear program (http://wornwear.patagonia.com) helps reduce waste by repairing, recycling, or reselling old clothing. Furniture retailer IKEA (www.ikea.com) buys back gently used furniture in participating locations.

» **Store it.** Consider storing any items that you don't want to part with, such as books, photographs, art, and family heirlooms. You can ask a trusted friend or family member to keep your stuff, or you can rent a storage unit while you're away.

To help you decide what to leave behind, compare the cost of storing an item with its current value and the cost of repurchasing it later.

» **Bring it with you.** Bring anything that you anticipate using in your new home abroad, such as clothes, medications, passport, wallet, important documents, and something that reminds you of home. See Chapter 7 for packing guidance. Check baggage fees and requirements with your travel provider before packing your bags.

Companies such as Luggage Forward (www.luggageforward.com) can ship baggage to your destination.

Shipping a palette or container of items can make sense if you're purchasing a home abroad or renting an unfurnished property. Consider shipping some items if your residency category comes with an import tax credit. Find out more about shipping in Chapter 7.

To help you decide whether to discard an item, ask yourself: Have I used this in the last year? Do I need this where I'm going? In the words of Marie Kondo, author of *The Life-Changing Magic of Tidying Up*, does this item spark joy? If you answer "No" to one (or more) of those questions about a particular item, it's probably time to part with it. Said Dave, who moved to Portugal, "We waited a long time to send our items in storage from the U.S. When they arrived, we ended up keeping less than half of the items. I wish we had sent the items sooner and not sent so much 'stuff.'"

You can do several things with cars that you own or lease before your move.

Selling your car (or not)

If you own a car, you can sell it to a dealership or a private party. You can also sell your car online through websites such as Autotrader (www.autotrader.com), CarMax (www.carmax.com), AutoNation (www.autonation.com), and Cars.com.

If you don't want to sell your car, you can rent it to others by using apps such as Turo (www.turo.com) or HyreCar (www.hyrecar.com).

Dealing with a car lease

If you lease your car, you can get out of your lease. List the car on sites such as LeaseTrader (www.leasetrader.com) or Swapalease (www.swapalease.com).

You can also donate cars to charitable groups such as Kars4Kids (www.kars4kids.org), where they arrange for a tow truck to collect the vehicle in exchange for a gift receipt that you can use as a potential deduction on your taxes.

Considering storage

As a last resort, you can store your vehicle. But vehicle storage leads to deterioration, loss of value, and additional storage fees for something you don't use. (If you're interested in buying a car abroad, see Chapter 9.)

Moving with Kids

Moving abroad can provide an enriching experience for you and your children. You get to bond as a family while immersing yourselves in a new country, language, and culture together. But moving with kids also adds a layer of complexity to your relocation planning, especially if you want to immigrate to a country long-term or enroll your children in school there.

If you intend to get a visa or residency permit, apply under the correct family category. Check with your residency attorney, relocation consultant, or destination country's consulate or immigration department about required documents. Birth certificates, health records, or school transcripts may be required to enroll as a local student or in a study abroad program.

REMEMBER

Involve your children in the decision to move abroad. Get their input on locations, encourage their excitement, and address their questions. Also, pay attention to their fears. They may be concerned about leaving their school, making new friends, communicating in a new language, and adapting to a new environment. Be transparent about how long you plan to stay in your new country and if or when they can expect to return home.

Finding new schools

Moving abroad presents exciting new educational opportunities for children, although changing schools can be challenging at any age. Discuss different education options with your children, including g public or private schools, international schools, and alternative methods of education, such as Waldorf schools, homeschooling, or world schooling.

Waldorf schools focus on helping children develop their imagination, creativity, and intellectual, spiritual, and emotional development. *World schooling* is a type homeschooling that you can do while traveling, living abroad, or working with a community of other world-schoolers. Look for a world-schooling hub by searching online for collectives, Facebook groups, and online learning portals.

Before moving abroad, investigate the laws and education requirements in the country you're moving to. Homeschooling and alternative education methods are illegal or restricted in many countries.

You can find out about schooling options by searching online, inquiring with a local relocation company, or contacting your embassy or the Ministry of Education website for your destination. When you uncover places of interest, contact schools directly to find out about the academic calendar, admission requirements, and tuition. You can read more about school and enrollment options in Chapter 9.

International expat websites and forums, such as Expatica (www.expatica.com), InterNations (www.internations.com), and GoAbroad.com, as well as Facebook groups, provide information on school options.

Keeping them healthy and safe

Put safety at the forefront of your move by choosing a safe destination, something Chapter 4 can help you with. Choose a home near parks and recreation areas and that has good public transit access. Think about how your child will commute to school: by walking, riding the bus, going with a private driver, or traveling on public transport. After growing up in Florida, where owning a car is the norm, I was surprised to see young children commuting to school unattended on metros throughout Europe.

Before departing, make sure your kids' vaccinations are up to date. You can find out about required vaccines through the health department or foreign affairs ministry in your home and destination countries. Prepare copies of medical records, find a doctor or pediatrician in your destination, and inquire about the availability of prescription medicines.

Choose a local or international health insurance plan that fits your family's needs. Find out more about insurance in Chapter 7.

Adapting to life in a different country

Like pets, children thrive on stability and routines. Upon arrival at your destination, make your new house a home by adding furniture, pillows, toys, and books that they like.

Co-create a new daily routine together, including bedtime and mealtimes. Include enough space in their schedule for extracurricular activities, sightseeing, friends, and downtime. Go for walks in your neighborhood, noting important landmarks and public transit stops to help your children feel comfortable in their surroundings and navigate with confidence as they grow older.

Consider enrolling your child in language and cultural adaptation classes to help them communicate better and understand the world around them. Ask whether they want to join a sports team or find a new hobby that might be unique to your new country. At home, watch videos and read books about your adopted country and discuss differences with your home culture as a family.

REMEMBER

A bit of homesickness is expected. But if your child is struggling to adjust to your new surroundings, consider hiring a child or expat therapist for help. You can easily lose touch with people when you move abroad. Help your kids stay in touch with friends and relatives through texts, phone calls, and video calls.

Moving with Pets

If you own a pet, it's natural to want to bring them abroad with you. Regulations for traveling with pets vary by transportation method and provider, so check with your bus, train, boat, or plane operator before bringing your furry friends on board. Fortunately, most countries allow pets that have proper paperwork, although exotic species, such as reptiles and monkeys, may be banned or strictly regulated. Other countries, such as Australia, New Zealand, and Japan, have mandatory quarantine periods for any live animals brought from other countries.

More accessible places to move for vaccinated pets, if you have the proper paperwork, include Canada, Mexico, South Korea, and the European Union.

Standard documents required when traveling with a pet include:

» **A recent veterinary health certificate:** A document issued by a licensed veterinarian that your pet is fit to travel. Ensure that you solicit this document within the right timeframe for your trip — usually within 10 to 30 days before departure.

» **Microchip and identification cards:** Many countries require pets to be implanted with an International Organization for Standardization (ISO)-compliant microchip. Include your pet's microchip number on all required forms and documents.

CHAPTER 5 **Planning Your Relocation Logistics** 83

>> **Proof of vaccinations, such as rabies:** Vaccine certificates often include details such as your pet's name, breed, age, microchip number, and the vaccination date and expiration.

>> **Shipper's certification for live animals:** If your pet is flying in the cargo hold, this certification may be required to demonstrate that your pet is in good health or to verify that a breed of animal is able to travel. For countries that have mandatory quarantine periods, an export quarantine certificate may also be necessary.

When moving abroad with your pet:

>> **Research pet import requirements in your destination.** Many countries have different requirements for differents types of animals.

>> **Look up the pet policies of the airline or transport provider that you plan to use.** Rules and fees vary depending on whether you bring your pet in cargo or the main cabin. Check with your airline to find out which species and breeds of pets are allowed.

>> **Check with your vet about the necessary paperwork.** Your vet can assist you with providing the documents mentioned in the previous list, such as a health or vaccine certificate.

>> **Consider hiring a company to help you move your pet.** Companies such as AirPets International (www.airpetsinternational.com) handle all the logistics of moving your pet across borders, including airport transfers, lodging, and care during travel delays. The company ships pets by using commercial airlines that have pressurized and climate-controlled cargo holds.

TIP

Make sure the company you use is approved by the Animal Transportation Association (ATA; www.animaltransportationassociation.org).

>> **Ensure your pet has everything they need.** Confirm you have the right-sized crate, ventilation, bedding, food, and hydration options. Airline websites offer exact specifications.

TIP

Help your pet acclimate to their crate during the days and weeks before your trip by letting them eat or sleep inside the crate, along with their favorite blanket, toy, or an item from home that has your scent for comfort. You can also take your pet on short car rides inside the crate and train them to use pee pads.

>> **Prepare for emergencies.** Keep a list of emergency contact numbers for local vets, emergency clinics, and your pet insurance provider on hand.

>> **Choose a pet-friendly airline that flies to your destination.** Japan Airlines provides a climate-controlled holding area for pets before loading them onto

the aircraft. Air France, KLM, and Martinair operate the Cargo Animal Hotel at Amsterdam Airport Schiphol, allowing pets to rest during long journeys.

Said Chase, who moved to Spain with his wife and their dog: "Moving with a pet is challenging but doable. Don't let paperwork and logistics hold you back. That said, if you have a larger animal that is older and somewhat temperamental, don't be naive to the challenges flying under the plane will cause them. It's a stressful event for them; don't take it lightly."

If you have the funds, you can also consider flying privately with your pet.

» **Set your pet up with their own airline.** BARK Air (http://air.bark.co) delivers a luxury, "white paw" experience to dogs traveling between New York, Los Angeles, London, and Paris, starting from $6,000 to $8,000 one-way, while K9 Jets (www.k9jets.com) offers canine charter flights to London, Geneva, Dubai, and more.

» **Consider alternative transportation.** The Queen Mary ship offers kennels for dogs and cats to travel by sea between New York and Southampton, England. Find more information at www.cunard.com.

After you arrive in your destination, give your pet time to settle in and acclimate to the local surroundings. Transition your pet to a new daily routine, take them for walks, and spend quality time together. Also, make sure to follow local laws. In some countries, pets must be on a leash when in public, while in other countries, unleashed pets may be allowed in restaurants and retail shops.

Read online reviews to find pet-friendly accommodations. Search for "pets allowed" on hotel and vacation rental websites, but don't hesitate to contact property owners directly to inquire whether they can accept your pet.

Evaluating Whether You Want Relocation Support

You might know the saying, "If you want something done right, you have to do it yourself." But that's not always the case. Getting help with a big project can allow you to accomplish your goals more quickly and easily than going it alone. When facing a challenge, especially one that you've never confronted, you can figure out how to do it yourself or get help.

I'm a professional who helps people move to different countries. But even with 20 years of experience in my field, I hire staff to help with various tasks, from property searches to research and administrative work. Whether I'm in the U.S. or abroad, I strive to reduce stress by delegating certain tasks. Likewise, there's no harm in getting support for some aspects of an international move.

Hiring a relocation consultant can save valuable time, ease your fears, and provide answers when you have questions. However, moving abroad isn't rocket science. You can do it on your own with the tools, resources, and information contained within this book and a bit of persistence and work. If you encounter a challenge, you can always get help.

To determine whether to outsource a task related to your move, ask yourself:

» Are you the only one who can do this task? Or can a professional do it better, faster, or more easily than you can?

» Do you like to do it? Perhaps you enjoy researching destinations but not navigating residency applications or interacting with local bureaucracy.

» Does accomplishing this task alone create value or waste time? It's easy to spend hours browsing forums and websites, which can often result in confusion and information overload.

Before-the-move tasks

Relocating internationally requires careful planning from the start. From selecting the right destination to managing financial considerations, these initial steps can help you set the stage for your move. Here are some important tasks to take care of before your big move, which a relocation advisor can assist you with. However, this book contains all the information you need to do things yourself:

» Applying for a visa or residency permit (Chapter 4)

» Booking travel (Chapter 7)

» Calculating your budget and taxes (Chapters 3 and 13)

» Choosing a destination (Chapter 4)

» Packing your home (Chapter 7)

» Selling your home and/or car (Chapter 5)

» Securing travel or health insurance (Chapter 7)

» Shipping boxes or containers of your personal items and home goods, such as artwork, clothing, furniture, and keepsakes (Chapter 7)

» Renting or buying a house abroad (Chapter 6)

- » Researching schools (Chapters 5 and 9)
- » Transporting pets (Chapter 5)
- » Updating your will (Chapter 13)

During-the-move tasks

While you settle into your new location, you need to address several practical matters to make your transition as seamless as possible and start building a comfortable life in your new home. See Chapters 7, 8, and 9 for information about what to do after you arrive abroad — from arranging airport pickup to activating your utilities accounts and getting oriented in your destination.

After-the-move tasks

After you arrive in your new home, your focus shifts to settling in and creating a sense of home in your new surroundings. From establishing daily routines, to integrating into the local community, Chapters 9, 10, and 11 provide guidance that can make your transition successful and comfortable.

Selecting a Relocation Expert

If you want to hire someone to help with any of the tasks I talk about in the previous section "Evaluating Whether You Want Relocation Support," here are some tips:

- » **Determine what you want help with.** Identify the tasks that you don't feel confident about or don't want to do.
- » **Ask about experience.** Read the About page of the relocation advisor and company websites. Inquire about how many years of experience they have helping people move to your destination.
- » **Check reviews.** Look up the company on sites and apps such as Google Maps (http://maps.google.com), Trustpilot.com, and Yelp to read public reviews.
- » **Verify licensing requirements.** Although few countries offer a professional license for providing relocation services, some organizations, such as WERC (www.talenteverywhere.org), offer global mobility certifications.

The cost of relocation assistance varies. A local relocation provider can charge as low as $10 to $20 per hour for small tasks, such as bill pay, booking travel, and researching information or $60 to $100 for a property viewing. Large companies, such as ARC Relocation (www.arcrelocation.com) or Crown Relocations (www.crownrelo.com), can charge five to six figures for a relocation package. I offer private consulting calls and a guided relocation training program called Ready to Relocate, which you can find more about at www.travelingwithkristin.com/relocation.

To find a local or country-specific relocation consultant, search online for "*city or country name* relocation services (or consultant)." You can also ask in Facebook groups and community expat forums such as InterNations (www.internations.org), Expat.com, and ExpatExchange (www.expatexchange.com). "Redditors," or users on Reddit threads, can also provide recommendations of service providers (try r/expats).

TIPS FOR WORKING WITH RELOCATION EXPERTS

When hiring someone to help with your move, you need to establish communication, set clear expectations, and understand the services that you're contracting for with your consultant:

- **Be realistic.** Relocation advisors can guide you through the relocation process and help with various aspects, but their support has limits. They can't make a bank open an account for you, guarantee your residency application will be approved, or otherwise influence companies, government agencies, or other third parties.

- **Set expectations and deliverables.** Understand what services you're signing up for and paying for. Ask specifics about what's included and excluded in your package.

- **Set a clear timeline.** Ensure your relocation provider is clear on your anticipated move date and can help you meet deadlines.

- **Stay organized.** Keep records of all necessary documents and legal papers for reference.

- **Provide timely responses.** Respond promptly to e-mails and messages from your relocation consultant. Communication delays can slow down the process.

- **Voice worries or concerns.** If you're confused or uncertain during the process, contact your rep to ask questions or get a progress update.

IN THIS CHAPTER

» Understanding principles of renting abroad

» Finding your perfect housing

» Checking off your to-do list

» Answering common housing questions

Chapter 6
Finding Your New Home Away from Home

Finding a home in a new country is one of the most exciting yet daunting aspects of an international move. You leave a place that's familiar to you for one where the location, surroundings, and principles of renting and buying are foreign to you. Even if you've traveled extensively, there's a difference between staying somewhere on vacation versus moving there long-term.

The process of finding your home away from home takes time. But after you sign on the dotted line and set foot in your new residence, it's worth it. In this chapter, I help you know what to look for when searching for housing abroad and equip you with checklists and strategies to prevent or resolve common hiccups.

Clarifying Your Property Needs

Before starting your property search, take a moment to define what you're looking for. Will you buy or rent? Do you want a house or apartment? Do you prefer living in the city or country? What are your must-haves and deal-breakers?

Your property requirements should include a property's type, size, price range, lease term, location, level of furnishings, and amenities. Also consider features you'd like to have, such as a washer and dryer, elevator, patio, yard, view, pool, gym, parking, or a pet-friendly property.

You should also identify what you don't want, such as a property with stairs.

TIP

Download a property search form and checklist at www.travelingwithkristin.com/moving-abroad.

Checking Out the Different Types of Accommodations

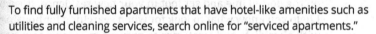

You'll encounter a wide range of property types in your housing search abroad — many of which you're familiar with in your home country. When faced with hundreds or thousands of housing options, however, you can feel overwhelmed. In this section, I share with you some of the most common property types available, so you can narrow your search and prepare to make smart choice that fits your needs.

The types of properties you may encounter during a search include:

- **Alternative housing:** Houseboats, sailboats, RVs, and tiny homes are a few examples.
- **Apartments (or flats) and studios:** Individual properties in a building or complex that has a community entrance.

TIP

To find fully furnished apartments that have hotel-like amenities such as utilities and cleaning services, search online for "serviced apartments."

- **Single-family (detached) homes:** Standalone houses, which you can find in city, suburban, or rural environments.
- **Shared housing and co-living:** Sharing a room or property with other tenants.
- **Student housing:** Dorms, rooms, and apartments for university students.
- **Townhomes:** Semi-detached homes typically found in cities and suburbs.
- **Villas and chalets:** Large, standalone residences, typically near water or mountains.

Any property type can come furnished or unfurnished, and for short- or long-term rentals.

Renting short-term vs long-term

When you move to a new country, renting a property (compared to buying one) provides a good first step while you find your forever home. It's lower risk and less expensive than investing in local real estate. As one traveler shared with me, "For those uncertain about long stays, I'd recommend starting with short-term rentals or serviced (furnished) apartments. It's a great way to test the waters before making any permanent decisions."

The length of time you can stay in a country and rent for depends on your passport's tourist authorization or the visa or residency permit you qualify for. (Chapter 2 goes into more detail about that.) After you know how long you can stay, you're ready to select your lease term:

>> **Short rentals:** Nightly, weekly, and month-to-month terms give you more flexibility and less commitment than buying a property or renting long-term. You don't need to sign contracts to stay in hotels or vacation rentals. Instead, you can book through secure, well-known websites — often without security deposits — and read others' reviews. But shorter terms come with higher costs per night and upfront versus monthly payments.

>> **Medium-term rentals:** Typically range from 3 to 6 months (the duration of most tourist visas). They can cost less than short rentals and more than long rentals. Websites such as Flatio.com specialize in medium-term rentals for digital nomads and travelers.

>> **Long-term rentals:** Rentals of one year or more tend to cost less while offering benefits such as a physical mailing address for proof of residency. If you plan to stay in one place long enough, a long-term rental lowers your cost of living and provides a more stable home base.

Some countries have unique lease term options, such as Italy's 3+2 lease — a rental term of three years with an option to extend for another two years. Five years sounds like a long time, but many landlords offer early exit clauses to terminate the agreement.

If you decide to end your lease early, give sufficient advanced notice per the terms of your agreement to increase the chances that you can recover your security deposit.

>> **Membership-based rentals:** Renting by using a housing service, where you pay a monthly or annual fee for access to a selection of properties. Examples

include Landing (www.hellolanding.com), Blueground (www.theblueground.com), and Selina (www.selina.com).

» **Sublets:** Renting a room or property from the current tenant for the duration or a portion of the lease term (can be short- or long-term).

Narrowing down a location

Beyond choosing a country location, which Chapter 4 helps you with, you want to narrow your search down to a city and neighborhood.

The best way to evaluate a neighborhood is to visit, but researching your destination from afar is a close second. Read books, blog articles, and watch videos about popular cities, towns, and neighborhoods in your host country. You can also learn a lot about prices, availability, and housing styles by browsing property websites. During your research, find out about the transportation options available, safety, and proximity to amenities and lifestyle considerations such as schools, restaurants, shops, hospitals, and entertainment. Once you find a few places you like, input the characteristics you're looking for into an AI website, such as ChatGPT, and see which similar alternatives it suggests.

TIP

Check out sites like Culture Trip to find more information ahead of your stay. Another site, Hoodmaps, uses publicly crowdsourced information to give you a (sometimes amusing) idea of what individual neighborhoods are like.

If getting around is important to you, look up your destination on Walkscore to understand how daily life looks from a transportation perspective. The higher a city's walk score, the more likely you won't need a vehicle for daily activities. For example, my home base in Miami has a walk score of 77. It's walkable, bikeable, and sunny year-round.

When searching locations, use Google Maps to zoom in and identify different areas where you can live. You can also search for "(City) + Neighborhood Guide" on Google to dig for clues before you make decisions.

Searching for property strategically

When to start searching for a place to stay depends on your arrival date abroad and whether you're renting short-term or long term. If you're renting for a short time, you can start searching as far out from your move date as you want because you can book hotels and vacation properties up to one year in advance. Like with the cost of airfare, prices for short-term rentals can increase as your arrival date gets closer and available inventory decreases.

EXPAT HOUSING TIPS

I asked my YouTube subscribers about their housing experiences abroad, and here's what they had to say:

- **Dave, Portugal:** We purchased a house in a small urbanization in the Algarve. The process took six months longer than expected as the house needed to be completed and registered. You need to be careful that the agent doesn't try to sell you on a place where they get special kickbacks and may not be in the best local versus tourist destination.

- **Richard, UK:** Finding rented housing as a fresh immigrant with no rental history in that country was an enormous problem! We had to get my employer to "vouch for us."

- **John, Italy:** Rent directly from a local to avoid high prices online. Before you travel, book a room at a family-owned hotel for about a week to be able to view properties in person with about five different local agencies. Don't expect huge American-style rooms or appliances. However, most have washer/dryer combos and, if you're lucky, a dishwasher.

- **Claudia, Canada:** [If I could do it again], I would not buy so quickly. I would rent for 1 year and then buy a house that I could rent out partially to make some extra income.

- **Mohammed, Digital Nomad:** The rental process varies by country. In some places, you can rent through online platforms, while in others, it's better to work with local agents or expat networks to find suitable accommodations. Language barriers and differing rental procedures sometimes make things tricky, but having a local contact or hiring a relocation consultant helped smooth out the process. Rely on trusted property agents and using reputable platforms for housing.

For long-term rentals, more properties become available closer to your arrival date. In that case, aim to start your property search a few months before you arrive. If you plan too far in advance, you miss out. Long-term rentals often come available 30 to 60 days before the occupancy date (or after they're empty).

Top ways to find a rental property abroad include:

>> **Classifieds sites:** Local marketplaces with a variety of goods, cars, and real estate for sale. You can search international sites, such as Craigslist and Locanto, or regional sites in your area. To find local classifieds sites, search "housing classifieds + [city or country]." For additional results, try searching "classifieds + location" in the local language. Examples of local classifieds sites

include Gumtree (Australia, Europe, New Zealand, South Africa), Inmuebles24 (Mexico), Rightmove (UK), and Kaidee (Thailand).

» **Expat sites:** Expat forums and websites often have housing directories. Examples include `Expatica.com`, `HousingAnywhere.com`, and `JustLanded.com`.

`Uniplaces.com` is a global platform with housing for international students.

» **Facebook groups:** You can find location- or housing-specific groups in most cities and countries worldwide. Search for "expats in [country]" or "housing in [city or country]" for results. Mining Facebook groups for housing opportunities can pay off in opportunities not available elsewhere. However, expect to invest time with this search method.

» **Local sources:** Find local deals by walking, biking, or driving around looking for "For Rent" signs. You can also ask people you know for tips.

» **Real estate and rental agencies:** For a traditional approach, contact estate agencies in your location, who have access to exclusive housing inventories and can help you with navigating property negotiations and contracts. Keep in mind that you may need to pay an agency fee if you rent through agents in some countries. To find them, search "real estate office + [location]" or "rental agency + [location]" in a search engine.

For additional results, search "real estate office" or "rental agency" in your phone's map app.

» **Vacation rental websites:** Book nightly, weekly, and monthly rentals on websites such as `Airbnb.com`, `Booking.com`, `Tripadvisor.com`, and `Vrbo.com`. Such sites offer 24/7 customer support. Airbnb also offers guests insurance coverage, known as AirCover.

If you have a flexible short-term rental budget, check out Plum Guide (`www.plumguide.com`) or Corporate Stays (`www.corporatestays.com`). You can find furnished homes, apartments, and other properties that offer plenty of luxury and comfort.

Searching for properties takes time and energy. If you want help, you can hire a real estate agent, relocation specialist, or virtual assistant to help. You can find remote assistants on jobs boards such as `onlinejobs.ph` or TaskRabbit, an app with people who can help by the hour. Once you choose someone, send them a detailed document of what you want, any websites or resources you want them to check, and a budget for how many hours you want them to spend.

Time your property search with your residency application if you need proof of accommodation for that application.

The following sections give you some other key considerations when conducting your search.

For a list of housing websites worldwide, download the bonus content for this book at www.travelingwithkristin.com/moving-abroad.

Budget

More money, fewer problems — at least when it comes to finding housing. Having an ample budget gives you more choices and flexibility. You get your pick of the market and can hire property assistants or relocation companies to search on your behalf. See Chapter 5 for guidance on hiring relocation experts.

If you're like most people, however, you want to stay within a housing budget. A popular guideline known as the "30 percent rule" recommends keeping your housing costs below 30 percent of your gross monthly income.

In addition to sources mentioned in the previous section, additional budget accommodation sources include:

- **Couchsurfing:** Good for short-term stays while you explore a new area. A community-centric platform where hosts offer their couches to travelers. Although you don't have to pay any couch booking fees, you do have to pay a membership fee to join.
- **Hostelworld:** A global website featuring budget-friendly accommodation, including hostels, dorms, and rooms for rent. A bonus: Staying in a hostel or shared housing gives you a good way to meet people fast.
- **Sublet.com:** A website to find short- and medium-term rentals worldwide. Landlords directly offer some properties, while others are sublets.
- **TrustedHousesitters:** This website connects travelers and house sitters with home and pet owners who need someone to help with maintenance or feeding your fur baby. You can register as a house sitter or home/pet owner for an annual fee of $149 to $299 per year.

In preparation for renting, save enough money to pay for the first and last month's rent plus a security deposit up front. In some cases, you may also need to present proof of income (bank or credit card statements) and references.

CHAPTER 6 **Finding Your New Home Away from Home** 95

AVOIDING COMMON HOUSING SCAMS

Avoid scams by using reputable websites and agencies. If you reserve a property through a classified site or a stranger, visit the property in person before you sign a lease or send money. If a property you see online looks too good to be true, it probably is.

If you're unable to view a property in person, send someone to view it on your behalf before you send money. You can also use sites such as PayPal (www.paypal.com) for payment that have vendor's insurance. If possible pay with a credit card so that you can dispute charges in case of fraud.

Avoid properties where landlords or agents tell you they'll mail you the key; and never send money to people you don't know and haven't met.

If you move to an affordable country, you can keep your housing costs low. See Chapter 4 for tips on choosing a destination and Chapter 16 for places to live under $1,500 per month.

Seasonality

The time of year or season when you arrive abroad affects the price and availability of your search results. For example, tourists from cold climates flock to warm destinations during winter, such as Mexico, the Mediterranean, and the Caribbean. Renting during high season typically costs more, and you have a slimmer selection of properties to choose from.

If possible, arrive during the low season (also called the *shoulder season*), when you have lower prices and more vacancies.

Also, place limits on the time and energy that you devote to your search. The longer, father, and wider you search, the more the market turns over. Properties you found a few days or weeks ago may no longer be available, but new properties may appear that fit your requirements.

Set up a property alert if the sites you use offer it. That way, you receive notifications, whether through an e-mail or text message, when properties that fit your specifications become available.

RENTAL PECULIARITIES AROUND THE WORLD

Some general principles of renting or buying change very little from country to country, no matter where you go. Landlords, rental agreements, security deposits, and Internet packages exist almost everywhere. But some countries do have their own particular housing requirements. In Germany, unfurnished rentals may not include appliances, but they usually do in Mexico. In Japan, some landlords expect a customary, non-refundable gift called *key money*, in addition to the rent and security deposit. In some European countries, tenants who rent through estate agents may pay a fee equal to half a month or one month's rent. However, in other countries, landlords typically pay such costs.

Buying Property Abroad

Many expats prefer to rent for their first year abroad to allow time to explore multiple locations before putting down roots. Renting offers you more flexibility and less commitment than buying. However, in some scenarios, buying a property makes sense.

Consider buying a property abroad if you want to:

» Establish a long-term home for stability (due to work, family, pets, retirement, or other reasons)

» Qualify for permanent residency or citizenship through a real estate golden visa program. (See Chapters 2 and 4 for more on golden visas.)

» Start a business, such as a bed and breakfast, farm, or other venture where having a fixed property is involved.

» Invest in a property to gain equity or to use it as a rental property.

» Rotate seasonally between properties you own in multiple locations.

» Buy a property that you might not be able to afford in your home country.

TIP

Your dollar can go further abroad (in certain countries and regions). If your home costs $500,000 in Austin, Texas, a comparable property could cost $366,000 in Italy. It's hard to find a beachfront condo in Miami for less than $1 million. But in Mexico, you can get one for $150,000.

PERKS OF INVESTING IN REAL ESTATE ABROAD

Owning foreign real estate can help diversify your investment portfolio when markets fluctuate around the world. When the housing market in one country slumps or crashes, it might thrive somewhere else.

Differences in exchange rates can work in your favor, although the opposite is also true.

Suppose you find a property in France for €100,000 in 2013; that property would have cost USD $133,000. But in 2025, the exchange rate between the U.S. dollar and the euro fell significantly. A €100,000 property cost USD $104,000 in 2025. Likewise, your property could lose value if the exchange rates favor the euro over the U.S. dollar (and you earn in dollars).

Your purchasing power may also be higher abroad than in your home country. The median price for a home in the United States was $420,400 in October 2024 (using an average home size of 2,000 sq. ft. [186 sq. m]) or $2,260 per square meter. In contrast, the average price per square meter for a home in Serbia, according to the local housing website Properstar (www.properstar.com), was €760 ($802). A comparable home in Serbia costs about €141,500 ($150,000).

Depending on the country, you may or may not be able to own a property outright. In some places, such as Thailand, Indonesia, and the U.K., foreigners can purchase leasehold property (which you own for a fixed number of years), but not titled (which you own outright). If you're unsure, verify local laws with a real estate attorney.

Choosing where to buy

When you start thinking about buying a property abroad, you first have to decide where you want to buy. Many investors choose a destination based on countries that they're familiar with, where they've visited before. However, many people also buy "sight-unseen," especially in the case of pre-construction properties. Do what you feel most comfortable with.

Many of my relocation clients cite "choosing a destination" as their biggest challenge when moving abroad. Chapter 4 helps you make a destination decision.

Annual reports such as the InterNations Expat Insider Survey (www.internations.org/expat-insider) can help you find the most- and least-liked places for expats to live worldwide.

After you know where you want to go, the Internet offers a ton of great sites to help you find out about real estate investment opportunities that cater to expats. Some sites include:

- ECI Development (www.ecidevelopment.com)
- Expatica (www.expatica.com)
- International Living (www.internationalliving.com)
- Live and Invest Overseas (www.liveandinvestoverseas.com)
- Global Property Guide (www.globalpropertyguide.com)

Many people want to buy real estate in countries where they can live well on Social Security or pension income. If you plan to retire abroad, you can find multiple videos that have suggestions on my YouTube channel, www.youtube.com/travelingwithkristin.

Getting help from professionals

After you figure out where you want to buy (see the preceding section), decide whether to work with a real estate agent or find properties for sale by owner.

Realtors offer the advantages of on-the-ground knowledge. They should have an eye for scams and a well-developed network of related professionals, such as attorneys, bankers, and in-home service providers (including plumbers, electricians, inspectors, and contractors).

On the downside, many estate agents would prefer to show you their exclusive inventory rather than sharing commissions with competitors. For the widest perspective on the market, take your time and shop around until you find a property that suits your needs. Seek opinions from different sources and research comparable options to know if you're getting a fair price.

Be sure to work with licensed agents when possible, but be aware that not all countries require professional licensing.

Upon making a purchase decision, hire a real estate attorney to review your contract, especially if you don't speak the language. For legal counsel recommendations, contact your local embassy or consulate, a title insurance company such as Stewart Title (www.stewart.com), or a reputable real estate broker.

CHAPTER 6 **Finding Your New Home Away from Home** 99

Paying cash or financing

If you've owned a home before, you may have purchased it with the help of financing. However, finding foreign financing abroad is challenging and expensive. In most cases, expect to fund your purchase and associated closing cost through a cash bank wire or escrow transfer.

If you find a bank, developer, or other provider abroad that lends to non-citizens, read the fine print and review the numbers carefully. Interest rates for foreign buyers frequently reach double-digits while requiring a large down payment of 30 percent to 50 percent or more.

Some countries require non-citizens to purchase life insurance policies as collateral to cover the mortgage balance. Your age and health affect the premiums that you pay on these policies, and a medical exam may also be necessary.

In addition to property taxes, transfer fees, legal and closing fees, budget for furniture and miscellaneous expenses when you move in, such as utility deposits, air conditioning installation, or a water filtration system. These expenses can add up fast.

To come up with a lump sum to buy a property abroad, consider

- Refinancing your current home
- Seeking a personal loan
- Buying from a developer who offers owner financing
- Using funds from a retirement plan, such as a 401(k) or IRA

You can purchase properties by using Bitcoin and other cryptocurrencies in some countries, such as the U.S., the UAE, Portugal, and El Salvador. You also can qualify for the St. Kitts and Nevis Citizenship by Investment program by using a cryptocurrency payment.

Buying leasehold property

When you own property in the traditional sense, it's yours forever and transfers onto your successors when you pass away.

However, some countries only offer leasehold, and not titled, property. If you buy a *leasehold* property, you may own the home but not the land it sits on. When the lease agreement ends, what happens depends on a country's laws. You may have the option to renew the lease or receive compensation from the original landowner. In other cases, ownership automatically reverts to the landowner or government.

Ownership regulations vary widely from one country to another. In some countries, foreigners can buy as much land as they want, while other countries impose restrictions.

For example, a high percentage of beachfront properties in Central America are leasehold. Only about 5 percent of beachfront property in Costa Rica is titled; the other 95 percent is concession land, available for 20- to 30-year periods. Be sure to research ownership regulations and know the risks. Buy where the laws align with your expectations.

Let the buyer beware: If the price of a property seems too good to be true, it probably is (or it's leasehold land).

Negotiating real estate abroad

Negotiating a property to rent or own in a different country can feel intimidating at first. But remember that an investment that's foreign to you is part of normal, everyday life for local residents. People are people everywhere in the world, although negotiating customs may differ.

The following sections give you some tips to face a negotiation process with confidence.

Research the market

Brush up on the cultural norms of the country that you want to buy in. Find out about the purchase process, whether it's a buyers' or sellers' market, and common negotiation tactics. Look up comparable properties online and talk to several property agencies to confirm your findings. Real estate agents can also give you tips and insights about negotiating. Make your buying or renting decision only after you have a good feel for the market prices and practices.

Perceptions and values vary by culture. A spacious suburban home might seem ideal in the U.S., whereas tiny apartments in Tokyo are in high demand.

Visit where you want to buy, if possible. Chapter 5 helps you plan an exploratory trip.

CHAPTER 6 **Finding Your New Home Away from Home** 101

Build a network

Get in touch with professionals who can help you during the purchase process, such as real estate agents, lawyers, property inspectors, and buyers' agents.

Connect with the expat community in person, or in Facebook groups or forums, for insights on their renting or buying experiences and things to avoid. However, check sources and remember that some people may exaggerate stories or have hidden motives for sharing information.

Wheel and deal

Depending on the culture that you're buying or renting in, you might ask for a price break or some added benefits, such as a flexible lease term, a better split on closing costs, or the inclusion of utilities, furniture, or appliances. When renting long-term, you can offer to pay multiple months of rent in advance for a discount (but make sure you visit the property first and know it's a good fit for you). Offer to pay U.S. dollars in countries that have weak or volatile currencies.

TIP

If renting, try timing your negotiation during the low season, when demand dips.

When buying, you can ask for a longer or shorter due diligence period, which is the time you have to investigate and inspect a property after placing a deposit and before closing and title transfer. In some countries, bartering and haggling are time-honored traditions, and sellers rarely expect to get the full price they initially quote. However, negotiating is frowned upon in other countries.

Be prepared

Acquiring a property abroad can be an exciting prospect. To prepare for the process and set yourself up for success, keep these suggestions in mind:

» **Have your funds ready.** Save money before starting your search. If you plan to buy, have enough saved so that you can pay in full because, as a foreigner, you have limited financing options. Use an escrow or title company to hold funds so they're safe until you complete the transaction.

» **Conduct due diligence.** Hire a local attorney or advisor to check your property's legal status and title history. Have an inspector check out the property. Ensure you understand local property ownership conditions and tax rates before buying.

» **Be patient.** Markets move at varying speeds. If a deal falls through, it could be for a reason. Keep an open mind and don't hesitate to walk away. Keep looking, and you'll find what you want.

>> **Dig deep.** Inquire about the seller's or landlord's motivation for selling or renting their home. The more you know about why a property is available, the more leverage you have in negotiations.

POPULAR PLACES TO INVEST ABROAD

Here's a look at some trending places to invest in real estate worldwide:

- **Brazil:** South America's largest nation has a stable economy and natural beauty. Foreigners can buy without a local address, but you do need a valid passport.

- **Costa Rica:** The land of *pura vida* (which translates as "pure life," a local greeting and philosophy of positivity and wellbeing) offers the same property ownership rights to foreigners as it does to its own citizens (but watch out for beachfront and coastal land leaseholds). Along Costa Rica's western shore, the regions of Guanacaste and Puntarenas are popular among investors, as well as the Central Valley that surrounds the capital of San José.

- **Dominican Republic:** Strong tourism appeal, tropical beaches, and low cost of living draw property investors from around the world. With a minimum investment of $200,000, foreigners can obtain residency through the Dominican Republic golden visa program.

- **United Arab Emirates:** The Emirati cities of Abu Dhabi and Dubai boast thriving luxury property markets. The country offers tax free zones in some areas, and you can find financing for foreigners.

- **Panama:** The home of the Panama Canal attracts investors with its stable, dollarized economy, warm climate, and tax-friendly policies. The country's government has developed a variety of visa and residency programs designed to attract foreign investment, such as the investor (golden) visa, *pensionado* visa for retirees, and the friendly nations visa.

- **Portugal:** Portugal is the most affordable countries to live in Western Europe, with a mild year-round climate and nearly 1,000 kilometers of beaches. Although the real estate portion of Portugal's golden visa was discontinued in 2023, foreigners continue to move there with the D7 and D8 visas for passive income residents and retirees. For city living, look to the capital of Lisbon. For a coastal lifestyle, search properties in the Algarve and Silver Coast.

- **Spain:** Spain's sunny climate and relaxed lifestyle appeal to investors, expats, and tourists alike. Popular cities for real estate investment include Barcelona, Málaga,

(continued)

(continued)

> and Valencia. You can also search for deals in the Spanish countryside, or consider the islands of Mallorca, Menorca, Ibiza, or the Canary Islands.
>
> - **Thailand:** Ranks among the top ten economies in Asia and the top ten tourism destinations in the world. Although the country doesn't have a real estate golden visa, it offers various residency-by-investment programs, such as the Thailand privilege card. Foreigners tend to settle in places such as Bangkok, Chiang Mai, Pattaya, Phuket, Koh Samui, and Koh Tao.
>
> Foreigners can't purchase land outright in Thailand, but they can own condos or apartments and rent leasehold properties.

TIP

Avoid scams and disappointment by getting a professional property inspection before closing a deal and hiring a qualified lawyer to review the contract and title to the property.

Solving Renting Problems

The most common setbacks and difficulties new arrivals face when they rent overseas is simply a lack of information. You don't know what you don't know. This section covers what to do about renting before you search for a property, sign a lease, or head for the airport.

REMEMBER

The first rule when you rent abroad is an old, familiar refrain: "An ounce of prevention is worth a pound of cure." Rental problems are much easier to resolve ahead of time, versus after you're on the ground in your host nation.

Here's a list of issues that may crop up when you rent properties abroad and what to do about them in advance:

- **Faulty Internet.** Check Internet speeds before you rent by requesting a speed test screenshot. Inquire about the possibility of upgrading the service, which you can read about in Chapter 8. Bring a backup travel Wi-Fi device with you in case of emergency.

- **Lack of accessibility.** If you need an accessible property, find out whether the property has stairs, an elevator, or handicapped access before you rent.

- **Lack of insulation or climate control.** Certain buildings may lack insulation, making them feel hotter in the summer and colder in the winter. Inquire about climate control options.

- **Loss of deposit or rent.** If you decide to break a lease early, you likely lose your security deposit. In some countries, you can be liable for paying the remaining months on your contract. Ensure you understand the conditions of your rental contract well and penalties for early termination.

- **Too much street noise.** If you dislike the noise of hustle-bustle cities, look at properties in suburban or rural areas. Properties that face interior gardens versus a street also tend to be quieter.

- **The property doesn't match the photos.** Ask for a video tour or send someone to snap pictures on your behalf before you move in. With many short-term rentals sites such as Airbnb (www.airbnb.com), you can request refunds if the property doesn't match what the listing advertised online.

WARNING

The sidebar "Avoiding common housing scams," in this chapter, gives you some tips, but sometimes you just can't see it coming. If this happens to you, cut your losses and move on.

- **Uncomfortable furnishings.** Look closely at the photos and reviews left by other renters. If you're staying long-term, you may want to visit a local store to supplement the furniture or add pillows and a mattress topper to your bed.

TIP

If you work from home, pay close attention to how comfortable the chairs look in photos or plan to buy an office chair.

- **Uncooperative landlords.** Every country has them. Some landlords may delay solving problems in your property or refunding your security deposit when you move out. Find out your rights as a tenant by seeking legal advice or contacting the local government's department of housing.

- **Unsafe property.** Buy international travel and local renters' insurance to protect your belongings. Hide valuables and documents in a home safe or safe deposit box. Rent in secure buildings on upper floors, where it's difficult to break in. Move out if you feel unsafe.

- **Utility outages.** Depending on where you live, consider installing a backup generator, batteries, and extra supplies during outages, storms, or natural disasters. Ask in advance about planned outages, and keep fresh supplies of food, water, power, and a mobile Wi-Fi device ready.

For a rental property and housing checklist, visit www.travelingwithkristin.com/move-abroad.

PAYING THE FOREIGNER TAX

Use local classified sites and local real estate agencies for the best opportunities to find fair, local pricing. If you prefer to deal directly with the landlord, call the numbers listed on For Rent signs written in foreign languages (and use a translator). In many developing countries, the *foreigner tax* (meaning a higher price charged to people moving in from other places) is simply part of the experience. But sometimes you can access local rates if you drive a tough enough bargain.

Research market *comps* (comparables; recently sold or rented properties similar to what you hope to find) on Airbnb (www.airbnb.com) and local classified sites so that you can figure out whether a property is overpriced (meaning you're paying the foreigner tax).

IN THIS CHAPTER

» Making sure you have the right insurance

» Researching and booking flights

» Packing your bags and shipping your stuff

» Getting all of your paperwork in order

Chapter **7**

Getting Ready to Hit the Road

This chapter can help you make your final preparations for the big day! Soon, you get to start a new chapter of your life in a faraway land.

In this stage of the relocation process, you focus on key logistical tasks to complete before you leave. I discuss how to select an insurance policy, book your flight, and decide what to pack and ship. I also cover how to organize your paperwork, bid farewell, and prepare for a smooth departure.

Applying for Insurance

You need appropriate insurance coverage if you plan to live abroad or travel long-term. The following sections go over five types of insurance to consider.

Emergency travel medical insurance

Travel insurance covers accidents, cancellations, and interruptions during your travel. It can include coverage for travel delays, lost baggage, canceled flights, natural disasters, double-booked hotel rooms, and accidents or sickness. Coverage may also include injuries or illnesses sustained before, during, and after your trip (depending on your policy).

Emergency travel medical insurance providers often offer health insurance plans as well, which you can read about in the following section. A few popular companies include:

- **Insured Nomads** (www.insurednomads.com): An insurance resource for remote workers, companies, and global travelers. Includes medical coverage, trip protection, group travel benefits, and coverage for professionals working in war zones.

- **Pacific Prime** (www.pacificprime.com): International health coverage, including vision, dental, maternity, and preventative care options.

- **SafetyWing** (www.safetywing.com): Worldwide health and travel insurance for nomads, retirees, and remote teams. They offer short-term (Essential) and long-term (Complete) policies. Rates start from around $56 per month and about $150 per month, respectively.

  SafetyWing has several coverage restrictions for U.S. citizens and for travelers going to or from the United States. Read the fine print and contact the company for details.

- **World Nomads** (www.worldnomads.com): Comprehensive travel insurance that covers more than 250 activities and scenarios, such as travel inconvenience, baggage delays, natural disaster evacuation, rental car, and emergency medical coverage.

- **Yonder** (www.insureyonder.com): An insurance marketplace offering protection for all forms of travel — business, family, senior, adventure, cruise, touring, student, journalism, and non-traditional travel.

TIP

Many credit cards come with travel insurance. Check the fine print of your card to find out.

You can compare companies, rates, and plans in a marketplace such as InsureMyTrip (www.insuremytrip.com).

Local or international health insurance

Consider getting a comprehensive health insurance plan outside of your home country if you expect to live abroad for long-term. You can opt for an international plan that covers you in multiple countries, or a local public or private plan for coverage in a single country.

Get a global healthcare plan if you want to travel long-term throughout multiple countries as a roaming retiree or digital nomad. Opt for a local plan if you intend to live full-time in one country.

If you plan to keep a home base in your home country, and travel back and forth from abroad, keep your home insurance plan active, especially if you're insured through your employer.

Travel insurance (discussed in the preceding section) covers you for accidents and emergencies. In contrast, a health insurance plan covers you for ongoing healthcare needs, such as prescriptions, vision, maternity, dental work, mental health, and primary care.

Here are the types of health insurance that you can get:

- » **Local:** To find a local health insurance provider, search online for "private health insurance + [country]." Examples of local insurers include Bupa (www.bupaglobal.com/private-health-insurance/mt) in Malta, Medibank (www.medibank.com.au) in Australia, and Samsung in South Korea.

- » Translate "private health insurance" into the local country's language or use a VPN connected to your destination's location for more relevant results. For example, search for *Seguro medico privado Chile* to find private insurance providers in Chile. You can also open your Maps app to Santiago, Chile, and search "private health insurance" for local offices.

- » **International:** To find an international insurance provider, search online for "expat health insurance." Examples of global expat health insurance providers include Allianz (www.allianzcare.com), Cigna Global (www.cignaglobal.com), GeoBlue (www.geo-blue.com), and IMG Global (www.imglobal.com/international-health-insurance).

  International and expat-focused healthcare plans are typically more expensive than local insurance plans. A local private insurance plan in Spain can cost you $100 per month, while an international healthcare plan can cost $300 per month and up. Get multiple quotes and compare rates before making a decision.

- » **Full-time traveler:** Specialized insurance products exist for digital nomads and full-time travelers. Genki (www.genki.world) offers worldwide health insurance for travelers in every country and for any doctor or hospital. Its Genki Native plan provides comprehensive worldwide health coverage for at least one year, while the Explore plan offers temporary travel coverage for up to 12 months.

CHAPTER 7 **Getting Ready to Hit the Road** 109

SafetyWing (www.safetywing.com) offers monthly and annual travel and health insurance plans. It has an Essential plan with standard travel coverage and a Complete plan for worldwide healthcare. Rates start from around $56 per month and about $150 per month, respectively.

TIP

Consider going through a broker to find an insurer. AOC (www.aoc-insurance broker.com) and Pacific Prime (www.pacificprime.com) are two examples, but you can find more by searching online for "expat health insurance broker + [your destination]."

In many cases, you can buy a travel or health insurance plan after you leave home, but if you set it up in advance, you're covered on the flight out. You can also purchase travel medical insurance policies while living abroad. If you're in the U.K., for example, you can even buy a travel policy at the post office.

Mohammed, a digital nomad, opted to invest in international health insurance plans that provided coverage across multiple countries. "Companies like Cigna Global and Allianz were invaluable," he said. "Their plans allowed me to access private healthcare facilities almost anywhere. I also kept a list of recommended hospitals and clinics in each country I spent time in, just in case of emergencies."

REMEMBER

You can opt into the public healthcare system in your new country if you have legal resident status. Brenden, who lives in France, said, "We're in the national insurance and it's easy to find and book bilingual doctors through a website called Doctolib. France's system is among the best in the world, and we LOVE it."

In some cases, you may opt to pay out-of-pocket for procedures. "In China," adds Brenden, "I had insurance. But medical care is so cheap compared to the U.S., that I just paid for anything I needed."

Emergency evacuation and repatriation insurance

If you're moving to an area with limited healthcare options or you want more comprehensive coverage abroad, consider adding emergency evacuation and repatriation insurance. This type of plan safeguards you against medical emergencies, security risks, extreme recreational activities, and global crises. It covers the cost of transporting you by ground, air, or back to your home country if you get seriously injured abroad. Coverage for hospital stays and repatriating your remains in case of death come standard in most policies.

Examples of medical evacuation (MEDEVAC) companies include:

- **Global Rescue** (www.globalrescue.com): Covers field rescue, medical evacuation, security, and health advisory during civil unrest, natural disasters, and more. The company is staffed by military veterans, intelligence experts, paramedics, and physicians.

- **Masa Medical Transport Solutions** (www.masaaccess.com): Offers emergency ground and air transport, extended hospital stays and private room upgrades, minor and pet return transportation, vehicle returns, doctor referrals, and emergency cash advances.

- **MedJet** (www.medjetassist.com): Premier global air medical transport and travel security. MedJet doesn't require a *hard trigger* (such as a government-issued evacuation mandate) to initiate a security response, unlike some other insurance plans.

- **DAN** (www.dan.org): Offers travel, accident, equipment, and liability insurance worldwide; good for incidents caused by participation in certain sports, such as diving.

Getting insurance over 65

Many seniors think about medical tourism while they decide where to live abroad. Countries throughout Latin America, Eastern Europe, and Southeast Asia offer low-cost, high-quality healthcare. You may be able to afford to pay out-of-pocket for specific procedures.

If you're looking for a comprehensive long-term plan, know that age can affect eligibility for some policies. Coverage is harder to find, more expensive, and often has limitations the older you are.

Here's a list of sites that can help seniors find coverage:

- **Freedom Travel Insurance** (www.freedominsure.co.uk): U.K.-based travel and holiday insurance for customers who have pre-existing medical conditions.

- **Generali Global Assistance** (http://shop.generalitravelinsurance.com): Has a premium plan that allows you to qualify for coverage if you have pre-existing medical conditions if you meet specific parameters.

- **JD Travel Insurance Consultants** (www.jdtravelinsurance.co.uk): Specializes in travel insurance for people who have serious illnesses or pre-existing conditions.

- **Saga Health Insurance** (www.saga.co.uk/health-insurance): Provides health insurance for over-50s. Includes a cancer care team, global access to general practitioners, and treatment for muscle/joint/bone pain within 48 hours.

- **Travelex** (www.travelexinsurance.com/travel-insurance/traveler/seniors): Covers seniors for emergency medical expenses, lost/stolen baggage, evacuations, missed connections, delayed baggage, and a travel assistance team available 24 hours a day.

- **Travel Guard** (www.travelguard.com): Similar to Travelex; it also offers health coverage for travelers who have pre-existing conditions.

Exploring other types of insurance

You can insure almost anything — and you may want to if you travel or live abroad. Here are some types of insurance that you might want to get to protect yourself:

- **Burial insurance:** Final expense or funeral insurance covers the costs and logistics of returning your remains home if you pass away overseas.

Check your travel insurance policy for accidental death and dismemberment coverage, which may cover these costs. For example, World Nomads (www.worldnomads.com) pays out for local cremation and the return of your remains to your country of citizenship.

Emergency evacuation insurance companies mentioned in the section "Emergency evacuation and repatriation insurance," earlier in this chapter, may also cover burial costs.

- **Business liability insurance:** Consider getting this type of insurance if you operate a company across borders or travel internationally as a digital nomad, freelancer, or remote worker. It can protect you from third-party liability claims, injury or death to employees, and travel to high-risk countries.

Clements Worldwide (www.clements.com) and The Hartford (www.thehartford.com) are two companies that offer multinational business liability insurance coverage.

- **Car insurance:** Always opt for comprehensive coverage when you rent a car abroad. Rental car agencies may charge a premium for damages, and you don't want to be held liable for injuries to another person. Your home car insurance plan won't cover you abroad. For information about buying or shipping a car abroad, see Chapter 9.

- **Credit card insurance:** Your credit card provider can include travel insurance coverage for canceled reservations, trip interruptions, delays, and lost or stolen baggage when you travel with the card that you used to book your reservation.

  Don't rely on credit card insurance as your primary provider abroad. Think of it as a backup plan, read the fine print, and know the coverage limits.

- **Personal liability insurance:** Protects you if you injure a person or property abroad. It can help cover foreign legal fees and medical bills. Check with your travel insurance provider to see if this feature is included in your policy.

- **Property or renters' insurance:** Protects your belongings from fire, theft, water, or other damage. The landlord or rental agency may require that you have it to rent a property abroad. Your landlord insures the building that you live in, but you're responsible for insuring its contents.

- **Tech and electronics insurance:** Many travel insurance plans cover loss or damage of electronics, but coverage limits are often low (think $500–$1,000). If you have a pricey laptop, cameras, or other professional equipment, consider getting a separate insurance policy.

The Professional Photographers of America (PPA; www.ppa.com) offers general liability, equipment, and drone insurance packages. You don't have to be a professional photographer to become a member.

Booking Your Flight

A booked flight makes your move feel real; now, if only you can find a great deal on the preferred route to your destination.

Finding a flight within your budget and timeframe takes patience. The following sections can simplify the process by offering top strategies, resources, and tips to help you find the best flight possible.

Weighing value versus convenience

Choose a flight that strikes a balance between value and convenience. Finding a low fare is just the beginning. Also, look for:

- **The most direct route possible:** Fewer connections means less risk of delays and lost baggage, and lower stress.

>> **An ideal timetable:** Pay attention to whether a flight leaves too early or late for your needs and whether the flight is a *red-eye* (arriving the next day) or has long layovers.

>> **An arrival airport close to your destination:** A city may have multiple international airports. London has three. Check the distance between the airport and your property address, considering that the closest airport may be in a different country. When I travel to Maastricht in the Netherlands, I prefer to fly into Brussels, Belgium, rather than the Amsterdam, because it's more than an hour closer by bus, train, or car.

WARNING

Avoid the temptation to save money by connecting multiple flights on different airlines. Although they appear cheaper, they add extra hassle and travel fatigue.

For journeys over 24 hours, where you can't avoid two or three layovers, consider booking a stopover to rest between flights. Look for private rooms and suites in major airports, such as Singapore Changi Airport, or get a nearby airport hotel. Treat it as a mini-vacation en route to your destination. It's much more comfortable than sleeping on the floor of an airport terminal — trust me!

Working with your airline

Airline apps make travel changes more manageable and communication more fluid. The app lets you change your seat, get up-to-the-minute notifications, track your bags, and chat with customer service in real time.

Before traveling, review your airline's baggage policy and associated fees, including for excess and overweight baggage. Baggage allowances vary by the fare class you purchase. Traveling with heavy luggage may be unavoidable when moving abroad, although some people manage to move with only carry-ons. Use packing cubes to condense the essentials, and travel as lightly as possible.

Find packing tips in the section "Packing Like a Pro," later in this chapter, and consider shipping luggage instead of checking it with a company such as Luggage Forward (www.luggageforward.com) or SendMyBag.com. (I talk more about shipping your things in the section "Shipping Your Stuff Internationally," later in this chapter.)

Staying organized

Keep travel details at hand by printing reservations, writing down important information, or saving everything in a travel organization app, such as TripIt (www.tripit.com). Double-check the following items before you book your flight:

- Average prices to your destination
- Baggage fees and allowances
- Change fees and cancellation policies
- Connecting flight or layover times
- Departure and arrival times
- Number of connections
- Seat selection fees
- Total travel time

When moving across countries, account for added transit time due to time zone changes; check-in and check-out times; security lines; and bus, shuttle, or rental car lines.

Save time at airports by enrolling in trusted traveler programs such as Global Entry and TSA PreCheck, which are available in the United States.

Booking flights online

Here are six websites that you can use to book flights and find deals on international travel:

- **Google Flights** (www.google.com/travel/flights): Has the largest selection of airlines and the most flexible and user-friendly tools and features. You can find numerous tutorials online that explain how to use it.
- **Kiwi.com**: Bare-bones, economy flights — international and domestic. Kiwi boasts a unique "Kiwi-Code" technology that helps you find the cheapest travel options available.
- **Momondo** (www.momondo.com): Has good deals on discount airfare with flexible filters that allow you to search by country, city, and cost.
- **Going** (www.going.com): Can help you save up to 40 to 90 percent off flights. This website charges a membership fee and alerts you whenever a great flight deal becomes available.
- **Daily Drop** (www.dailydrop.com): A travel resources website with a membership site (Daily Drop Pro) that helps you save up to 80 percent by using fare alerts and points program deals.
- **SkyScanner** (www.skyscanner.com): Has strong search filters, like Google Flights, that can help you get granular and specific in your deal search.

TIP

Install an ad blocker on your web browser to minimize annoying pop-up ads that some flight booking sites try to push.

Before making your flight selection, check the results from flight booking portals against airlines' websites. Sometimes, the airline offers a price match or the lowest fare guarantee.

REMEMBER

Read the airline's or booking platform's change fee, refund policy, and cancellation policy to ensure you know what to expect.

Going roundtrip

If you don't have a long-stay visa, residency status, or citizenship in your destination country, buy a roundtrip or additional one-way ticket. Most countries require proof of onward travel for tourism purposes and may ask to review your outbound reservation at check-in, boarding, immigration, or all three.

A bus, cruise, ferry, or train ticket serves as proof of onward travel, as does an airline reservation. If your travel plans aren't set in stone yet, other strategies include:

» Booking a roundtrip ticket, but changing your return date after you land.

» Buying two one-way tickets if you plan to country-hop. One ticket is for your current destination, and the second is for the following destination.

» Buying two one-way tickets (there and back) and making the return ticket changeable or fully refundable. After you arrive at your destination, you can alter or cancel it.

» Using a service that provides a temporary confirmed flight/passage itinerary, such as Onward Ticket (www.onwardticket.com). Reservations are valid for up to 48 hours.

WARNING

Whatever you decide, respect the limits of your visa and don't overstay your welcome.

Packing Like a Pro

Packing to move somewhere is different than packing for vacation. This section helps you know what to pack and what to leave behind.

116 PART 2 Mastering Your Move — Relocation Logistics

First, decide whether you want to ship most of your belongings or pack the essentials into a few suitcases. If you plan to bring everything except the kitchen sink, review the section "Shipping Your Stuff Internationally," later in this chapter.

If you want to bring only a carry-on bag and a suitcase (or two), the following sections provide a packing list and tips.

You can purchase many items at your destination after you arrive. Mohammed, a digital nomad, agrees. "My advice is to pack light," he told me. "Focus on essentials, such as tech gear, important documents, and a few personal comforts that aren't easy to replace abroad. Anything else can usually be purchased locally, often at better prices and suited for the destination."

Whether you're packing big or small, take the following factors into account before you start:

- » **Climate:** Pack for multiple temperatures if you're moving somewhere that has four seasons. If you're retiring in the tropics, you can focus more on warm-weather clothes.
- » **Seasons:** Consider the time of year when you're moving. Perhaps you want to bring articles for one season and purchase more clothing after you arrive.
- » **Location:** If you're moving to a city or urban area, you can probably find everything that you need or get it shipped there. If you're going to a more remote location, you may have fewer retail options. In that case, bring essential clothing, medicine, tech tools, and anything that you can't live without (literally and figuratively).
- » **Your personal needs:** You may not *need* to move with your espresso maker, favorite stuffed animal, or leopard-print Christian Louboutin heels. But if you want to bring it with you, do so.
- » **Your timeline:** If you plan to move permanently, you may want to bring more personal items with you. If you're living abroad on a short timeline, such as a school semester, you can likely make do with a suitcase, a carry-on bag, and a backpack.

Making your list and checking it twice

To make sure you don't miss anything, separate your packing list into groups. The following sections can help keep you organized.

You can download a relocation packing list at www.travelingwithkristin.com/moving-abroad. You can also find more ideas of what to pack in my Amazon Travel Shop (www.amazon.com/shop/travelingwithkristin).

CHAPTER 7 Getting Ready to Hit the Road 117

Travel essentials

The following items make your travel day smoother. Bring these items (along with anything you can't be without) with you in your carry-on or personal bag:

- **Clear bags:** Pack liquids and gels in airport security-approved bags.
- **Electronics:** Your phone, tablet, laptop, camera, cables, chargers, hard drives, and adaptors.
- **Charging devices:** A portable charging device to juice up on the go (or if you can't find a free outlet to plug into). I like to travel with one adaptor and a power strip to plug into.

  Lithium-ion batteries can't go in checked luggage. Check your airline's luggage policy before traveling.
- **Noise-cancelling headphones:** Drown out noise by using ear plugs and/or noise-canceling headphones.
- **Over-the-counter medicines:** You may want to bring over-the-counter pain relievers, motion sickness pills, and melatonin for sleep.
- **Prescriptions:** Enough months' worth of prescription medicines until you can get a refill locally or internationally.

  Bring a doctor's note or written prescription with you, especially if medicines are stored outside of the original container.
- **Money:** Credit and debit cards (make sure they don't expire for at least one year). Download any apps that you need to manage your finances. Bring some cash in the local currency (an amount that you feel comfortable with).

  When crossing borders, you must declare cash and *financial instruments* (meaning any type of currency, travelers' checks, money orders, or bearer investment securities) greater than $9,999.
- **Kid items, if applicable:** A supply of diapers, baby formula, bottles, blankets, toys, games, puzzles, and other activities.
- **Luggage locks:** TSA-approved locks or luggage that has built-in locks.
- **Packing cubes:** Keep your items organized in packing cubes of multiple shapes and sizes.
- **Packable bags:** Light, foldable bags or a compact day pack for carrying items that you may purchase in transit.
- **Personal items:** Trinkets, keepsakes, or family photos that you value.
- **Refillable water bottle:** A slim metal, durable plastic, or foldable travel water bottle.

- **Snacks:** That won't melt or spoil, such as nuts, dried fruit, and granola bars.
- **Travel pillow and eye mask:** If you don't have these items, you can purchase them at the airport.

Documents

Ensure you have all the necessary documents for your travels and after you arrive in your destination, such as:

- **Your passport:** Valid for at least six months, ideally longer.
- **Personal documentation:** Including an insurance policy, birth certificate, college records, or financial statements. Says Richard, who moved to the UK, "Packing important documents like a birth certificate and university diploma is helpful because you never know when you might have to prove something."
- **Travel reservations and booking info:** Print or keep this info in a trip organization app, such as TripIt (www.tripit.com).
- **Vaccine records:** Some countries require proof of vaccinations for entry. Find out which vaccines are necessary by contacting your airline, state department, or the health department in your destination.
- **Visa or residency permits:** Keep a physical and digital copy of your travel visa or residency permit, as indicated by your residency advisor or host country's consulate.
- **Driver's license:** You need your driver's license (or international driving permit, which I talk about in Chapter 9) if you want to buy or rent a car.

  Notarize, certify, or apostille any documents that you need for your residency application.

TIP

See the "Checking Your Paperwork" section below for more about preparing your documents.

Clothes

Pack enough clothes to last one to two weeks and ensure that you pack the proper clothing for your destination's climate and season. However, if you plan to travel internationally from your new country, you might want to bring a few items that you don't want to repurchase, such as an expensive jacket (even if you're moving to the tropics).

Here's a list of the basics for a variety of destinations:

Everyday Basics:

- Belt
- Bras and/or underwear
- One or two blouses or dress shirts
- One to two pairs of jeans or lightweight, quick-dry travel pants
- One to two sets of workout clothes
- Pair of walking shoes
- Pajamas or sleepwear
- Rain jacket and/or poncho
- Two to four basic T-shirts
- Variety of socks

Warm or Tropical Destinations:

- Bathing suit(s)
- Pair of sandals or flip flops
- Sarong or packable travel towel
- Shorts or skirts
- Sun hat

Cold or Variable Weather:

- One or two long-sleeved shirts
- Hat, gloves, and scarf
- Hoodie, fleece, or sweater
- One to two pairs of leggings
- Pair of boots
- Packable down jacket
- Thermal base layers
- Other jackets or outerwear

Specialty Items:

» A watch and basic jewelry

» Nice dress, evening wear, or business attire

» Pair of dressier shoes

» Slippers

» Sunglasses and/or reading glasses

REMEMBER

The 80/20 rule applies to clothing — most people wear only 20 percent of what's in their closet. It can also apply to packing — remove 20 percent of what you pack before zipping up your suitcase.

Toiletries

Buy full-sized toiletries in your destination to save space and weight in your luggage. However, consider bringing the following items in a travel-friendly size, if possible:

» Antibacterial gel and wipes

» Brush and/or comb

» Contacts and lens solution

» Deodorant

» Feminine hygiene products (if applicable)

» Lip balm and lotion (airplanes are notorious for having dry air)

» Nail grooming set
  Scissors and sharp items can't go in carry-on bags

» Shampoo and conditioner bars

» Toothbrush, toothpaste, and dental floss

» Travel first-aid kit

What not to bring

Unless you're moving permanently, or buying or renting an entirely unfurnished property, you probably don't need to pack the following items (you can purchase them in your destination):

» **Cookware:** Provided in furnished properties. It's also heavy, bulky, and easily replaced.

CHAPTER 7 **Getting Ready to Hit the Road** 121

- **Food:** Fresh fruits and vegetables, and meats generally can't go through Customs (although you can bring some packaged and processed foods). Check Customs requirements before you travel. But if a certain food item is significant to you (and allowed), bring it. Two of my French real estate clients arrived in Nicaragua with a suitcase full of chocolates and cans of pâté.

- **Linens:** Most furnished rental properties provide sheets, towels, and pillows.

- **Toiletries:** They weigh a lot, and many are liquid; you can buy them at your destination. Bring just the basics with you.

- **Valuables:** Store valuables and family heirlooms in a safe deposit box in your home country if you plan to return. Otherwise, bring them, but use caution.

Sorting through your excess baggage

Ultimately, you must decide how much luggage you want to take with you.

Check your airline's excess and overweight baggage policy before packing, especially if you want to bring oversized items such as athletic equipment (golf clubs, surfboards, and snowboards), strollers, pet crates, furniture, and desktop computers.

WARNING

Measure and weigh your bags before heading to the airport.

Carrying it all on the plane

While living abroad and traveling as a digital nomad, I've always been an overpacker. At my worst, I traveled with two large suitcases (right at the maximum weight limit), a carry-on item filled with camera and video equipment, and a backpack for my laptop, purse, and other items. If you can, pack lighter than I did. Plenty of people move or travel abroad with a single carry-on.

Here are some tips to help you pack carry-on only:

- **Roll as many clothes as you can.** Folded clothes take up way more space.

- **Use packing cubes.** Packing cubes keep everything tight, organized, and compressed.

TIP

- **Vacuum-seal your clothes.** If you're headed somewhere with cold weather, compression or vacuum-sealed bags can significantly reduce the space taken up by bulky sweaters, jackets, and snow pants.

- » **Wear your thickest gear on the plane.** If your destination involves bulky gear such as hiking boots, pack your smaller street shoes in the bag and wear the boots on your feet.
- » **Keep cosmetics and toiletries to bare necessities.** You can always stock up for variety after you get settled.
- » **Stock up on travel clothing.** Look for companies specializing in lightweight, wrinkle-resistant clothing for travelers.
- » **Create a capsule wardrobe.** Wear a copy of the same outfit daily. It's one less thing to think about!

TIP

"Travel light," recommends John, who moved from the U.S. to Italy. "It may seem counter-intuitive, but even if you're moving overseas for a year, pack enough for three days of travel and buy anything else you need after you get there. In over 40 years, I've never traveled with more than a carry-on and a laptop bag."

Checking Your Paperwork

Ensure all your paperwork ducks are in a row so that you can arrive as smoothly and seamlessly as possible.

Before heading to the airport, check the following items on your pre-departure checklist and arrival itinerary:

- » **Update all documentation.** Update travel visas and permits, passports, and driver's licenses with a minimum six-month window before you need to renew them. Getting an International Driving Permit (see Chapter 9) can allow you to drive for one year in some countries.
- » **Check how long you can stay in a country with your passport.** All countries offer some tourist or visa-free travel authorization to citizens of certain countries. Search your home or destination country's consulate or government travel portal to find out how long you can stay with your passport and if you need an additional visa or other authorization.

  Sites such as VisaHQ (www.visahq.com) offer this information for multiple countries in one portal.

  You can't reside in a country for any length of time without a residency or other valid permit. If you don't have one yet, you would enter as a tourist who's visiting.
- » **Avoid banking and financial issues.** Confirm international ATM and transaction fees with your bank before you travel. Alert them if you're going abroad. Download apps for your bank accounts, and renew any expiring cards early.

CHAPTER 7 **Getting Ready to Hit the Road** 123

>> **Check health restrictions.** Check with your airline, embassy or consulate, or your destination's tourism board and public health department, to meet any necessary health requirements for travel.

>> **Draft your itinerary.** Details you should have on your itinerary include flight number, home emergency contacts, and hotel or rental address.

Before moving abroad, draft an emergency plan with a trusted family member or friend. Provide your travel itinerary, contact info abroad, and who to contact if they can't reach you. Also, designate a cadence for check-ins and your preferred method of communication, such as a phone call, video call, or messaging app. Your loved ones also need to know how to reach you in an emergency.

Consider creating an emergency file stored securely in the cloud, including your emergency contact, insurance policy, living will or last will, trust, and other important info. You can also store such info in a safe deposit box and give someone power of attorney so that they're authorized to access it in case you become incapacitated. Update this information on an annual basis.

Add beneficiaries to all your financial accounts before you depart.

Here's a list of items to write down and provide to someone before you go:

>> The address and contact info of your property manager or host abroad.

>> Your home country's embassy or consulate in your destination.

>> Personal contacts (friends, family, work colleagues, or employer) in your host country.

>> Local civil authorities, such as law enforcement and emergency services.

>> Local health and safety facilities, such as hospitals, clinics, and your local pharmacy.

Register with your embassy to receive emergency alerts regarding terror threats, natural disasters, and other risks.

Add emergency contacts to your airline or other transportation provider. You can add an emergency contact to your profile if you have a frequent flier account with the airline. You can also add someone during the check-in process.

Shipping Your Stuff Internationally

One word says it all when it comes in international shipping: expensive. Whether you use the postal service, FedEx, UPS, DHL, or a container ship, overseas shipping costs an arm and a leg.

After nearly two decades of helping folks move abroad, I've had very few clients who decided to ship a Full Container Load (FCL) of home goods. However, it happens sometimes, especially when people are moving permanently or for work, own expensive furniture, or want to furnish a property abroad.

You have three methods of moving your stuff without bringing it with you on a plane or train:

- **Mail shipments:** Good for sending small boxes of non-valuable items that you don't want to carry. You can send packages internationally through your country's postal service or a company such as FedEx or UPS.

- **Luggage shipments:** Optimal for sending packed suitcases that you don't want to carry. Get quotes from companies such as Luggage Forward (www.luggageforward.com) or SendMyBag.com.

- **Sea freight:** Applicable for sending large palettes of furniture or home goods, or for shipping cars, containers, and other large objects.

Looking into international movers

Here's a list of well-known international moving companies:

- **AGS** (www.agsmovers.com): International removals and storage services on five continents.

- **Allied** (www.allied.com): One of the largest and oldest moving companies in the world, Allied helps with packing and unpacking, loading, storage, and Customs clearance.

- **Mayflower** (www.mayflower.com): Helps with international moves, car shipping, and insurance. The website offers an online planner to help coordinate your move.

- **North American** (www.northamerican.com): Provides various corporate and personal worldwide moving services, including furniture assembly and appliance installation.

- » **Ranier Overseas Movers** (www.rainieros.com): Offers relocation services and moving guides and handles Customs forms.

- » **UPakWeShip** (www.upakweship.com): Offers affordable, do-it-yourself shipping solutions in various sizes, from palettes to containers.

Coordinating an international shipment

Gather at least two to three quotes from moving companies before you decide on one to ensure that you find the best option for your move. Ask each company about Customs duties and other fees. And request binding quotes to avoid unexpected costs at your destination.

TIP

Check with your residency attorney if your visa category comes with Customs allowances for cars, boats, and personal items, as this can reduce your overall shipping costs.

Whenever possible, arrange for an in-person estimate and ask for a breakdown of how they calculate the price. Many shipping companies use container shipping, and they often base their charges on cubic meters.

TIP

If you don't need a FCL, consider splitting it with someone else to save money. You can find potential people to share a container with through expat Facebook groups or InterNations (www.internations.org).

REMEMBER

Get insurance to protect your valuables. If it's not included in your shipping quote, you can add it separately through a company such as Clements Worldwide (www.clements.com).

Downsizing

The biggest tip I can give you about moving your stuff is to downsize as much as possible before you leave. Shipping internationally can cost thousands of dollars and is a time-consuming ordeal. You may be better off selling, storing, donating, or discarding most of your belongings before you depart. Says John, who moved to Italy, "I've lived all over the world, and trust me — you can find anything you need in almost any country you visit." Abir, who moved to Switzerland, agrees. "After moving so many times, I've learned to travel light. Nothing's worse than hauling a ton of stuff with you overseas."

Look, people have stuff. It's part of being human. But you'll thank yourself later if you downsize the quantity of items that you own. It also feels good to shed stuff (perhaps better than the dopamine boost of buying it). Adds Claudia, who moved to Canada, "Take the absolute bare minimum along. Don't move the entire household (thankfully, we didn't)."

When deciding what to get rid of, give yourself time. According to Marie Kondo, the inventor of the KonMari Method of decluttering and tidying, you may need one year or more to tidy your home and discard anything that doesn't spark joy. It's never too soon to start. On the flip side, starting too late can really stress you out. For help downsizing your belongings ahead of your move, see Chapter 5.

Saying Your Goodbyes

I can't offer you an easy way around this part, and it doesn't get easier after the first few times you do it. It's time to say goodbye to family, friends, and everything that you know.

According to travel blogger Melissa Parks, the best tool to navigate awkward, painful farewell moments is mindful acceptance of them. Don't run away or avoid them, but don't let them stop you, either.

She offers a few ideas and tips to process the transition:

>> Write a goodbye letter that records your memories.
>> Get rid of physical objects that keep you tied to your old life.
>> Give yourself permission to cry and experience emotions.
>> Walk through empty rooms and old haunts, and whisper "goodbye" to them.

REMEMBER

Every season of life comes and goes, including this one. Even if you buy a retirement home in your destination and have no plans to return, other than for short visits, you still have a few seasons to come.

AIRPORT AND TRAVEL DAY TIPS

You have a lot to process, go through, and think about when embarking on your journey.

These tips from travel insurance company WorldTrips (www.worldtrips.com) can prevent you from getting bogged down in minutiae and keep you grounded, even while you're in the air:

- Activate international data roaming on your phone. Purchase in-flight Wi-Fi, too.
- Take along a travel journal. Write down whatever thoughts, emotions, or journey markers you encounter.
- Arrive at the airport two to three hours early, particularly for international flights.
- Avoid airport food. It's expensive, unhealthy, and generally of poor quality. Bring your food with you or eat before you go to the airport.
- Download books, movies, or shows before you travel.
- Register with your embassy or consulate nearest to your destination.
- Bring snacks, chewing gum, and a water bottle. You definitely want to avoid dehydration or hunger on long plane rides.
- Listen to podcasts and other content relevant to your destination.
- Bring a pillow, a sleep mask, and a small blanket. A good pair of noise-canceling headphones are worth every penny, too.

USING TRAVEL CREDIT CARDS OR REWARDS PROGRAMS

Ignoring travel rewards programs is one of the top mistakes expats make. Sign up for them when your overseas finance plan takes shape. Most major airlines, hotel chains, and travel providers (such as Travelocity [www.travelocity.com] or Expedia [www.expedia.com]) offer travel credit cards, as do the big banks.

Whether at home or abroad, daily life costs money. If you already spend money on everyday purchases such as groceries, gasoline, and rent or a mortgage — you may as well accumulate cash or points-based rewards while doing it.

Travel cards have features that standard credit or debit cards don't offer, including

- Additional travel or car rental insurance
- Easy dispute resolutions and reimbursements for fraudulent purchases
- Emergency funds through a cash advance

You can cancel and replace cards quickly; most companies can send you replacement cards anywhere in the world.

You can choose between:

- **General travel cards:** Good for budget travelers, these cards have low or no annual fees. You accumulate points while you pay for necessities such as groceries, gas, and living expenses.
- **Airline cards:** Accumulate travel mileage and offer perks such as elite status on the partner airline, seat upgrades, and lounge access.
- **Hotel cards:** Rack up points for free stays, early/late check-in/out, room upgrades, and concierge services.
- **Platinum cards:** Offer extra perks such as 24/7 concierge assistance, airport lounge access, no spending limits, and priority boarding, seating, and service.

    Platinum cards have high annual fees (usually around $500 or more). Don't sign up unless you're comfortable with those costs.

Daily Drop (www.dailydrop.com) can help you find up-to-date information so that you can compare the best cards and plans.

(continued)

(continued)

In the new age of *cryptocurrency* (decentralized, borderless digital currencies such as Bitcoin), some companies jumped on the bandwagon and now offer credit card rewards. You can get a card from `Crypto.com` with zero annual fees and 8 percent cash back on spending, which you can reload with *fiat* (government-issued money) or cryptocurrency. Check out NerdWallet's list of the best crypto cards (`www.nerdwallet.com/article/credit-cards/credit-cards-with-crypto-rewards`).

Personally, I use two credit cards for travel: the American Express Delta Reserve card and the Chase Sapphire Preferred Visa card. The Amex card benefits have helped me achieve Diamond Medallion status on Delta. In return, I get free access to Delta Sky Clubs, earn bonus frequent flier miles for each dollar spent, and receive spending waivers that help me to gain elite status faster. I tend to use the Chase Sapphire card for everyday purchases abroad when Amex isn't accepted. Through the Chase card, you can earn Ultimate Rewards points that you can exchange for cash back or apply to book travel.

Consider your situation to figure out which kind of card works best for you:

- If you don't expect to use your card often, get one that has zero annual fees.
- Treat your card like a debit card. Spend only what you can afford and pay the full bill monthly. (If you begin to accumulate interest, you defeat the purpose of the rewards savings.)
- Carry a Visa or Mastercard as a contingency if Amex is your primary card. Not all cards are accepted everywhere.
- Ensure that your credit card company doesn't charge foreign transaction fees. They add up!

3
Leaping Into Your New Life Abroad

IN THIS PART...

Adapt to life in a foreign country.

Find your way with local transportation.

Design your daily life abroad.

Avoid and solve common problems.

Handle banking and paperwork.

Find a local doctor and fast Wi-Fi.

IN THIS CHAPTER

» Arriving in a new country

» Getting acclimated to day-to-day life

» Figuring out your first month

» Keeping your finances in order

Chapter 8
Landing in Your Adopted Country

Because you have to put so much effort into planning your relocation (which you can read about in Part 1 of this book), it's possible to overlook what happens *after* you move. In this chapter, I share how to spend your time in your first days and weeks abroad so that you hit the ground running.

From whizzing through the airport upon landing to arriving safely at your destination, this chapter gives you tips on what to do for a seamless arrival.

You also get a roadmap for how to spend your first month abroad — from the logistics of activating your cellphone to meeting your first new friends, navigating public transport, and making the place that you're staying feel like home.

Navigating Your First Day in a New Country

Your first day abroad can invoke a mixture of feelings. Anticipation, excitement, fear, and apprehension are a few that I've experienced in the past. Whatever emotions you feel on your first day on foreign soil, it's normal. The following sections can help you overcome common hurdles and keep your sanity when emotions run high.

If you don't have a strict timeline with regards to how you spend your first days in a new country, take your time with tackling your to-do list. There's no need to rush — especially if enjoying a relaxed pace of life is one of the reasons that you're moving.

As Mohammed, a digital nomad in Dubai told me, "The first week in a new country is always a mix of excitement and unexpected lessons. It's a reminder that flexibility and a sense of humor go a long way when settling into a new place."

Getting through the airport and immigration

Ensure that you can successfully pass through airport customs and immigration before your plane lands by having the right paperwork to get into the country. To visit short term, you may need a passport that has visa-free travel authorization, a tourist visa, or another short-stay visa. Find out which type of visa you need for travel by researching online, contacting your airline, embassy, or consulate, or by visiting a site such as `VisaHQ.com`. Also check if your destination country offers automated, self-service kiosks for passport control (also known as eGates), which allow you to bypass long immigration lines. In that case, you may walk through without getting your passport stamped.

Staying somewhere as a tourist is different than *living* there. To live in a country, you need proper permission. Find out more about visas and residency permits in Chapter 4 and read up on preparing your travel documents in Chapter 7.

If you're traveling as a tourist, you need proof of onward travel. Onward travel can be in the form of a train, bus, or plane ticket that departs before your stay expires. If you have a visa or residency status, have your paperwork with you or ensure that you have the stamp or document affixed to your passport.

If you don't have the proper paperwork, visa stamp, or permission to stay in a country that you travel to, that country can refuse you boarding onto the plane headed there, refuse you entry when you arrive, or deport you.

Some countries offer a known traveler program for expedited entry, such as Global Entry in the U.S., the EU Smart Borders program in Europe, and Canada's NEXUS system. Apply for clearance in advance, because processing times can take months.

After deboarding the plane and passing through immigration, you arrive at the baggage claim belt. Before leaving this area, inspect your luggage for damage. If you notice a rip, tear, or broken wheel, you could qualify for compensation from your airline or travel insurance company. For assistance, go to your airline's baggage customer service desk.

Before exiting baggage claim, you must clear customs. You have two options, with signs indicating whether you have something to declare (usually red) or nothing to declare (typically green).

Choose the appropriate line for your situation.

Common items that you should declare include (but don't take this as an exhaustive list): animals or animal products, cash or monetary instruments over $9,999 or equivalent in the local currency, and fresh foods and produce.

Not declaring necessary items can result in hefty fines, deportation, or even incarceration. Know what you need to declare and follow the rules.

For information about preparing for arrival, refer to Chapters 5 and 7.

Activating your cellphone

If you want your phone to work when the wheels of your plane touch down, plan ahead with the tips in Chapter 7.

If you keep your home country phone plan, you can simply turn on your phone upon arrival, turn on your Cellular Data and Data Roaming, and wait until your phone connects to local networks.

If you installed an eSIM, follow the activation steps according to your provider's instructions — most companies offer an app with help guides and step-by-step tutorials. Contact their support team with questions.

Here are the general steps to activate an eSIM:

iPhone:

1. Open Settings > Cellular.
2. Tap on the eSIM you want to activate.

3. Turn on Data Roaming.

4. Start Web surfing, texting, and/or calling!

Android:

1. Go to Settings > Connections > SIM Manager.
2. Turn your eSIM on.
3. Turn off any other installed eSIMs.
4. Return to Connections > Tap on Mobile Network.
5. Turn on Data Roaming to begin your plan.

If you don't have an eSIM, you can purchase one online using your cellular data or after connecting to the airport Wi-Fi. Popular eSIM ompanies include: Airalo, Holafly, and Saily.

You can also purchase an eSIM or physical SIM at an airport kiosk or store if your flight arrives during regular business hours. In most countries, you can also pick up a free SIM at convenience stores or cellphone stores, which you activate online or in-person.

If you plan on using your new SIM card as a Wi-Fi hotspot, confirm that the provider you're considering allows tethering.

If you use your domestic cellphone provider abroad, 4G and 5G data speeds may be capped. Contact your provider to know what your plan includes.

For additional details about how to prepare your phone plan for your international departure, see Chapter 7.

Accessing your cash

Before departing from your home country, make a plan for how to access your money abroad. Chapter 5 helps you with banking and finances, but here are a few tips:

» Notify your bank and credit card providers before traveling to prevent fraud or other transaction blocks on your card.

» Bring more than one credit or debit card with you in case one gets blocked, lost, or stolen. Store them in separate places in your luggage.

- » Carry cards from different providers, such as American Express, Mastercard, and Visa, in case one isn't accepted in certain places.
- » Choose credit cards that don't charge foreign transaction fees.
- » Travel with some local currency (how much depends on your personal spending habits and what you anticipate you might need cash for, such as tipping, transportation, and emergencies). You can also withdraw or exchange some cash at an ATM upon arrival.

You can withdraw money at the airport or city center upon arrival. Airport currency exchange booths don't offer the best rates, but they are convenient.

Decline the proposed currency conversion at ATMs and points of sale in retail outlets to save on exchange rates. Accept the charge in the foreign (local) currency. If you're in Europe, transact in euros. If you're in Japan, transact in yen.

Another way to receive cash abroad is to use a money transfer or remittance service, such as Western Union (www.westernunion.com), Remitly (www.remitly.com/), or OFX (www.ofx.com).

Check out Chapters 5, 7, and 9 to find out more about exchanging or using money abroad.

Arriving at your destination

After you pick up your luggage, clear immigration and customs, and confirm that your phone is working (see the preceding sections), it's time to make your way to your first destination, whether that's at a hotel, a rental property, or a home that you purchased.

Exiting the baggage claim to a sea of unknown faces can be intimidating, especially if the airport is crowded and you're in a foreign country for the first time. But you'll soon be on your way.

You can compare different routes from the airport to your destination address by using a map app, such as Google Maps (http://maps.google.com) or Apple Maps (www.apple.com/maps), or the website Rome2Rio (www.rome2rio.com). Rome2Rio shows you different routes and booking options for getting anywhere by bus, train, plane, car, or ferry, as well as prices and travel times.

Your primary transportation methods include:

» **Buses:** Often the most affordable methods of travel, search online to see whether you can find an airport bus in your area. A one-way fare from Barcelona BCN airport to the center with Aerobus (www.barcelona-aerobus-tickets.com) costs €7.25 ($7.60) versus $45-60 for a taxi.

» **Metro:** Taking the subway, tube, or metro is another budget-friendly option. Look for signs in the terminal to find the airport metro station or ask at an information desk. Purchase a ticket from a vending machine or ticket counter and double check your map and destination before boarding to ensure you're traveling in the right direction.

» **Planes:** If you're traveling far from a major hub, see whether a domestic airline can take you from one part of a country to another. Sansa Airlines (www.flysansa.com) in Costa Rica has offered domestic routes around the country since 1978.

» **Taxis and rideshares:** Hail a cab from the airport taxi line or pay in advance at a taxi desk inside the terminal. To book a rideshare, use an app such as Uber or Bolt. And look up local apps such as Careem (www.careem.com), Grab (www.grab.com), and Yandex Go (http://taxi.yandex.com). Tip your rideshare or taxi driver according to the local custom.

Before entering a taxi, confirm the fare and payment method.

When booking a rideshare, ensure you request pick up at the correct terminal and baggage claim number. In some cases, rideshare pickup is located in a dedicated, shared area that you must walk to.

» **Trains:** Most major hubs have a high-speed train from the airport to the city center, such as the Heathrow Express (www.heathrowexpress.com), which takes you from London Heathrow Airport (LHR) to Paddington station in 15 minutes for £25 (about $31 at the time of writing).

Depending on your comfort level in your destination and how much luggage you have with you, consider arranging an airport transfer in advance. Booking a ride with a friend, guide, or private driver gives you one less thing to worry about when you land.

Here are a few sources that you can use to find a ride from the airport:

» Ask one of your local contacts for a recommendation, such as your landlord, real estate agent, or relocation consultant.

- Look up transportation options on your arrival airport's website.
- Hire a driver from a travel and tourism website, such as TripAdvisor (www.tripadvisor.com).
- Search for "airport transfers" in your location on Google (www.google.com) or another search engine.

TIP

Read reviews and compare rates before selecting a transport option.

Checking into your new home

Depending on how far you travel to get to your final destination, you might be tired or jetlagged when you arrive. Rest assured, your work is almost done, but make note of a few things before your head hits the pillow (and see Chapter 6 for information on how to find and secure your new digs):

- Ensure that you can access the property okay and contact your landlord with any issues.
- Conduct a walk-through upon arrival. Check for any home damage, such as a faulty lock, ripped carpet, marks on the walls or floors, or broken furniture and appliances. Also, note if you smell mold or mildew, or if you notice any safety concerns or the presence of pests.
- If your property is furnished and you have a copy of the home inventory (list of items included with the property), check whether anything is missing or broken, such as tableware, decorations, or linens.
- Connect to the Internet and test the speed by using a website such as Speedtest (www.speedtest.net). If the connection is slower than promised, or if you can't connect, notify your host.
- Test the plumbing and water temperature in the kitchen, shower, and laundry.

TIP

Report any damages as soon as possible to your host or rental website — definitely within 24 to 48 hours of arrival — for the best chance of a quick resolution or refund. If you're moving into a long-term rental, communicate damages to your landlord or rental agent.

For information about buying or renting a home abroad, see Chapter 6.

EXPATS SHARE THEIR FIRST DAY ABROAD

Everyone has a different "first day abroad" story to tell. What will yours be? Here are a few experiences from people in their own words:

- **Dave, Portugal:** Everything went very smoothly. The most memorable moment was when my wife opened the door to our new house and started crying from the surge of emotions. It truly was a joyful moment.
- **John, Italy:** Just get on the bus, Gus. Get a bus pass and ride around for a couple of hours. Start walking and stop and talk with people in their native language. Everyone and anyone will talk with you.
- **Karl, Mexico:** When I first arrived, I lived with locals in their homes. I went to their family events. I helped people to learn English at the library.
- **Joe, Costa Rica:** The first weeks and months were so fulfilling, happy, and validating. The sights, sounds, food, people, and routines were exactly as I'd hoped.
- **Richard, U.K.:** At first there was a bit of "buyers remorse." Little things — the different smells, the lighting, the climate — at first reminded us that we were somewhere "not home." Knowing it would be a while was stressful . . . until we adjusted.
- **Mohammed, Dubai:** Upon arriving, I realized how different even simple things like getting around or setting up a bank account could be. I spent the first day trying to navigate public transport before realizing ride-hailing apps were far more efficient. A mishap I vividly remember was not having enough local currency on hand. I assumed card payments would be accepted everywhere, but a few small shops and taxis only accepted cash. I had to hunt for an ATM late at night, which added unnecessary stress to an otherwise smooth day. Overall, the first week felt like controlled chaos but was full of rewarding experiences and quick adaptation.

Getting Settled During Your First Month Abroad

Your first weeks and months in a new country can feel like a roller coaster. Your emotions are a product of culture shock and adaptation to a new place, which I discuss more in Chapter 10.

Whatever you feel, it's normal — and it'll pass. The following sections can help you make the most of your first month abroad. Before you know it, you'll feel like a local!

Exploring your new surroundings

Take it easy during your first few days abroad, especially if you're tired from the move and jet lag. Today is the first day of the rest of your life, and you have plenty of time to seize the day after getting some much-needed rest. How you feel (and what you have planned) can determine how you spend these days:

- » **If your energy is low:** Sleep in, putter around your new home, take your time unpacking, and scope out the neighborhood.

- » **If you feel energetic:** Take on more tasks faster and get into a daily routine more quickly.

- » **If you're not in a rush:** Use the first few days like you're on a vacation or holiday. Walk around, do some sightseeing, and be present. Tackle your to-do list later — unless you have something urgent to address, such as registering your visa or residency paperwork, installing public services, or visiting a healthcare provider.

Take this time to learn basic words and phrases to greet and interact with local people in their native language. Also, attend a local event or meet-up to connect with people in your community from the beginning.

PREPARING FOR AN EMERGENCY

Before or upon arriving abroad, identify emergency services in your area. Save important contacts to your phone or in a Notes app with the following information:

- **Emergency number:** The number to dial in an emergency varies by country. In the U.S., it's 911. In Europe, it's 112. In Australia, it's 000. You can find the emergency number in your location by searching online, visiting your local embassy consulate website, or visiting the government portal in your destination country. You can dial an international emergency number from a foreign phone.

  You can also download an app that allows you to call emergency numbers in countries worldwide, such as SOS Global Emergency Numbers, World Emergency Call, or EchoSOS.

- **Hospitals:** Hopefully, you don't have to go to a hospital, but knowing which ones are nearby can help if you do. Use your maps app or search online for the nearest hospital, then save the number on your phone.

(continued)

(continued)

- **Information:** Search online or contact the local tourism board for a general information number.

- **Police:** To contact law enforcement when it's not an emergency, call the station directly. You can find this number on the police website or by looking up the nearest station on a maps app.

- **Other issues:** Find out the local warning system for natural disasters. Chile has an earthquake warning system. Thailand has a tsunami warning system that includes sirens and voice messages in multiple languages. And the U.S. offers hurricane alerts through FEMA, wireless emergency alerts, and the National Hurricane Center. Most countries have mobile alert systems to advise about floods, fires, and other risks.

You need a local phone number to receive local alerts. See the section "Activating your cellphone," in this chapter, for more information.

Learning the lay of the land

Figuring out your way around a new place can be disorienting at first, especially if you move to a big city. I've been visiting Amsterdam for ten years and still get lost in the maze of canals, bridges, and curved streets.

Browse the area in your maps app and note how it's designed. Is your new town a neat grid of well-labeled or numbered streets, such as Las Vegas, Nevada? Is it a medieval (often circular) city center, such as Tallinn, Estonia? Is it a beach town with one main road, such as Jaco, Costa Rica? Spend a bit of time absorbing the layout of your new location to help you find your way around without always relying on GPS.

One way to familiarize yourself with a new place while getting your daily steps in by walking around. You can roam alone or join a free walking tour. Find free tours in your area on sites such as Free Tours by Foot (www.freetoursbyfoot.com), Free Tour.com, and GuruWalk (www.guruwalk.com). You can also hire a private guide on TripAdvisor (www.tripadvisor.com), ToursByLocals (www.toursbylocals.com), and GetYourGuide (www.getyourguide.com).

You have many options for how to get a feel for your area:

>> **Take the bus.** If you're in a city, board a hop-on, hop-off bus for a quick lay of the land. To save money, inquire whether you can get a tourist transportation card that you can use for your first few days or week. As a bonus, these cards often come with discounts and other benefits.

- » **Ride a bike.** See a city by bicycle, as long as the topography is relatively flat and safe. Look for bike rental agencies that have hourly, daily, or weekly rates. You can also buy a bike, new or secondhand. If you buy a used bike, purchase the lock separately. (I once had a bike stolen this way by its previous owner.)

- » **Keep a map handy.** Download maps for offline use. If you don't use a smartphone, carry a small, printed map or pick one up at a tourism information center.

- » **Look into public transportation.** If you don't have a car, research public transit options in your area and buy a monthly pass. Locate your home transit stop and the number or color of the bus or metro line near your home.

Always follow local laws regarding helmet use.

You can figure out your way around organically over time, so don't stress if you feel lost for a while. Taking a wrong turn can result in finding a new favorite restaurant, seeing a new sight, or making a new friend.

Becoming a navigation whiz

Living like a local starts with using public transportation like a local. Download the rideshare and transit apps for your area and create an account on each one, linking your bank card. (See Chapter 5 and the section "Receiving Your Paycheck or Pension Abroad," later in this chapter, for banking tips.)

With local transportation apps, you can purchase bus, train, and metro tickets, look up routes, find out about scheduling delays and service stoppages, and receive push notifications. If you have questions, contact the operator by phone or email. You can also clarify information at a station customer service desk.

A local transport card can save you money (and time) compared to buying individual tickets. In some locations, you can use your bank card, Apple Pay, or Google Pay to scan in and out of buses or metros without buying a ticket at a machine.

Identifying important places and contacts

After you settle into your new location, search in your maps app for nearby amenities. For example, find the closest bank and ATM, bus stop or metro station, doctor and dentist, and schools. Save each place to a list in your phone's maps app. Label them as Important Places or something similar so that you can find them easily later.

> **UNIQUE TRANSPORTATION OPTIONS WORLDWIDE**
>
> Many countries offer unique forms of local transport. Medellín, Colombia, Funchal, Madeira, and Bergen, Norway have funicular cable car systems. Venice, Italy, is famous for its gondolas, while Thailand is known for its colorful longboats. In Bocas del Toro, Panama, you can island hop in a water taxi.
>
> By land, Southeast Asian countries have "tuk tuks" and ferries, while Japan has a high-speed train system. Peru's overnight buses are the perfect solution for traveling long distances from the Amazon to the Andes. When in the Netherlands or Denmark, rent a bicycle to experience life through the local people's eyes.

I also like to save lists of restaurants, hotels, famous sights, and places that have free Wi-Fi so that I can get some work done. You can also make a wish list of places you want to go.

TIP

If you want to use your phone's GPS without constantly staring at the screen, pop in Bluetooth headphones, turn on navigation guidance, and let the audio cue guide you.

After you identify some points of interest, get out and explore!

Setting up your utilities and Internet

When you're in your home country, transferring electricity into your name could be as easy as setting up an account online with the local utility company. But it's not always that straightforward.

In some countries, public services can remain in the property owner's name, even if they don't live there. You may (or may not) get the bill delivered to your home each month. However, you can usually pay the bill online, regardless of whose name is on it.

If you're renting short-term on a nightly or weekly basis, your rental agreement may include some or all of the utilities in your rent, but always verify with the landlord before signing on the dotted line.

For long-term rentals or contracts lasting at least 1 to 12 months, you often have the additional cost of electricity, on top of the monthly rent price.

Some services, such as water and gas, may require a deposit or work on a pre-paid meter. Inquire with the property owner or rep to know how to operate them.

When you move into a rental property, your water, electricity, gas, trash collection, Internet, cable, and maintenance may be set up as ongoing services. But if you move into a property that's been vacant for a while, you may need to activate some services yourself.

In any case (if you rent), the Internet connection that's installed when you move in (if there is one) may be slower than you want (or need). If so, negotiate an upgrade with your landlord before you move in. In most countries, foreigners are allowed to contract Internet, cable, and phone services by using their passport for identification.

A local personal or corporate ID number may be required to install water or electricity in your name, such as a *Codice Fiscale* (tax number) in Italy. Check with local utilities providers for up-to-date information in your location.

Follow these steps to set up Internet and phone service in your new country:

You can solicit internet or phone service before or after you arrive. If you won't have Wi-Fi set up yet, consider scheduling your installation in advance. Installing services could take one to two days or one to two weeks. Plan accordingly so that your installation appointment falls on or just after your arrival date. You can also schedule it before you arrive if someone who has a key can meet the technician at the property on your behalf.

1. **Search online for Internet service providers in the area that you're moving to.**
2. **Look at each provider's website to compare plans and prices.**
3. **Contact each company through live chat or the customer service number.**
4. **Choose a provider and plan.**

   You can save money with bundled Internet and cellphone packages.
5. **Complete the onboarding process to become a customer.**

   Ensure they offer coverage at your exact address. Ask about the requirements for foreigners to become customers, the minimum contract length, cancellation fees and policy, and estimated installation time.

TIP

To contact toll-free customer service numbers in a different country, dial the exit code for your country, followed by the country code of the destination company plus the phone number. To dial a 0800 number in the U.K. from the USA, dial 011-44-0800-(number).

TIP

If you're staying in a country on a passport, you may only have access to purchase pre-paid phone data and not a monthly plan. If you can't get a cellphone plan in your name, you may be able to get one through a local company name instead. Contact a local legal advisor for how to set up a foreign company.

WARNING

Utility prices abroad can be higher than you're used to. Check rates for your estimated consumption and adjust your budget as needed.

REMEMBER

Whether you rent or purchase a property abroad ask your real estate agent or lawyer for more specifics about installing services at your property. If you own a property abroad, services must be installed in your name or the holding company through which you purchased the property.

Chapter 6 explains more about finding housing abroad.

Making your house a home

After you move into your new home, you may notice a few things that you want (or need) to add, such as extra linens, pillows, or appliances. To make your new house feel like home, buy anything you need. However, remember that you'll have to sell, donate, leave, discard, or recycle such items if you move again.

In the spring of 2023, I rented a house in Manchester, U.K., for six months. Within 24 hours of moving in, I spent more than £500 ($631) at local shops on new linens, dinnerware, candles, cutlery, a coffee press, and a yoga mat.

Within the first month, I'd also acquired a standing desk, a computer monitor, a bicycle, new knives, a bamboo cutting board, a heavy-duty frying pan, and two Himalayan salt lamps. Could I have lived without the salt lamps? Sure, but they made my living room and bedroom cozier on the chilly nights in Northern England.

Sourcing home goods can take time and effort in certain countries. Try as you might, you won't find big box stores in the fields of Provence, France or on Indonesia's Gili Islands. To get what you need, you may need to visit multiple shops.

You have options when it comes to finding things you need in your new home:

>> **Local stores:** Start your search by looking for home goods stores, shopping malls, or other retail options on your maps app.

- **Amazon around the world:** Check whether Amazon is available in your country. For example, there are different websites for Amazon UK, Amazon NL (the Netherlands), and Amazon MX (Mexico).

- **Online purchasing:** Ask in Facebook groups or forums whether anyone has recommendations for finding what you want. Or browse classified sites such as Craigslist (www.craigslist.org), eBay (www.ebay.com), Facebook Marketplace (www.facebook.com/marketplace), OfferUp (www.offerup.com), Locanto (www.locanto.com), or local sites.

- **Local marketplaces:** Most countries have a local online marketplace, such as Malta Park in Malta, Mudah in Malaysia, Tutti.ch in Switzerland, and Sahibinden in Türkiye.

Hiring domestic help

During my younger years as a stereotypical broke college student in the U.S., I never considered hiring someone to clean my dorm room. However, shortly after graduating from university, I moved to Costa Rica, where I could afford a part-time maid to cook, clean, and do laundry. She also helped me with food prep as well, chopping up fruits and vegetables, dicing onions, and mincing garlic to add to my weekly meals.

A cleaning service can cost $50 to $100 per hour in the U.S., but the going rate for domestic help in Central America is $20 to $30 per day. It could cost €10 to €20 per hour in Europe ($10.50-21), which still provides a significant savings over the U.S. costs. When I stayed in Amsterdam for a month in 2023, it cost €15 ($15.70) to have someone clean my studio apartment. In Miami, I pay $150-200 for a two-hour cleaning.

TIP

Find a maid or private chef through an online search, on classified sites, or through companies that provide such services.

I most often found help around the house through referrals from local residents that I know in person or through Facebook groups and online forums. If you don't know anyone yet, go through a cleaning or staffing agency; or just wait until you feel comfortable and settled before hiring help.

WARNING

Before inviting someone to work in your home, do a reference and background check, and collect their ID. Consider getting insurance for your belongings or inquire if your helper or their agency carries liability insurance. Also, have them sign a contract or services agreement. Check with a lawyer to see whether the local law considers this person a contractor or an employee. You may be liable for providing benefits and severance pay to your home helper.

CHAPTER 8 **Landing in Your Adopted Country** 147

Registering with your embassy

Upon arrival at your new destination, register with your embassy or consulate. Doing so allows you to opt into updates and safety alerts about natural disasters, emergencies, and political unrest.

TIP

The Smart Traveler Enrollment Program (STEP; `http://step.state.gov`) is a free program for U.S. citizens, while Canada has a similar program, Registration of Canadians Abroad (ROCA; `http://travel.gc.ca/travelling/registration`).

Meeting your new neighbors

You might not know a soul when you arrive to a foreign country, but you can make friends fast. If you feel comfortable, consider walking next door to meet your neighbors or leave them a letter introducing yourself (translate it into the local language, if it's different from yours).

Here are other tips for meeting people in your new country:

» **Go international.** If you're interested in meeting fellow internationals, join local groups and events on sites such as Facebook (www.facebook.com) and Meetup (www.meetup.com).

» **Shop (and eat) local.** Rather than ordering groceries and meals through delivery services, go out to eat at locally owned restaurants and shop at farmers' markets.

» **Get help from HR.** If you're working abroad, make an effort to meet coworkers or talk to your Human Resources department about ways to connect.

» **Do what you love.** Join clubs or activities that you're interested in. You can find groups for various hobbies and interests online, from wine aficionados to hiking groups, book clubs, and sports teams.

TIP

For more tips on making friends, flip to Chapter 11.

Sourcing food and water

In the section "Identifying important places and contacts," earlier in this chapter, I recommend locating the nearest supermarket to you. Looking for restaurants that can either help you feel at home or adapt to the local culture is also a good idea. You're in luck if you love Mexican food and move to Mexico. But you may find tamales hard to come by in other countries. Finding where to get your favorite foods can provide you a source of comfort and familiarity upon arriving in a foreign country — or anytime. After all, there's no such thing as too many tacos.

Can you drink the water? Check whether you can drink tap water safely before you try it. Harmful bacteria such as E. coli and cholera, as well as parasites such as Giardia, can lurk in tainted water. I found out the hard way that the term *Bali Belly* exists for a reason. I'll never brush my teeth at a Balinese sink again. But I digress.

Check with the local health department to find out whether water is potable. You can find information through forums, Facebook groups, and Google, but be sure to verify information with local authorities.

If you can't drink the tap water, install a water filtration system or look for a water delivery company in the area. Replacing one large refillable bottle per week costs a few dollars in Rosarito, Mexico, for example.

Make buying cases of single-use plastic bottles a last resort because they're not the best for your health, your wallet, or the planet. You can also find lugging heavy water bottles around tricky if you don't have a car.

Travel with a water filtration straw or bottle to use in an emergency. LifeStraw (www.lifestraw.com) is one popular brand.

Settling into a routine

Moving to a different country is an opportunity to disrupt your daily routine by establishing new habit cues in a new environment. However, if you love your routine, you don't have to change it (much). You may naturally resume familiar habits by default, wherever you live, or you can be intentional about creating new ones.

To design your new routine, envision what you want your daily life to look like. Then, set anchor habits around which you can build a routine. *Anchor habits* are activities you do each day on autopilot, such as waking up, brushing your teeth, and making coffee or tea in the morning. To start a new habit, do it right before or after one of your anchor habits.

Your environment can support or detract from your goals. Chapter 4 helps you choose a destination that supports the habits that you want to create.

Example habits include:

>> **Timing when you wake up:** If you want to wake up early, living near the equator can help naturally because the sun rises year-round at 5 or 6 a.m.

CHAPTER 8 **Landing in Your Adopted Country** 149

However, you may find getting up early more challenging if you live in higher latitudes during the winter, such as Northern Europe or Canada, when the sun rises at 9 a.m. or later in some areas.

» **Running errands:** If you used to drive to the supermarket or membership warehouse clubs for large weekly or monthly purchases, you might now adopt a different strategy. Perhaps you change your routine to shop for fewer, fresher items daily by walking to your local corner market.

» **Exercising:** Consider what type of exercise you want to do and how your surroundings play a part. When I lived in Costa Rica, I used to surf or take yoga classes. When I stayed in Bulgaria, I attended an outdoor bootcamp class in the summer and went snowboarding in the winter.

When designing your daily routine, consider

» What time you want to wake up
» How you want to start your day
» Which hours you want to work (if you're working)
» Where to work, if you do — at home, in an office, or at a coffee shop
» Whether you prefer to cook at home or eat out
» Your wind down/evening routine and ideal bedtime

REMEMBER

Feel free to adjust your daily routine as needed and remember to be flexible and compassionate with yourself. Humans aren't robots. Sometimes, things come up — whether you stayed up late watching Netflix or you jaunted off for a weekend getaway in Strasbourg and drank a few too many mulled wines. Rules were made to be broken (or so I've heard).

Receiving Your Paycheck or Pension

You worked hard for your money. Fortunately, today's technology makes it easy for you to collect it almost anywhere.

When you move abroad, you may or may not need to change how you get paid or receive your pension. If you maintain and retain access to your home country's bank account, you can continue receiving funds by direct deposit.

The types of payments you receive depend on your situation:

» **Self-employed freelancers and business owners:** If you're an independent contractor, own your own business, or work for yourself, you can continue to receive funds in the bank account that you use for your business if you're abroad. The same goes for your payment processing setup.

However, you may want to open a local corporation or limited liability company to comply with local regulations and your visa or residency permit requirements. Opening a local company gives you a local corporate tax ID number, enabling you to file taxes, open a bank account, and process payments with a regional provider. For guidance on opening a company in a foreign country, consult a local attorney.

» **Pensions and Social Security payments:** So long as you retain access to the bank account where your pension is deposited, you can spend those funds overseas with a credit or debit card. You can also transfer your funds to another account. Some countries can even send your monthly Social Security check to your offshore bank account. For instance, Panama, Ecuador, and Costa Rica allow U.S. retirees to receive Social Security payments in their local banking systems. Check with your home country's Social Security website or your pension provider for more information.

» **Remote employees:** Your employer should still be able to pay your salary to your home country's bank account, even if you're traveling internationally or living abroad. However, some companies require employees to remain in the same country as the company for tax reasons. Before moving abroad, consult with your employer or HR department.

» **Traditional employees:** If you get an in-person job with a company abroad, it likely sponsors your work visa or permit. In this case, you can open a local bank account by providing proof of your permission to work there and a local address and resident ID card.

Regardless of your occupation, you may need to file extra tax forms if you move abroad. Chapter 13 has more about paying taxes abroad. Ask your accountant or CPA about double tax treaties between your home and destination countries.

If you move abroad permanently, your domestic bank may freeze or close your account. Check your bank's policies and open an account in your destination country if needed.

TIP

Services such as as TruResidence by Virtual Post Mail (www.virtualpostmail.com/) offer you a U.S.-based home address for use with banking and financial accounts. For more ways to access your funds abroad, see Chapter 5.

Consider opening an online account with Revolut (www.revolut.com) or Wise (www.wise.com) to reduce international transfer fees on payments. You can find out how in Chapter 5.

Wiring money internationally

You can send money between two countries by wiring them from a bank in one country to another. This method requires outgoing and incoming fees.

To send an international wire, you will need the following information: the account holder's name and address, the bank name and address, the bank account number or International Bank Account Number (IBAN), and the Society for Worldwide Interbank Financial Telecommunications (SWIFT) code. Optionally, you can include intermediary bank Info if you have more than one bank involved in sending the transfer.

Depending on your bank, you can send a wire through your online banking, in person at a bank branch, and sometimes with a request by fax or a phone call to your bank's customer service.

Wise and Revolut offer wire transfer capability with lower fees than traditional banks.

Opening a local bank account

Before opening a local bank account, ask yourself if you need one. If you're living somewhere long term, you probably do. But perhaps not if you're there part-time or short term.

If you have a national ID number through your residency, visa, or work permit, opening a bank account in your host country should be easy-peasy. It's more complicated (or impossible) if you're abroad on a passport or tourist visa, although some countries allow it. Depending on where you live and banks' policies, you can open accounts in multiple currencies, such as the national currency plus U.S. Dollars, British Pounds, and the Euro.

To open a bank account without visiting a physical branch, search for online banks in your host country. Examples include Ally Bank and Capital One in the United States, Bunq in the Netherlands, KOHO in Canada, N26 in Germany, Nubank in Latin America, and Starling in the U.K. International online accounts, such as Revolut, Varo, and Wise, are also popular options for managing money internationally.

To open a bank account as a foreign citizen, you will generally need a valid passport or local ID and/or a tax or social security number. Proof of address is required, which can be a utility bill, paycheck stub, or rental agreement. Proof of income is also necessary, which may include an employment contract, previous bank statements, or a letter from an accountant. Additionally, a minimum deposit is required, which can range from $20 to $100,000, depending on the bank and account type.

Some international banks, such as HSBC, offer a "premier" international expat or non-resident account that lets you keep your money in a foreign country while living anywhere. However, income and minimum balance requirements to open an account can be high. Find out more at Expat.hsbc.com.

Due to FACTA — the Foreign Account Tax Compliance Act — U.S. citizens abroad without a local ID find it harder to open bank accounts than foreign tourists from other countries. Since it was enacted in 2010, many international banks have begun declining U.S. customers due to increased scrutiny and reporting requirements.

IN THIS CHAPTER

» Getting plugged into the local infrastructure

» Driving around and buying a car

» Enrolling kids in schools or daycare

» Finding healthcare providers

» Receiving mail abroad

Chapter **9**

Going Farther Afield: Additional Considerations

After you spend the first few days and weeks acclimating to your new country, consider some of the more long-term aspects of living abroad.

This chapter focuses on the roots that you put down during your first few months in a destination — things such as buying a car, receiving mail, and handling healthcare and residency paperwork. It can help you manage the small logistics of life so that you can focus on the more fulfilling parts of your move.

Adjusting to the Infrastructure

Getting familiar with a country's banking, communication, and transport networks takes time. But you have to adjust to a new system if you want to integrate smoothly. You may find amenities better or worse than in your home country.

Abir, an expat who moved from Canada to Switzerland, told me, "Everything was quick and efficient overall. I never felt safer, either. It's such a convenient place to be when everything works as expected."

On the flip side, here are a few challenges to anticipate:

- » **Lack of reliability:** Developing countries may have delicate infrastructure, with planned or unplanned electricity and water blackouts. You might experience unreliable public transportation, with buses or trains running late (or not showing up) and intermittent Internet outages.
- » **Limitations in access:** Rural areas may have limited public transport options and access to basic utilities. Ensure that you have access to food, water, and a vehicle if you plan to live in such places.
- » **Crowds in the city:** You may have to deal with heavier traffic and congestion than you're used to.

Although you may find infrastructure issues frustrating, it's part of adapting to life in a new place. The experience of being able to live in a different country makes these challenges worthwhile.

Outsmarting power and water outages

Utility blackouts can happen anytime, anywhere — especially if you're in a developing country. Consider purchasing a portable backup generator if you expect frequent outages. A generator can also help you out in case of a strong storm. You can find a suitable one online or in a hardware store.

If you work remotely from home, invest in an Uninterruptible Power Supply (UPS) battery. These batteries can protect your devices against power surges and fluctuations. They can keep your computer, router, or other electronics powered for 5 to 60 minutes, depending on the capacity and number of devices connected.

If you live somewhere that has water restrictions, keep a supply of clean water readily available.

Contact your local municipality or health department for instructions during a utility outage. When you get your water supply restored, check with the authorities to find out whether you can safely drink it.

Make a list of emergency contact numbers for local utility providers and keep that list easily accessible. Ask your neighbors or online in Facebook groups and forums for tips on what to do when the power or water goes out.

Regardless of where you move, keep an emergency kit that contains essential supplies, such as food, water, flashlights, and batteries.

Keeping fast Wi-Fi

Internet outages can especially cause problems for digital nomads, remote workers, and those who work from home. To prepare for seamless connectivity, check internet speeds before you arrive. You can ask your host or landlord for a speed test screenshot from a site such as Speedtest (www.speedtest.net).

If your internet is slow, find out whether you can upgrade the speed or set up a separate account in your name. Chapter 8 has more details on setting up your utilities.

 If you get a new connection, use a different Internet Service Provider (ISP) than the landlord to prevent confusion and give you a backup plan if your primary connection goes down.

Also consider a satellite Internet connection. It's affordable and widely available almost anywhere in the world, including remote areas. Starlink (www.starlink.com) now offers roaming Internet packages for $50 per month for up to 50GB of data or $165 per month for unlimited data.

Getting from here to there

Taking public transportation is a quick way to get a feel for a new place. You can get around most major cities on buses, trams, trains, subways, and taxis.

Pay attention to how locals use the different options. Figure out the best routes for your needs and learn basic phrases in the local language so that you can ask people for directions.

 Download apps specific to your destination's transport system, such as Transport for London (http://tfl.gov.uk) or GoTokyo (www.gotokyo.org). Citymapper (www.citymapper.com), Google Maps (www.google.com/maps), and HERE WeGo Maps (www.here.com), also help you plan your routes.

I cover local transport options in Chapter 8.

As a new resident, respect transportation laws and customs. For example, drivers in the Bahamas, the U.K., Ireland, Australia, and South Africa use the left side of the road, while drivers in most other countries stay on the right. Jaywalking is tolerated in some places but strictly enforced in others (both Singapore and Switzerland fine jaywalkers).

CHAPTER 9 Going Farther Afield: Additional Considerations 157

Before you drive on foreign roads:

WARNING

- » **Find out about tolls.** Buy a pass, bring cash and coins, and figure out any toll-by-plate options.

- » **Check for driving restrictions.** Some historic city centers ban large vehicles. Other places restrict certain license plate numbers on certain days of the week. And many cities, including London, enforce low-emission zones in some areas.

- » **Get a tune-up from a mechanic.** Before setting out on a long journey, check your car's lights, battery, fluids, and fuel.

- » **Get insurance.** If you're renting, get the maximum insurance coverage. Your home country's policy doesn't cover you in a foreign country.

To Own or Not to Own a Car: That Is the Question

Whether to purchase or import a vehicle depends on your budget, goals, and the cost to ship a car or buy one locally.

The decision to own a car also depends on where you live. If you move to a European city that has plentiful public transportation, you likely don't need one. However, you can't easily access some regions, such as the Alps, without a car. And get a vehicle that has four-wheel drive if you live on a remote beach in Central America.

Before moving, research costs to see which option makes more sense. Think about the sights and experiences you want to enjoy in your destination and how you plan to reach them. Richard, who moved from the U.S. to the U.K., told me, "I wish I brought my motorcycle, but bringing our American car was a dufus move!"

Bringing your car

Shipping your car to a foreign country takes money, time, and a heavy dose of patience. But in some circumstances, it may be your best option. Consider keeping your car if you're moving long-term and you need a vehicle. Perhaps you plan to drive your kids to school and take family road trips; or maybe you're relocating to a rural area, and having a car can make your life easier.

A reason to ship your car is if you have one that's suitable for the road conditions where you're going. You don't want to bring your Ferrari to the bumpy, dusty roads of Nicaragua. (Although driving your Ferrari down the Autobahn would be fun if you move to Germany.)

Keeping an eye on cost

Keep cost in mind. You have to pay shipping fees to move your car, as well as import taxes, insurance, and registration fees in your destination country.

A vehicle's CIF (cost, insurance, and freight) value determines its customs duty (rates vary by country and a car's make, model, and year):

CIF = Car Value + Shipping Insurance Cost + Freight Cost

In Europe, budget for paying Value Added Tax (VAT), which can range from 8 to 27 percent.

TIP

Depending on your destination country and residency category, you can move your car at a reduced cost. For example, Belize allows retirees in the Qualified Retired Persons (QRP) program to import a vehicle, boat, or small aircraft duty-free. Some countries offer exemptions from customs fees for diplomatic personnel, non-profit organizations, or vintage and classic vehicles.

Gathering what you need to import a car

REMEMBER

Check with your immigration attorney for timely information about bringing a car or container of goods to your destination.

To import a car to a foreign country, you need:

- **Proof of ownership:** The original vehicle title and registration.
- **Bill of sale:** Your original purchase invoice.
- **Customs declaration:** Details about your car and its value.
- **Import taxes and fees:** By importing your car, you may have to pay import duties, VAT, excise tax, and customs processing fees. Research local fees and taxes on imported vehicles or ask your shipping agent.
- **Import approval or permit from your destination:** These documents may include emissions testing and compliance, which can vary at state, provincial, and nationwide levels.

WARNING

You may need to modify your car to make it road-worthy abroad. Check whether the headlights, license plate frames, and speedometer need adjustment. There's a big difference between miles and kilometers per hour!

Before shipping your car abroad, consider the age, make, and model of your car, the total shipping and import costs, and the time to receive your car abroad.

Buying a car

Buying a car abroad makes sense if you want one and can't be bothered with shipping yours. By purchasing a car locally, you can choose from makes and models that might not be available in your home country. You also get a car configured for local conditions, such as paperwork, plates, and insurance.

Set your budget and research the market before you buy a car, new or used. Here are some of the basics you need for your purchase:

» **Bill of sale:** Provided by a dealer. If you buy from a private party, ensure you have a secure contract. Hire a lawyer to review the terms, especially if the agreement is in a foreign language.

» **Identification:** A valid government-issued ID and driver's license.

» **Proof of address:** Rental agreement, utility bill, or other documentation.

» **Title transfer documents:** Verify whether the seller includes title processing fees in the price.

» **Financing:** Find out whether you qualify for financing. Check interest rates and note that foreigners may not have access to the same deals, depending on your residency status.

If you buy a used car, make sure to do the following:

» **Negotiate wisely.** Research prices ahead of time on local car websites, such as Autoscout24 (www.autoscout24.com) in Europe, Mercado Libre (http://autos.mercadolibre.com.mx) in Mexico, and Carro (www.carro.co) in Southeast Asia. Investigate the local negotiation customs before accepting the sticker price.

» **Get it checked out.** If you want to buy a used car, hire a trustworthy mechanic to evaluate it.

» **Confirm ownership.** Check a car's title history and legal owner, and ensure the title doesn't have any liens.

160 PART 3 **Leaping Into Your New Life Abroad**

REMEMBER

Always carry insurance for your vehicle. Although global companies such as Allianz (www.allianztravelinsurance.com) and AXA (www.axatravelinsurance.com) may offer coverage options, getting a policy from a domestic insurer is often more affordable. You can find options online, or ask local friends or car dealers.

For help acquiring a car abroad, check out companies such as International Autosource (www.intlauto.com), which provides long-term rentals, leasing, and purchase assistance. Expat Ride (www.expatride.com) offers multiple services, from airport transfers and chauffeurs to car rental and leasing.

Driving Abroad

Most countries allow you to rent a car and drive with the license that you already have, issued by your home country. But after living there for some time (usually a year), you need a local driving permit.

Figuring out what you need to drive abroad

Find out whether you need an International Driving Permit (IDP), in addition to a valid license, in order to drive in the country that you're moving to. You can check through an online search or with your embassy, consulate, or car rental agency abroad.

You can get an IDP through an issuing authority or auto club in your country, such as AAA in the U.S., a post office in the U.K., or a Regional Transport Office (RTO) in India. IDPs are valid for one year, and you must renew them annually.

IDP requirements include a valid driver's license, application form, processing fee, and passport-sized photos.

WARNING

Even if a car rental agency fails to ask for your IDP when you rent a car, you may need to present it if you get stopped by police (if you don't have an IDP, you can receive a fine).

REMEMBER

If you travel internationally on a passport, you must always keep it with you while driving unless you have a local license.

CHAPTER 9 **Going Farther Afield: Additional Considerations** 161

Getting a local driver's license

After an initial grace period — typically one month to one year — you must transition from a foreign or international license to a local one.

Sometimes, your home and adopted countries offer reciprocity, where the license you have in one country remains valid in the other. Often, however, you need to pass a driving test in the local language to qualify for a foreign permit, which can be a formidable challenge.

Says Chase, who moved from the U.S. to Europe, "Getting a driver's license in Spain is a huge pain and expensive. Once you've lived there for six months or more, you have to get a Spanish license, and it's very complicated."

To apply for a license in your destination, you need:

- **Residency status:** See Chapters 4 and 5 for details on getting a visa, residency, or citizenship abroad.
- **Proof of address:** A utility bill, lease agreement, or bank statement in your name.
- **Medical tests:** Countries often require a medical exam or vision test before issuing a license.
- **Translation requirements:** You may need to have your license translated or pass a driving test in the local language.
- **Vehicle registration:** If you own a car, they may ask to see proof of registration and insurance.
- **Vehicle transmission:** Some countries offer different licenses, depending on your ability to drive a manual (stick) versus an automatic transmission.

To apply for a driver's license in your new country, follow these basic steps:

1. **Find out the requirements for obtaining a license from the relevant government agency.**

   You may need to get in touch with the local motor vehicles department.

2. **Gather your identification and any necessary forms.**

   You probably need your residency permit and a medical exam.

3. **Complete and submit the application and pay any associated fees.**

   In Ireland, a new driver's license costs €65 ($67). However, medical exams and driving classes cost extra. Expats and immigrants in Spain report spending over €1,000 ($1,025) to get a license.

4. **Study for the driving exam, and then pass the test (with flying colors, of course).**

   After you complete all these steps you receive your provisional permit or official license.

If you need, turn to local professionals for help. Enroll in a driving school or take language classes. Chapter 10 helps you get started in a foreign language.

Enrolling in Schools or Daycare

If you have children, overseas relocation provides them with an education all its own. Kids who are exposed to new customs, languages, cultures, and traditions gain unique perspectives. However, as a parent, you may want them to have a traditional education in addition to the school of life.

The following sections review the main types of schools that you can find in different countries.

Public versus private education

Whether to enroll your children in public or private schools when your move abroad is a personal choice has pros and cons on each side. The quality and curriculum of public and private education systems vary by country.

Private and international schools typically offer an English-speaking curriculum and charge tuition. Public school classes are often taught in the local language and are free or low-cost to attend for residents.

Paying for private school

Prepare to shell out cash if you choose a private school. Tuition fees alone can start at $5,000 to $10,000 per year. In addition, most private schools charge fees for registration, uniforms, extracurricular activities, and technology. However, private schools have some benefits:

>> Greater flexibility in curriculum, teaching methods, and admission standards

>> More likely to offer specialized programs, advanced placement, or alternative educational philosophies

CHAPTER 9 **Going Farther Afield: Additional Considerations** 163

Going to public school

Public schools cost significantly less than private schools (and some public schools are free). They tend to follow a more standardized national- or state-mandated curriculum and typically don't charge tuition fees for residents. That's good news if you're moving long-term and qualify for a residency permit, which you can read about in Chapter 4. If you have kids younger than ten years old, a public school may give you a good place to start, as young children pick up foreign languages quickly. Studying in a public school allows them opportunities to socialize and adapt to local customs.

Considering an international school

TIP

If you anticipate significant challenges adapting to a public school consider enrolling your children in an international school. International schools may follow a different curriculum than a local private school. They cater to students from various countries, presenting an intercultural experience. They can also offer specialized learning tracks, diverse clubs and sports, and classes in multiple languages.

On the downside, international schools often have lengthy waiting lists. Some administrators charge fees with no admission guarantees. International schools often operate in urban areas. Consider a school's location when you choose a city, town, or country that you want to move to, or prepare for a potentially lengthy and pricey commute.

TIP

The International Schools Database (www.international-schools-database.com) lets you research over 3,600 international schools in 306 cities worldwide. You can also browse schools on Smapse Education (www.smapse.com).

Navigating the enrollment process

Enrolling your children in foreign schools often requires documentation such as transcripts or certifications of equivalency. For instance, a high school diploma in the United States is equivalent to A levels in the U.K.

Here are some key details to consider when you search for schools:

» **Assess your language needs.** If your child isn't bilingual, consider enrolling them in an international school, where teachers or staff can communicate in a common language, such as English.

» **Contact schools directly.** Go to the source to determine availability, admission requirements, and paperwork. Ask ahead about wait lists.

- » **Gather all the required documents.** You need paperwork such as passports, visas, immunization records, transcripts, and any other information the schools need.

- » **Prepare a list of questions to ask administrators and teachers.** Ask them about the curriculum and educational structure that they use.

- » **Get outside input.** Read online reviews of schools, if you can find some. Talk with parents whose kids attend the same school.

- » **Visit the school(s), if possible.** Arrange tours to get a firsthand look at class sizes, atmosphere, and facilities.

Moving abroad affects each child differently. For tips on overcoming culture shock, see Chapter 10.

Homeschooling abroad

Homeschooling offers flexibility to parents who want to direct the depth and pace of their child's education. You can conduct classes from a sailboat, your family's RV, or inside a museum.

Homeschooling can make sense if you change locations throughout the year while slowly traveling the world, which makes it hard to start and stop traditional schooling. You can also consider homeschooling if you work from home and have a flexible schedule. Some students can finish an entire day's schoolwork between breakfast and lunchtime.

Check the laws in your destination country before homeschooling. In some cases, you can homeschool your child only if you're associated with an accredited institution.

A challenge for homeschooled students is having fewer resources than those in public and private schools. Certain types of technology and sports equipment are expensive and not-so-practical to travel with. If you choose to homeschool, ensure that your kids get plenty of opportunities to interact with the local culture and community. That's where alternative types of schooling (online or in-person) can help.

Alternative education options include:

- » **Montessori schools:** Founded in the early 1900s by an Italian physician, mixed-age Montessori classrooms focus on hands-on learning and real-world skills more than tests and grading. You can find public and private Montessori schools in more than 100 countries.

» **Waldorf (or Steiner) schools:** Encourage unique and immersive learning styles for kids of all ages, from early childhood through secondary education. Students learn through art, music, storytelling, and human connection, in addition to a core curriculum that includes language, math, and science.

» **Worldschooling:** A way of educating children through travel, food, art, and cultural experiences. You can teach your kids alone or with a network of other families.

» **Unschooling:** A philosophy of teaching children according to their interests and needs without a formal curriculum.

Connect with homeschooling parents through online groups and conferences. Find a community on Homeschool World (www.home-school.com), the official website of *Practical Homeschooling Magazine*.

Finding daycare abroad

You can find public, private, and alternative childcare options abroad. Public daycare is more affordable than private options. Either way, the experience allows your little one to acclimate to your host country's culture and language from a young age.

When you choose a country or city to live in, find out the types of childcare available. Germany is famous for its childcare offerings, *Krippe* (for infants), *KiTa* (ages 3-5), *Tagesmutter* (in-home daycare), and *Schulhort* (after-school daycare for elementary children). Japanese daycare providers take a structured approach to early childcare, whereas Swedish daycare centers may encourage more playtime.

Regardless of your chosen establishment, ensure it's accredited and meets local health and safety standards. When in doubt, ask for recommendations from trusted contacts and tour the facility before enrolling your children. Ask questions about cleanliness, meals, activities, and the caregiver-to-child ratio.

Most daycares require incoming children to have a health check, vaccination records, and proof of address or residency documentation.

If you have little ones who require daycare, here are some helpful places to search:

» **Apps and aggregator sites:** At the time of writing, Care.com helps people find daycare in 17 countries. AuPair.com is a global matching service for au pairs and host families. Looking for a nanny or babysitter in Europe? Download Sitly (www.sitly.com) from your app store.

- **Expat forums and Facebook groups:** Search for family-friendly groups in your destination and ask for referrals (while also doing your due diligence).
- **Government resources:** Contact your local town hall or department of education for recommendations.
- **Sitter sites:** AuPairCare (www.aupaircare.com), GreatAuPair (www.greataupair.com), and Tripsitta (www.tripsitta.com) can help you find affordable and diverse options.
- **Word of mouth:** After you move abroad, ask people in your community for recommendations and visit locations in person.

Your local embassy or consulate can frequently connect families living abroad with services unique to their needs. You can also inquire with local relocation companies.

You can also look into in-home care by hiring a nanny or au pair. Depending on where you're from and where you're moving, the low cost of in-home care may surprise you. Prices range from $1 to $2 per hour in India, to $10 to $20 per hour in Europe, up to $25 hourly or more in the United States. Room and board may be additional for live-in nannies.

Hiring a full-time helper may require compliance with local employment laws. For information in your area, seek professional legal counsel.

Booking Your First Healthcare Appointment Abroad

Visiting a doctor in a foreign country can be daunting, but you can find high-quality hospitals and clinics in many parts of the world. If you live in an urban area, you probably are never too far from the care that you might need. Depending on where your travel takes you, you can often encounter better, more affordable healthcare options than you're used to at home.

You can choose between receiving public or private healthcare abroad. Public healthcare systems are taxpayer-funded, and private care is funded through private insurance plans or patients paying for treatment out-of-pocket. Typically, all legal residents can access public healthcare systems, often with little to no direct cost when they receive the service. Private systems can offer faster access and broader services, but only to patients who can afford it.

Public systems tend to be free or low-cost but have longer wait times. Private systems usually offer faster access, but the higher price tag is a trade-off.

If you're a resident or citizen of the EU, EEA, or Switzerland, you can qualify for healthcare in other European countries if you have a European Health Insurance Card (EHIC). Find out more on the EU Employment, Social Affairs, and Inclusion website. From the main web page (http://employment-social-affairs.ec.europa.eu).

Finding a doctor

You can find a doctor in a number of ways:

- » **Ask your insurer.** Whether you have a local or international insurer, they can help match you with providers in your location.
- » **Check with your embassy.** Your country's embassy or consulate can provide resources for citizens abroad who are navigating foreign healthcare systems.
- » **Contact local medical facilities.** I've often found doctors and specialists by calling or emailing a facility and asking whether they accept new international patients. Most hospital websites have an online directory of practitioners. Before booking your appointment, ask about prices for care.
- » **Look into online directories and associations.** You can often find English-speaking doctors through the International Medical Association for Medical Assistance to Travelers (IAMAT; www.iamat.org/medical-directory) or the International Society of Travel Medicine (www.istm.org).

For access to quick care while you're abroad, search online for a "hotel doctor." You can find English-speaking websites offering home or hotel visits for reasonable prices.

Preparing for your appointment

Keep these tips in mind before you book your first office visit with a doctor:

- » **Contact your insurance carrier.** Getting reimbursed usually goes more smoothly if you get insurance pre-approval. Also, review your policy's deductibles and coverage limits.
- » **Prepare your medical history.** Collect your medical records and prescriptions. If necessary, have them translated into the local language.

>> **Leverage local contacts.** Facebook and online medical tourism groups can help you find a good doctor and know how to approach your first appointment. Don't be afraid to ask for recommendations.

If necessary, bring a medical interpreter to your appointment. Always clarify if you don't fully understand a prescription dosage or care instructions.

Going to the dentist

Follow the tips in the preceding sections if you need to find a dentist. For minor care, such as dental cleanings, you may pay out of pocket and go to the closest dentist, which you can find on your map app. One of my friends traveled from the U.S. to Costa Rica for dental work. She received about $20,000 worth of procedures for $2,700.

As always, read reviews and research providers before receiving care.

Finding a telehealth doctor

Telehealth can give you a convenient option for minor injuries, mild sickness, questions, and preventative care that don't require in-patient visits. Visiting a doctor online saves time and offers at-home convenience.

Providers such as Teladoc (www.teladochealth.com), Amwell (http://business.amwell.com), and Doctor on Demand (www.doctorondemand.com) offer virtual consultations by phone or video call. You can also find telehealth options by searching locally online. After getting a painful sinus infection one year in Amsterdam, I found a company called Mobidoctor (www.mobidoctor.eu) that allowed me to book an appointment and fill a prescription the same day.

Telehealth has some limitations. Some treatments necessitate in-person care. If you have an unstable Internet connection, telehealth might not be the best option. Some insurance plans don't cover telehealth appointments, so ask first.

Getting emergency care

In case of an emergency, always contact emergency services first. Most countries offer emergency response through a dedicated phone number: 112 and 911 are the two most common numbers used worldwide. 112 is standard in the EU, and 911 is often found in North America, Latin America, and the Caribbean.

CHAPTER 9 **Going Farther Afield: Additional Considerations** 169

Table 9-1 shows a few more emergency numbers — keep in mind that some countries have different numbers for police, medical, and fire response.

TABLE 9-1 **Emergency Numbers by Country**

Country	Police	Medical	Fire	Traffic Accidents
Australia	000	000	000	000
Bahrain	999	999	999	999
China	110	120	119	112
Hong Kong	999	999	999	999
Japan	110	119	119	110 or 119
Nicaragua	118	128	115	118
Switzerland	117	144	118	117
Thailand	191	191	191	191
U.K.	999	999	999	999

Response times and service availability might not be what you're used to. Research the speed and reliability of service in your destination, particularly if you have a medical condition that requires a fast response. Remote areas don't offer ambulance services, so plan ahead.

Some countries may require identification and insurance information before a doctor or facility can treat a patient, while other countries provide care regardless. Find out about the billing practices and ID requirements in your destination.

Making health insurance claims

All insurance policies have restrictions and limitations. Before filing a claim for treatment that you receive at a facility outside your home country, make sure to know about:

- **Coinsurance:** The percentage of a total bill (minus deductibles) that you have to pay out of pocket; the insurance policy covers the balance.

- **Deductibles:** Your out-of-pocket responsibilities before insurance coverage applies.

» **Exclusions:** Medical conditions or occurrences that your policy doesn't cover treatment for.

» **Coverage limits:** The total amount that your insurance company agrees to pay.

Global Healthcare Accreditation (www.globalhealthcareaccreditation.com) has a helpful guide to understanding how coverage for expats abroad works.

To file a claim, follow these general steps:

1. **Notify your insurer as soon as possible that you need or needed medical assistance abroad.**

    Some companies require pre-authorization for services.

2. **Follow your insurer's instructions.**

    Fill out the necessary forms to submit your claim and provide the insurer with any requested documentation.

3. **Keep detailed records for any treatment or procedure related to your claim.**

    Include originals or copies of documents, bills, receipts, and medical records.

4. **Check your claim's status periodically and follow up with your insurer, as needed.**

    Set reminders for when to contact your insurer for information until they approve or deny your claim. If your claim is denied, you can appeal the decision.

Receiving Your Mail Overseas

If you expect to receive physical mail while abroad, have a plan for retrieving it. Chapter 5 helps you build your relocation plan and organize your paperwork before you leave home, and this section builds on that premise.

Download apps or sign up for email updates on the status of any packages headed your way. You can also track your item's progress to its destination in real-time.

The following sections offer some strategies to receive your mail as smoothly and seamlessly as possible.

CHAPTER 9 Going Farther Afield: Additional Considerations   171

Know your local mailing address

Have your full mailing address abroad, including the postal code. If you don't have an address, consider getting a post office (PO) box from the local mail service.

Many countries lack formal addresses that include numbered buildings and street names. One of my former Costa Rican addresses started with *del palo de mango, 200 metros al oeste*, which translates to *200 meters west of the mango tree*. While I lived in Nicaragua, I noticed that residents used past landmarks to give directions, such as "*donde fue la estatua...*" — where the statue in the roundabout *was* (before the civil war).

In Ghana, the government developed a system called GhanaPostGPS (www.ghanapostgps.com) to overcome this problem and designate addresses, especially in rural areas.

Get a courier

To increase the chances that your mail reaches you, consider paying a courier to bring it to you. Couriers are popular in places where it's complicated to receive goods ordered online. Items may be subject to customs delays and duties, so if you want to receive your Amazon package ASAP, look for a local mail courier service.

Such companies provide a physical address in your home country or abroad where you can receive mail and packages. They then deliver them to a central location or your door.

Examples of couriers include:

» **Aeropost** (www.aeropost.com): This company operates primarily in Latin America and the Caribbean. It offers a U.S.-based PO box for mail and a physical address for packages. Aeropost expedites customs clearances and can deliver to one of its local offices, a central bus station, a post office, or your home.

» **Aramex** (www.aramex.com): Offers domestic and international shipping services and e-commerce delivery throughout Africa, Asia, and the Middle East.

» **Parcel Monkey** (www.parcelmonkey.com): Global discounted shipping provider in more than 200 countries.

» **USA2Me** (www.usa2me.com): Mail, packaging, and virtual mailbox services for expats and businesses that require a U.S.-based address.

TIP If you struggle to receive packages to your residential address via snail mail, consider having items sent to a local post office or mail store, such as Mail Boxes Etc. (www.mbeglobal.com), The UPS Store (www.ups.com), or a local equivalent.

You can often use DHL (www.dhl.com), FedEx (www.fedex.com), and UPS for international shipping. However, it can be expensive.

Set up a virtual mailbox

Virtual mail scanning services provide you with a real street address or P.O. box where you can receive mail. They provide convenience by opening and scanning paper mail for you. You can sort through your mail digitally, select any that you want forwarded to your international address, and discard or store the rest.

Popular mail-scanning services include:

» **Anytime Mailbox** (www.anytimemailbox.com): Offers virtual mail and business services at more than 2,500 locations in the U.S. with plans from $9.99 per month.

» **Traveling Mailbox** (www.aramex.com): Virtual mailbox, mail forwarding, and check deposit services designed for travelers and RVers. Plans start at $15 monthly.

» **US Global Mail** (www.usglobalmail.com): Get a U.S. street address to receive mail with same-day processing and scanning. Forward mail from different locations to one, permanent address. Plans range from $19.95 to $85 per month.

» **Virtual Post Mail** (www.virtualpostmail.com): Offers virtual mailbox, check deposit, and physical address services under its TruLease and TruResidence products. Can also help you form a U.S. limited liability corporation (LLC) and maintain legal compliance for your company. Plans start at $20 per month.

4 Living Your Life to the Fullest

IN THIS PART . . .

Get familiar with foreign languages.

Combat culture shock and loneliness.

Make friends and find community.

Discover places to go and things to do.

Manage your taxes, paperwork, and finances.

Plan your expat exit strategy.

IN THIS CHAPTER

» Working through the inevitable culture shock

» Embracing the adjustments and changes

» Becoming part of your new community

» Keeping your expectations realistic

» Solving problems when things go awry

Chapter **10**

Embracing Culture Shock Like a Pro

When planning a move abroad, many folks focus on the logistics of how to get there. But succeeding in your new life after you arrive is equally (or more) important. The reality of adapting to a new language, society, and different customs is easier said than done.

Understanding and processing your emotions takes different skills than finding a place to live, packing your stuff, and booking a flight. Although you can (and should) see moving abroad as an exciting experience, in this chapter, I address an often less-considered aspect of a big move: the emotional rollercoaster that comes with such a significant change. It's helpful to figure out how to confront these inevitable challenges in the months and years ahead and know where to get further support.

Understanding Culture Shock

Culture shock expresses itself in various ways. It can come on quickly — a veritable shock — or it may seep into your awareness over time. When you experience culture shock, you may feel all the things — anxiety, loneliness, frustration, sadness, and more. You may experience physical, mental, or emotional symptoms (or a combination of all of them). You might notice changes in your appetite and sleeping patterns, a loss of motivation, and withdrawal from society. Whew! That doesn't sound like fun, does it? But if you know the symptoms, you can prepare to overcome them and grow stronger because of the experience.

Don't let culture shock discourage you. It's an evolving feeling that dissipates with time. Your emotions ebb and flow — and they won't last forever. It's a bit like the rollercoaster of life. Some days, everything goes wrong, while other times, life is sweet. Life tests us, but in the words of entrepreneur Marie Forleo, "everything is figureoutable."

When you exit your comfort zone, you feel *dis*comfort at times. That's what you signed up for, and it's a good thing. When culture shock hits, acknowledge it and use the suggestions in this chapter to process your feelings in healthy ways.

Riding the Curve of Cultural Adjustment

Although *culture shock* has been a buzzword in modern-day society since the 1950s, philosophers have pondered the difficulty (and stages) of adjusting to unfamiliar cultures since ancient Greece.

Various scholars have attempted to illustrate the phases of cultural adaptation — what academics call the *curve of cultural adjustment*, which follows a progression toward integration:

- **The honeymoon phase:** Where everything is wonderful.
- **The frustration phase:** Where everything is horrible.
- **The adjustment phase:** When you start integrating with the culture.
- **The adaptation phase:** Finally, you emerge into the stage of accepting differences and figuring out how to thrive in your new surroundings.

Anthropologist Kalervo Oberg (1901–1973) likened culture shock to "an occupational disease of people who have been suddenly transplanted abroad." However, like other ailments, you can find a cure.

According to Oberg, the cause of culture shock is losing touch with the social cues and norms that guide your daily behavior, causing you to feel like a fish out of water. You sense that the way things are done in your host country are somehow wrong because they make you feel bad or uncomfortable. Oberg's curve, developed in 1954 and shown in Figure 10-1, describes the various stages of adjusting to culture shock.

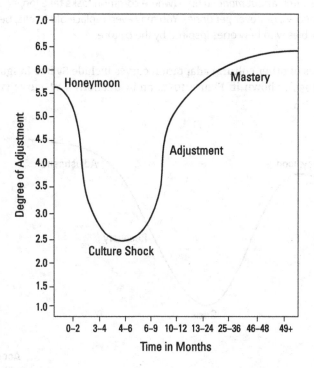

FIGURE 10-1: Oberg's curve of cultural adjustment.

Here's a deeper explanation of the curve's phases:

>> **Phase 1 — The Honeymoon:** You find everything in your new home fascinating and novel. This phase can last from a few days to six months or more.

>> **Phase 2 — Culture Shock and Frustration:** You begin feeling negativity and having trouble with daily activities, from grocery shopping to ordering your daily coffee. In this phase, you can decide whether to stay and work through your struggles with the people, language, and customs or leave.

CHAPTER 10 **Embracing Culture Shock Like a Pro** 179

>> **Phase 3 — Adjustment and Turning the Corner:** If you stay and face your culture shock crisis, you begin recovering. You start to learn from mistakes, embody new ways of doing things, and maybe even gain a sense of humor about the situation. If you accidentally head-butt someone while leaning in for a cheek kiss (a customary greeting in France and Argentina), you can laugh about it.

>> **Phase 4 — Adaptation and Feeling at Home:** You accept and adapt to the way of life in your adopted country. You don't feel like everything is perfect, but you experience less of an emotional reaction to problems. You begin to appreciate the cultural differences, learn some of the language, and complain less often about *mañana* time (where common tasks take longer than expected, or never get done). You may even replace old habits, beliefs, and hobbies with new ones inspired by the culture.

Examples of other cultural adaptation curves include Sverre Lysgaard's U-shaped curve (1955), shown in Figure 10-2, and Gullahorn's W-curve (1963), shown in Figure 10-3.

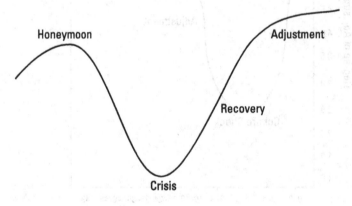

FIGURE 10-2: Sverre Lysgaard's U-shaped curve.

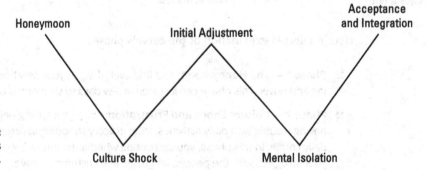

FIGURE 10-3: Gullahorn's W-curve.

Your curve might look and feel nothing like a research study, and your phases and feelings can change if you move countries again.

Culture shock can affect you even if you've traveled to a country many times and feel familiar with its culture or have parents or family members who are from there. For example, may be of Mexican ancestry and speak Spanish with your relatives, yet struggle to adapt if you move to Mexico.

Tracking Your Own Cultural Adaptation Curve

Everybody's experience of cultural adaptation is unique. To help you recognize your own phases while they happen, pay attention to your feelings and how they help you identify the stage you're in. Journal how you feel throughout your move, starting anytime from when you begin planning your relocation.

Log your emotions, whether you're feeling excited, panicked, uncertain, selfish, or anything else. Know that what you feel is normal, and nothing you feel is wrong or weird.

The following sections provide some questions to ask yourself at each stage of your move.

Preparing for take-off

Here are some pre-departure questions:

» How do you feel about your upcoming move? What are you most looking forward to?

» Is anything worrying you?

» What will you miss about home?

» What's one pending thing that you can tick off your to-do list right now?

» What's a goal that you hope to achieve in your first month abroad?

Initial shocks and the honeymoon phase

Ask yourself these questions during your first month after arrival:

> » What do you love about your new country?
>
> » What shocked you the most?
>
> » What has frustrated you the most?
>
> » What's a small win that you've achieved?
>
> » What's one new habit you can adopt to help with your adjustment?
>
> » Who can you call or meet with to connect?

Feel free to answer the questions above before your arrival to predict how you'll feel. Then, answer them again after your move.

Frustrations and adaptations

Three months after arriving, ask yourself these questions:

> » How do you feel compared to your first month abroad?
>
> » Which phase of cultural adaptation do you think you're currently in?
>
> » What have you changed about your daily routine?
>
> » What culture shock coping strategies work for you?
>
> » What do you still struggle with?

Finding your rhythm

Here are questions to ask yourself after six months of living abroad:

> » What's your daily life like?
>
> » Does your new country feel like home to you?
>
> » What still bothers or annoys you?
>
> » What new friends and contacts have you made?
>
> » How do you feel about your progress?

Transformation and integration

After a year of living abroad, ask yourself these questions:

- What have you learned about yourself this year?
- What do you feel proud of?
- What cultural differences do you embrace?
- What's a moment when you felt like you belong in your new country?
- How have your perspective and mindset changed since you first moved?
- What's next in your expat journey?

Coping with Change

How you face the challenges of moving abroad defines your experience. To anticipated cultural challenges, inform yourself before you go. Preview the cultural differences between your home and destination countries by using The Culture Factor Group's Country Comparison Tool (www.theculturefactor.com/country-comparison-tool). This online tool can help you visualize how countries differ on various cultural dimensions.

PRIORITIZING WELLBEING ABROAD

Although moving abroad is a wonderful and enriching experience, it can also create some new challenges to your wellbeing. If you find yourself in need of mental health support, you can connect with therapists remotely on BetterHelp (www.betterhelp.com) or search online for an expat counselor by using a website such as the International Therapist Directory (www.internationaltherapistdirectory.com).

If you're married, coupled, or have kids, moving abroad could change the dynamic of your relationships. Approach your move and adjustment period as a team, while giving each other space to go on your own journeys. Schedule intermittent times to check in with each other and share doubts, questions, and wins during the process.

If you feel frustrated or overwhelmed, remind yourself of your why. Reflect on why you moved and the goals that you hope to achieve. Chapter 1 helps you set your living-abroad goals.

Below, you can see the cultural differences between the United States, Mexico, and Portugal.

REMEMBER

Adapting to a foreign country is a natural process that takes time. Even if you struggle a little, don't give up! Speed up the process of learning about your adopted culture through classes (online or in-person) or books that discuss that culture. Search online for "cultural awareness training + *location*" or "intercultural training + *location*" to find opportunities.

Learning the Language

If you move to another country where few (if any) people speak your native language, you can greatly benefit from learning the local tongue. Speaking the language helps you communicate better, find your way around, understand the culture, and make friends with local people. But learning a second language is no simple feat.

After taking five years of Spanish classes in high school and college, I was dismayed to arrive in Mexico, unable to understand a thing. I remember struggling so much to decipher what a supermarket clerk said to me that I held up the check-out line.

Many people want to learn a foreign language, but it can feel like an overwhelming task when life gets busy. Despite my initial challenge in learning Spanish, I eventually became fluent through time, patience, and effort. I can't offer you any short cuts. Think of it as a lifelong pursuit.

After you decide on a destination, start small. Sign up on a language app or website, and start practicing before you leave home. Here are a few platforms that you can use:

>> **Babbel** (www.babbel.com): If you like learning through conversation, this option offers courses in Italian, Dutch, Norwegian, and many additional languages. Its technique focuses on everyday vocabulary and audio from native speakers.

>> **Duolingo** (www.duolingo.com): Start learning 30-plus languages for free. The site and app offer short lessons backed by scientific research to help you learn fast. Stay motivated with the game-like streak feature and reminders.

>> **HelloTalk** (www.hellotalk.com): A free phone and web app that connects you with real people through text chat, voice notes, and video messages. You

can practice more than 150 languages by talking with millions of native speakers worldwide.

» **Lirica** (www.lirica.io): This app helps you learn Spanish, English, or German through music. Reading song lyrics from the Mexican singer Natalia Lafourcade helped me understand Spanish while studying abroad, so this strategy may work for you, too! You can rock out to superstars such as Shakira and P!nk while learning new words.

» **Rosetta Stone** (www.rosettastone.com): Founded in 1992, Rosetta Stone offers three-month, one-year, and lifetime access to single or multiple language plans in 25 languages. Rosetta Stone's research-backed method helps you master a language through reading, writing, speaking, and listening. I especially like the pronunciation feature and phrasebooks that help you discover the culture (or cultures) while getting familiar with common phrases.

Practicing with locals

After you arrive at your destination, you pick up new words naturally through constant exposure. You read street signs and menus and hear people speak the language around you. However, if you want to become fluent, it helps to stay with the locals in a homestay situation or take in-person classes:

» **Homestays:** During a homestay, you live with a local family to better understand their culture, customs, and traditions. Although you may find living with strangers who speak a foreign language uncomfortable or awkward initially, I've found it's one of the most effective ways to improve your speaking and comprehension skills. You can find homestays through websites such as Home Language International (http://hli.co.uk), Lingoo (www.lingoo.com), or through brick-and-mortar language schools.

TIP

Check out more tips about immersion and homestays on the *Traveling with Kristin* Podcast, Episode 151, "The Best Way to Learn a Foreign Language (Fast)." You can listen or download episodes for free on all podcast apps, such as Apple, Spotify, or at https://www.podcast.travelingwithkristin.com.

» **Language classes:** Find language classes in your destination by searching online or by using a map app to locate schools close to you. You can also ask for recommendations online in Facebook groups and expat forums. Attending in-person classes is also a great way to meet new people.

TIP

» **Private tutoring:** Consider hiring a private language tutor to come to your home.

Tips for language learning

Here are some tips that help me learn languages when I travel abroad:

>> **Buy a book of local phrases and slang.** I can't stress enough the benefits of learning the local slang, which helps you understand people and culture on a deeper level. In Dutch, *lekker* translates to "tasty," but you soon come to find that anything pleasant or nice can also be *lekker*, from the weather to a song to your new pair of shoes. Even a situation can be *lekker*. It's similar to how Americans say "cool" or "sweet," or how Spanish speakers use *rico* (rich) to describe food, weather, situations, and sleep.

>> **Carry a small dictionary (or download an app).** So that you can look up words that you don't know and write them down. My Spanish teacher once told me that you can more easily remember words if you find and define them, rather than asking someone, "¿Cómo se dice . . . ?" ("How do you say . . . ?").

>> **Partner with a local.** Many people report that they can learn languages fast by conversing with friends or mates from another country. You learn their language and they learn yours. It also helps if you speak the same language and study a second language together.

>> **Download language translation apps to your phone.** Examples include the old faithful Google Translate (http://translate.google.com), as well as iTranslate (www.itranslate.com), a leading translation and dictionary app.

TIP

Most translation apps have a camera feature, which allows you to scan a label or snap a picture to translate. This option can help you interpret nutrition and ingredient labels in grocery stores and instructions for operating your foreign washing machine.

>> **Listen to local radio or news programming.** You can hear local reporting about important topics in your adopted country while improving your language skills.

>> **Listen to podcasts.** Search in your favorite podcast app for "Learn *language*," test a few out, and listen consistently to one that you like.

>> **Talk to strangers.** Strike up conversations with locals to practice your skills and meet new people. Remember that they may also want to practice their English with you (or a third language that you have in common).

>> **Translate street signage and restaurant menus.** Try to recognize words that you see often and practice ordering food in the local dialect.

>> **Watch TV with subtitles.** You can turn subtitles on in different languages in your streaming app or go to a movie theater to watch a new English-language release that includes local-language subtitles.

Although you naturally want to browse social media, call your loved ones back home, and meet people who speak your language, be wary of spending too much time online and in the *expat bubble*, which is a social circle made exclusively of foreigners. The more time you spend around expats and immigrants, the longer it takes to adapt to the local society.

Be consistent, and don't give up, even if you miss practicing for a few days (weeks or months)! You never know when your language breakthrough will occur.

Overcoming Loneliness

Occasional loneliness is a natural part of life, whether you live abroad or not. However, your first few weeks and months in a foreign country can exacerbate such feelings while you adjust to the culture and language, and build a support network.

Stave off loneliness before it starts by trying to meet people in your early days living abroad. If you want to make friends fast, search online for local interest groups or expat. Also, look up networking apps and membership sites for travel-minded people, such as ASmallWorld (www.asmallworld.com).

Even if you want to avoid the *expat bubble* (which occurs when foreigners spend more time together than with local citizens), talking about your experiences with people who've been through similar situations can help you relate to each other's journeys. Connect with foreigners online or attend in-real-life (IRL) meetups through the options below:

» **Dating and friendship apps:** Some apps, such as Bumble (www.bumble.com), Hinge (www.hinge.co), OkCupid (www.okcupid.com), and Tinder (www.tinder.com), are available worldwide. You can also search your app store for popular dating apps in your country or region. To find friends, Bumble has a BFF mode. Additional friend apps include Friender, Yubo, and language apps such as HelloTalk.

Bumble BFF (www.bumble.com/bff) lets you search for friends, and Bumble Bizz (www.bumble.com/bizz) can help you with networking connections.

» **Local clubs:** Join groups of people who have shared interests. Meetup (www.meetup.com) has more than 330,000 groups for everything from hiking to wine tasting to meditation. Internations (www.internations.org) helps expats connect in 420 cities worldwide.

CHAPTER 10 **Embracing Culture Shock Like a Pro**

- » **Local events:** Search Facebook Events (www.facebook.com/events) and websites such as Eventbrite (www.eventbrite.com) for your location's music, cultural, and sporting events. You can also learn new skills through Eventbrite. I've attended craft workshops and writing classes that I found there. ASmallWorld (www.asmallworld.com/), a free and premium membership site for travel enthusiasts, hosts 1,000+ events annually.

- » **Volunteering:** Research indicates that helping others improves your physical and mental health. Generous acts boost feel-good chemicals such as dopamine and serotonin, which are soldiers in your battle against culture shock and loneliness. You can find international volunteer programs on Go Overseas (www.gooverseas.com) and local opportunities through religious institutions, community organizations, animal shelters, and volunteer centers.

- » **Local sports:** Look up sports lessons, clubs, and teams online. If you like golf, join a country club. If you're into pickleball, find a league. To practice your dance moves, enroll in salsa classes.

Choose a popular sport in your location to combine exercise with cultural immersion. For example, you could try lawn bowling in Australia, cricket in England or India, or surfing in Sri Lanka. Or, if you prefer to watch sports rather than play them, attend a game in person. Soccer (football to everyone outside the U.S.) and Formula 1 racing are popular worldwide.

Staying busy also helps with loneliness. Joe H., who moved to Costa Rica, said "My life here is full. I spend half of the day doing work, research, or personal admin. I make time to exercise, play pickleball, explore the local area, and meet with my support network. I've made friends locally and usually meet for food or drinks to stay connected. There is no loneliness or homesickness at all."

One digital nomad I know recommends "finding at least one 'comfort spot' — a café, park, or library that you can visit regularly and that provides a sense of familiarity. Over time, you find that homesickness fades as you create new memories and relationships."

If loneliness becomes a chronic problem, you can get support. Flip to the sidebar "Mental Health Considerations," in this chapter, for some suggestions.

Managing Your Expectations

I once heard a saying that every story has three sides: your side, the other person's side, and what *really* happened. Living abroad is similar. First, you have expectations. Then, you have an experience. Your perception of how it went may be slightly different from reality. Of course, how you feel about what you're going through is significant, even if it's through an ever-changing emotional lens.

Before setting off for Italy, you may envision yourself sipping wine and slurping pasta in the golden sunlight of a Tuscan backdrop; or maybe you picture waltzing through the streets of Paris with a chocolate croissant in hand. Either of those scenarios may realistically occur — I've often pinched myself that I was living my dream life while sailing the Mediterranean, hiking Peru's Machu Picchu, and watching the sunset from a surfboard in Costa Rica.

But in between the peaks of presence and elation you feel during a special moment, you have to deal with valleys. You may find it hard to feel grateful when your neighbor is having a fiesta at 3 a.m., you're waiting for hours in a bank line, or you're missing a loved one's birthday or wedding. Some disappointments and surprises are par for the course.

Here are a few misconceptions about life abroad:

- **Culture shock won't affect you.** Despite understanding the nature of culture shock, you can easily underestimate the differences between your home and adopted countries. Traveling somewhere on holiday feels different than moving there. Check out the section "Understanding Culture Shock (and How to Navigate It)," earlier in this chapter.

- **Every day will be exciting.** The longer you live abroad, the more it feels like normal life. This is a good thing because it means you're adapting. But it also means some days will be tedious, frustrating, or downright rotten, or you'll have some off days.

WARNING

Beware the urge to move to a new place every time the sheen of a country wears off. Try as you might, you can't live in the honeymoon phase forever (see the section "Riding the Curve of Cultural Adjustment," earlier in this chapter, for more about the honeymoon phase of a move).

- **Everything will be Insta-worthy.** The marketing images of destinations often differ from reality (thanks, Photoshop!). The pristine beaches that you expect to see in Bali are filled with plastic and trash. The remote Icelandic waterfall that you travel to is jam-packed with tourists toting selfie sticks. When you live in a country, you see behind the façade. The true authenticity of a place isn't a carefully curated image — it's the good, the bad, and the ugly rolled into one.

- **The locals will love you.** I've never met an expat or immigrant who didn't want to make friends with the local people. But you have no guarantee that the residents you encounter feel the same. Don't take it personally if the locals you meet seem hesitant to get to know you or if they ignore or reject you. It takes time to build trust. Be patient. Accept your role as an outsider. Connect with other foreigners until you learn the language and can really bond and build relationships with the local citizenry.

CHAPTER 10 **Embracing Culture Shock Like a Pro** 189

» **Moving abroad can solve all your problems.** Before you arrive in your destination, you can easily see things through rose-colored glasses. You might think life will be simpler, cheaper, better, or more fulfilling than it is at home. In some cases, you'd be right. But the grass isn't always greener. Living abroad can be like playing Whack-a-Mole with your problems — you solve some and create new ones.

REMEMBER

Remain flexible and open-minded about your experience abroad. When you feel frustrated or uncomfortable, remind yourself that it's part of the journey. Keep this chapter handy for encouragement and tips on how to get unstuck.

MENTAL HEALTH CONSIDERATIONS

Feelings of culture shock and loneliness can turn into long-term burnout and mental health challenges if left unchecked. If you feel persistent sadness, hopelessness, or depression, get help:

- **Find a therapist.** Contact your insurance or healthcare provider for mental health practitioners covered by your plan. You can connect with talk therapy counselors anywhere in the world on BetterHelp (www.betterhelp.com).

- **Get active.** Exercise has profound benefits for your well-being. It can help improve your memory, sleep, mood, and mental state. Even 20 minutes of activity per day can have an impact. Whether you like walking, yoga, or high-intensity activities, every little bit helps.

- **Keep cool.** Ice baths, cold showers, and cryotherapy can also improve your mental state. Cold therapy boosts endorphin levels while decreasing cortisol, a stress hormone.

- **Get outside.** Spending time in nature helps you feel calm, connected, and more present. According to The Pew Charitable Trusts (www.pewtrusts.org), researchers from various institutions have found that being in nature reduces stress, loneliness, and depression symptoms while enhancing overall well-being.

- **Stay off screens.** Spending excessive time on your phone or computer can harm your mental health. Set up screen time limits and notifications on your phone. Use an app such as Freedom (www.freedom.to) to block addictive apps and websites or a physical device such as Brick (www.getbrick.app) to turn apps off.

Solving Problems When Things Go Wrong

When problems inevitably arise, remember that you have solutions. The following sections discuss some possible challenges that you may face and how to deal with them.

- » **Buyer's remorse.** If you begin to second guess your decision to move, journal what you're feeling. Reflect on your reasons for moving (which I can help you determine in Chapter 1). Write down the main things bothering you and ideas for how to resolve them. Use the resources in this chapter to talk to a therapist who can help you make decisions.

- » **Financial stress.** If money is tight or unforeseen expenses crop up, refer to Chapter 3 for budgeting tips.

To manage cash flow, use travel expense tracking apps such as Apple's Tripcoin (available at http://apps.apple.com) or TravelSpend (www.travel-spend.com) for Apple and Android users. You can also consider hiring a financial advisor to help balance your books.

Use an international money transfer and currency app such as Wise (www.wise.com) to save money on international transfers and ATM fees.

- » **Homesickness.** Even if you love your life abroad, you might feel homesick sometimes. When the feeling strikes, phone a friend or family member, watch a TV show or movie that reminds you of home, cook one of your favorite meals, or attend a meet-up with people from your home country. If all else fails, a visit back home might be just what the doctor ordered.

Stay in touch with friends and family through video calling apps such as FaceTime, WhatsApp, and Zoom. Use a website such as WorldTimeBuddy (www.worldtimebuddy.com/) know what time it is for friends and family in different time zones. Most smartphones also allow you to add locations to your world clock.

For more ways to meet people and make friends, see Chapter 11.

- » **Physical Danger.** If you find yourself in actual danger while abroad, contact the local authorities and your embassy or consulate. Chapter 13 has resources on staying safe abroad and preparing for disasters, emergencies, and conflict.

If you've exhausted all resources or feel it's time to end your expat journey, Chapter 13 guides you in crafting your Expat Exit Strategy.

THE HARDEST THINGS ABOUT LIVING ABROAD

I scoured the Internet, both in forums and Reddit, for the most common gripes about living abroad. Although you might not experience any or all of these, they're worth mentioning so that you know you're not alone:

- **Being far from family:** Missing important milestones such as birthdays, weddings, and funerals can take a toll on you and your loved ones. Stay in touch with family and friends through regular texting, phone, and video calls. Plan trips to visit on occasion. See Chapter 11 for more tips on staying in touch.

- **Navigating bureaucracy:** Applying for visas, keeping track of immigration deadlines, and dealing with delays can be a hassle. To avoid stress, organize your documents well, add reminders to your calendar, and hire professionals to help.

- **Language and cultural barriers:** Despite your best efforts, you may struggle to learn a new language and fully fit into a foreign country. Although you may never look or sound exactly like the locals, you can still have a meaningful and transformative experience. Refer to the section "Learning the Language," in this chapter, for help.

- **Loneliness and loss of community:** Many people feel torn between their familiar life in their home country and their new life abroad. Although you can't be in two places simultaneously, focus on what you hope to achieve by moving abroad. Prioritize your current life and stay in the present. Focus on building new relationships while remaining connected with those who stayed behind. Invite people to visit you and let them into your new world. See the suggestions in Chapters 10 and 11 for more tips on fitting in abroad.

- **Logistical challenges:** Flight delays, housing issues, and unforeseen problems and expenses can crop up during an international move. Keep calm and check Chapters 5, 6, and 7 for help building and executing a flexible relocation plan.

- **Work and career difficulties:** You may find challenge in adapting to a different salary, job responsibilities, and office culture. Choose a job that fits your work style and career goals. Communicate well with your employer or HR department. Seek mentorship inside the company or hire a business coach for additional support.

If you're struggling to adapt, consider becoming self-employed or finding a remote job. My book *Digital Nomads For Dummies* (John Wiley & Sons) can guide you in how to generate online income while traveling.

> **IN THIS CHAPTER**
> » Meeting new people
> » Forming cross-cultural connections
> » Growing your professional network
> » Staying connected to your home country

Chapter 11

Finding Your Community

Creating a new life abroad has much to do with the people you meet. Making new friends and integrating with the local community is the difference between traveling somewhere and living there.

Moving to another country gives you a chance to meet people from different cultures in one place. In this chapter, I share how to build a support network that includes both locals and foreigners. You can find practical suggestions for cultivating new friendships, meeting romantic partners, and expanding your professional reach — all while staying in touch with friends and family back home.

Meeting the Locals

You may have seen chatter online about how to fit in with the local population when you move abroad. At first, you may feel intimidated by the perceived differences in your cultures, languages, and backgrounds. But you soon find that people are people. You meet people abroad like you do at home — through your daily life and routines. From frequenting your corner café to going grocery shopping or picking your kids up from school, you meet people through everyday interactions.

The following sections offer some ways to seek out local friendships.

WARNING

Always take safety precautions when meeting new people and building trust. For tips on staying safe abroad, see Chapter 13.

Putting work (or school) into making friends

One of the best ways to make new connections is on the job or at school, where daily interactions and shared experiences lead to natural friendships. Here are a few ways you can transform working or studying into growing your social circle:

» **Apply for a job:** Research suggests that most people have a close friend (or two) at their workplace.

Receiving a job offer in a foreign country helps you qualify for a work permit, which can give you a good way to stay abroad long-term. See Chapter 4 for more about visas and residency permits.

If you work remotely or from home, you consider changing your environment to be near others. You can locate a coworking space to join on Coworker (www.coworker.com).

» **Enroll in school:** With a study permit, you can move abroad and meet people who share a common interest. Twenty years after studying abroad in Costa Rica and Australia, I remain friends with people I met during that time. You don't have to enroll in a university to obtain a permit, either. Taking language, cultural, or vocational classes can qualify you to study in countries such as Hungary, Italy, Spain, Thailand, and others.

Moving to a small town

If you move to a place where you're the only foreigner, you meet local residents by design. I once spent time in the small village of Þingeyri, Iceland (population 326 in 2020). I rented a house with a Finnish woman who worked remotely from our coworking space, The Blue Bank. In the mornings, we swam laps in the community pool and sipped coffee in the hot tub with neighbors. After a week, I felt like I'd lived there for a year.

I had a similar experience in Aposentillo, Nicaragua — a town so small that I couldn't find population data for it! As one of the few foreigners living within a one-hour radius, I spent most of my time with Nicaraguans.

REMEMBER

You really can make friends in cities and towns of all sizes, so don't let that dictate where you move.

Moving to a friendly country

Although friendliness is subjective, expats rate some countries higher than others regarding the ease of settling in abroad.

Over 12,500 people worldwide participated in the 2024 Expat Insider survey by InterNations (www.internations.org). Costa Rica, Mexico, and the Philippines topped the list of most welcoming countries, with Costa Rica winning first place for having the nicest people. Expats also found it easy to befriend locals in Brazil, Panama, and Mexico. However, foreigners reported struggling to fit in in Austria, Kuwait, and Switzerland.

You can discover the most amicable places to live in the world by searching online for friendliest countries rankings. For instance, the U.S. News Best Countries report (www.usnews.com/news/best-countries/rankings) rates Canada, Spain, and New Zealand in its top three. You can also find friendly places by searching on Reddit (www.reddit.com) and Quora (www.quora.com) threads. Or check out Nomads.com, where you can see how a city or country scores in categories such as "community," "friendly to foreigners," "female friendly," and "LGBTQ+ friendly."

Learning the lingo

Speaking a few words of the local language goes a long way, and Chapter 10 provides resources to help you learn them. However, you don't need to become fluent to communicate. According to psychologist and professor Albert Mehrabian (author of the book *Nonverbal Communication* [Routledge]), people may rely more on non-verbal cues in certain situations. When there's inconsistent or conflicting in-person communication, words can account for a scant 7 percent of the message, compared to 38 percent for tone of voice and 55 percent for facial expressions and body language.

Although you may feel awkward or self-conscious at first, don't shy away from saying hello (or *hola*) to strangers. Take every opportunity to speak with people, whether you're riding a bus, sitting on a park bench, or walking down the street. You might be surprised how open people are to conversation.

TIP

Look for a language exchange opportunity where you can help a local person speak your language while learning theirs. You can find a language buddy online by using a website such as HelloTalk (www.hellotalk.com) or Tandem (www.tandem.net).

CHAPTER 11 **Finding Your Community** 195

Setting up your social life

The longer you live abroad, the more you'll meet people organically. But there are ways to jump-start your social life:

- » **Adopt a dog.** Walking around with a furry friend can give you an effective conversation starter and an excuse to hang out in dog parks!

- » **Join local clubs.** Let your interests lead you to new friendships. Dive into a hobby or interest shortly after arriving at your destination. Take a pottery class, join a gym, go for a group hike, or whatever suits your fancy.

  Claudia, who moved to Switzerland, suggested a range of ideas: "To make friends, I joined the Swiss Society, networking groups, talked to neighbors, and made some connections at work. I also joined a ladies' group for women over 35 without children. I enjoy being part of a community and usually integrate quickly."

- » **Host a dinner party or event.** Invite your neighbors for a housewarming party or register an event on Eventbrite (www.eventbrite.com) or Meetup (www.meetup.com). I once attended a memorable dinner party in Berlin that included a mix of international and German residents, which I found through ASmallWorld (www.asmallworld.com).

  Strangers are friends you haven't met yet.

REMEMBER

Putting down roots and branching out

After moving to a new country, it can take time for your mind and body to feel at home. The following are a few ways to adapt quickly to your surroundings:

- » **Live with locals.** Rather than moving straight into a private home or rental property, consider staying with a local family. In addition to helping you with your language and cultural skills, your new housemates can introduce you to their neighbors, social circles, and places to hang out. A typical homestay lasts anywhere from one week to a few months. Find more about homestays in Chapter 10.

- » **Dive into the dating pool.** If you're single, dating a local person can help you learn more about the culture and language. I talk more about dating in the section "Meeting a Mate or Life Partner," later in this chapter.

- » **Live your life.** Go about your daily routine, greeting your neighbors, commuting to work, playing sports, or dining out. You're bound to meet people through chance and serendipity.

- Find out where people hang out in your area. Visit parks, bars, public gardens, farmers markets, and community events.
- » **Stay long-term.** The best way to make friends is to stay in one place. The more you move around, the more often you start over with new relationships.

In some cultures, family comes first, and long-term friendships trump making new acquaintances with outsiders. Before arriving abroad, research the social structure of the country. Don't take it personally if you find it hard to make friends with locals at first; building relationships takes time.

Offering a helping hand

Volunteering helps you meet like-minded people and community leaders. Participate in a beach cleanup or help build houses with Habitat for Humanity. Contact food banks, homeless shelters, nursing homes, and religious organizations to see whether they accept volunteers. Find more tips in the section "Volunteering Opportunities," later in this chapter.

Making Friends Across Cultures

If you want to encounter expats, immigrants, and travelers hanging out together — a sort of international community that speaks your language — try the solutions I suggest in the following sections.

Choosing a foreigner-friendly destination

International residents flock to some places more than others. For instance, Bali, Indonesia is popular for tourists, nomads, and retirees alike. Chiang Mai, Thailand, and Tulum, Mexico are hubs for digital nomads. Lisbon and the Algarve, Portugal are popular places for expats to settle. San Miguel de Allende, Mexico attracts many retirees from the United States and Canada.

To find international communities abroad, search online for surveys, rankings, and blogs of the "best countries for expats." Part 5 of this book lists ideas for the best places to retire abroad, live cheaply, or travel as a digital nomad.

My YouTube channel, Traveling with Kristin, features hundreds of videos about the best places to live in the world. (Just go to www.youtube.com and enter "Traveling with Kristin" into the search text box to find my channel.) Chapter 4 also helps you with destination inspiration.

CHAPTER 11 **Finding Your Community** 197

Finding your people

Follow your interests for ways to meet people and participate in your new society. Whether you connect with others through sports, fitness, the arts, or spirituality, engaging in activities you enjoy will naturally lead you to make new connections.

Dave, who moved from the U.S. to Portugal, shared his experience with me: "We connected with people through communities of friends, local events, and passion points such as padel tennis, golf and surfing."

Here are a few ways to meet people with shared interests:

» **Look for international meetups.** Search Facebook groups, events, and Meetup (www.meetup.com) to find foreigner-friendly events in your area. During an InterNations-hosted happy hour in Manchester, U.K., I once met people from 23 different countries. Find expat meetups in 420-plus cities worldwide on the InterNations website (www.internations.org).

» **Attend conferences and events.** Look online for events related to your career or interests. Web Summit (www.websummit.com), an annual tech conference in Lisbon, Portugal, attracts more than 70,000 attendees worldwide. For music festivals and parties, you can find events on websites such as Eventbrite (www.eventbrite.com), Ticket Source (www.ticketsource.eu), or Shotgun (www.shotgun.live).

» **Join expat clubs.** Find strength in numbers by being part of an expat organization. Hanging out with foreigners who've spent a few months or years in a country lets you meet people who know what it's like to live there as an expat. Specialized websites such as Expat.com, Expat Exchange (www.expatexchange.com), and Just Landed (www.justlanded.com) host forums and support groups where you can find upcoming events in your area. Type in your location and dive in!

TIP

If you're interested in politics, consider uniting with members of your political party abroad. You can find chapters of Democrats Abroad (www.democratsabroad.com) and Republicans Overseas (www.republicansoverseas.com) in various countries.

» **Try co-living.** Choosing shared housing over a private rental saves you money on rent and comes with a built-in friend or two. Find affordable co-living opportunities from $100 per month in 70+ countries at Coliving.com. You can also find rooms for rent in shared houses on Airbnb (www.airbnb.com) and sublet and classifieds websites.

» **Be a tourist.** As a guest or new resident of a foreign country, don't be afraid to let your tourist flag fly sometimes. Take a guided tour around town, hang out at a hostel, or sign up for Airbnb Experiences (www.airbnb.com/experiences). You can also meet travelers through Couchsurfing (www.couchsurfing.com).

TIP

For even more ideas, make a list of your hobbies and interests. Copy and paste this list into an AI website, such as ChatGPT (www.chatgpt.com), and ask for suggestions about events, groups, activities, and organizations in your area.

Making the most of technology

Join destination- or interest-centric websites, apps, and messaging groups. You can typically find WhatsApp (www.whatsapp.com), Telegram (www.telegram.org), or Signal (www.signal.org) groups for a location by asking in Facebook groups (www.facebook.com) or searching forums such as Nomads.com and Reddit (www.reddit.com).

TIP

Create a profile on friend and networking apps that you find in your app store, such as BumbleBFF (www.bumble.com/bff). The UK's Tagme app (www.tagmeapp.co.uk) helps you meet a range of people. Check it out if you want someone to drink coffee or walk your dog with, or if you're seeking a sports team or band to join.

Meeting a Mate or Life Partner

With more than 8 billion people in the world, your soulmate could live anywhere! Moving to a new place presents opportunities for finding love. You can meet a future significant other (S/O) through new friends, visiting the corner pub, or by following some of the suggestions I give in the sections "Meeting the Locals" and "Making Friends Across Cultures," earlier in this chapter.

You can meet a mate abroad in the same ways that you might in your home country, although you may have additional communication and cultural challenges. The following sections provide ways that you can meet romantic partners or strengthen your existing relationship.

REMEMBER

If your relationship turns serious while you're living abroad, plan to extend your residency permit or explore partnership options, such as a marriage or fiancé visa. If you get married abroad, you may also want to file a foreign marriage certificate in your home country.

CHAPTER 11 **Finding Your Community** 199

Swiping left and right

Dating apps are an increasingly popular way to meet mates worldwide. Research collected by Statista (www.statista.com) shows that a growing number of people connect via online dating and social media sites.

Between 1995 and 2017, the number of couples who met online jumped from 2 percent to 39 percent, while the proportion of people who met at work, school, or through friends and family declined.

According to Statista, Tinder is the largest app by revenue, followed by Bumble, Hinge, Grindr, and Badoo (see Figure 11-1):

» **Tinder** (www.tinder.com): The world's largest app for dating and meeting new people. You can choose from free or paid tiers, including Tinder Plus, Gold, Platinum, and Select. Tiers offer varying benefits, such as unlimited likes, Go Incognito mode, and the ability to Passport to any location (meaning you can match with people in other places).

» **Bumble** (www.bumble.com): An app that allows you to date, find friends, and meet business contacts. A unique feature of Bumble is that women can message their matches first, whereas either party can contact people first on other sites. Like with Tinder, you can customize your profile by adding photos, videos, gender pronouns, and the type of relationship or connection that you seek.

» **Hinge** (www.hinge.co): The founders of Hinge say that they want you to go on your "last first date" and delete the app quickly. It's built on a Nobel-Prize-winning algorithm that encourages better matches and in-person connections through detailed profiles and conversation prompts.

» **Grindr** (www.grindr.com): Founded in 2009, Grindr is the most popular LGBTQI+ dating and social networking app in the world. Like many dating sites, it offers free and premium features. With location filters, you can find people to date as close as zero feet away. It's suitable for casual dating or finding a long-term partner.

» **Badoo** (www.badoo.com): This free, Bumble-owned app lets you log in with your e-mail, phone number, or Google or Facebook account. With Badoo, you can message people before matching with them. And the app's Safety Centre helps you date safely.

Couples also report meeting through social networks, such as Facebook, Instagram, and gaming sites.

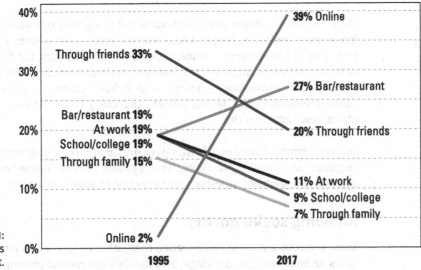

FIGURE 11-1: How couples meet.

Source: https://www.statista.com/statistics/1359421/top-grossing-dating-apps-worldwide/ CC BY 4.0/accessed on March 31, 2025

Dating across cultures

You may meet a variety of people abroad. You could end up dating someone from your home country, marrying a local, or meeting a fellow third-country national. In researching this book, I came across many stories, such as a French woman who met her Dutch husband while living in Japan. She disclosed on Reddit that they're raising their children in Germany.

You may find dating someone from a foreign country challenging, however. You're getting to know a new person while having different language, cultural, and social norms to navigate. To avoid misunderstandings, be forthcoming about what you're looking for in a relationship. Ask your partner about their expectations and preferred communication style so you can better understand them.

I talk about common cultural barriers to anticipate when dating in the following sections.

Decoding communication styles

Every couple argues sometimes, but your culture and communication style can influence how you handle conflict. Identify your cultural biases and talk with your partner about theirs. Anticipate potential misunderstandings and discuss solutions while on good terms. Set healthy boundaries and always treat one another with respect.

CHAPTER 11 Finding Your Community 201

Minimize miscommunications by finding out about your new country's culture. In low-context cultures people value direct verbal and written communication. Examples of low-context cultures include the U.S., Canada, the Netherlands, and Germany. However, high-context cultures are those which prioritize subtler cues such as tone, expression, gestures, and indirect communication. High context cultures include China, Japan, Russia, and many countries in the Middle East, Africa, and Latin America.

Someone from a different culture can easily misinterpret your tone of voice, body language, and facial expressions. What appears passive to one person may seem aggressive to another, whether you're texting or speaking face-to-face.

Knowing social norms

Some societies are more conservative than others. Find out about the traditional views on commitment, marriage, and family involvement in your adopted country. Also investigate a society's take on public displays of affection. In some countries, holding hands or kissing in public is frowned upon or illegal.

Considering gender roles

In some cultures, men and women have defined gender roles, but that's not the case everywhere. For example, women still handle most household tasks in Italy, Poland, and the United States, while men do more housework in Denmark and Slovenia. Some countries prioritize equality between sexes, while others have high rates of gender-based oppression, violence, and forced marriage or human trafficking. (See Chapter 13 for ways to stay safe internationally.)

Although no country boasts complete gender parity, equal rights are available to men and women in Belgium, Canada, Denmark, Norway, Sweden, and the Netherlands. Australia, Iceland, Germany, and Portugal also recognize non-binary and transgender rights.

WARNING

Women, minorities, and the LGBTQI+ community remain at risk in many countries. Find out about the legality of issues that you care about before moving abroad, such as abortion, contraception, gay and religious rights, and the treatment of women and minorities.

Moving abroad can potentially enhance your safety and freedom compared to what you experience in your home country.

Dealing with money and finances

Expectations regarding sharing or separating finances vary by culture. From debating how to split the bill at dinner to buying a home together, discuss this topic early in your relationship. That is, before you propose, open a joint bank account, or sign a prenuptial agreement.

Going to the matchmaker

Matchmaking services can help you connect with people internationally or in a certain demographic. However, they come at a cost — typically at least $1,000 per month or more.

International matchmaking sites include:

- **Elite Connections International** (www.eliteconnections.com): Professional matchmakers from this site aim to help you find long-term, meaningful relationships. Although it's based in the United States, this company offers international services with one- and two-year membership options.

- **Kelleher International** (www.kelleher-international.com): A high-end matchmaking service that has offices in New York, Chicago, London, and beyond. The company boasts an 89 percent success rate based on its practice of making hand-picked connections over letting an algorithm do the work.

- **ML Introductions** (www.mlintroductions.com): This Brussels, Belgium-based company has offices in the U.S., Dubai, Singapore, and Australia. Its team helps clients find love on five continents. The matchmaking process starts with a one-on-one interview, followed by an introduction within as little as two weeks.

You can also find local matchmakers in your area by searching online or through a map app for "matchmaking services."

Relating in your current relationship

Moving abroad with your mate presents new challenges and opportunities for growth in your relationship. Maintaining a positive attitude, sharing reasons and goals for moving, and relating well after you arrive abroad can help strengthen your relationship. But don't expect all smooth sailing; some days will test your patience.

Coping with relocation logistics is the first hurdle to overcome together. Applying for visas, downsizing your belongings, or flying your pets across the ocean is enough to stress anyone out — alone or coupled. Anticipate such situations and approach planning and problem-solving as a team.

Here are some tips for strengthening your relationship while abroad:

» **Communicate well and often.** Discuss how your relationship dynamic might change before you move. Perhaps one partner moves for work while the other puts their career on hold. Or maybe you want to move abroad but your partner prefers to stay home, so a long-distance relationship is in the cards. Try to anticipate any friction and brainstorm solutions in advance and express concerns before they become problems.

Navigating a move abroad can test your relationship. To minimize any feelings of bitterness or overwhelm, divide up tasks and responsibilities related to the planning. Perhaps you're in charge of finding housing while your partner takes care of visa documentation.

If needed, seek relationship counseling online or in person.

» **Enjoy the experience.** Living in a foreign country together can strengthen your bond as a couple. Attend language or cultural classes and social events together. Go sightseeing in your new location or take side trips to nearby destinations.

» **Seek solo time.** Living together abroad doesn't mean you have to do *everything* together. Although you undoubtedly want to make memories as a couple, embrace this opportunity for personal growth. Sign up for classes and activities that pique your interest, go on solo travel trips, or take yourself on a date in your new city or neighborhood.

Volunteering Opportunities

Giving back to your local community can provide you with a great way to meet people while learning more about the culture and language of your adopted country. It also gives you a good way to experience a place briefly and decide whether it's somewhere you want to live someday. An easy way to start is to search online for "volunteer opportunities + [*your location*]."

TIP

Search in the local language to get more specific results. For example, search "vrijwilligerswerk + [*Dutch city*]" to find volunteer opportunities in the Netherlands, or "oportunidades de voluntariado + [*Portuguese city*]" to get ideas for helping in Portugal.

You can also contact local or international organizations that help causes that you care about:

- **Refugees:** Look up the United Nations Refugee Agency, also called the United Nations High Commissioner for Refugees (UNHCR), to help displaced people worldwide.

- **Disaster relief:** Contact the Red Cross to see how you can help in a disaster.

- **Animals:** If you love animals, seek out a local pet shelter or farm animal rescue sanctuary.

- **The environment:** Enroll with a global non-profit such as Greenpeace.

If you have athletic skills, consider coaching a team sport. While living in Costa Rica, I volunteered to teach surf lessons at an annual event benefitting an orphanage.

TIP

Contact your country's consulate abroad or visit government portals for more ideas. In Great Britain, the website www.gov.uk/volunteering lists volunteer opportunities throughout the country.

You can also find free and paid volunteer options through providers that cater to an international audience. However, you may meet more travelers than residents this way. Here are some good international volunteer organizations:

- **Nomads Giving Back!** (www.nomadsgivingback.com): Founded by a digital nomad, this organization aims to help long-term travelers and expats get more involved in the communities they spend time in. Participate in group events, social impact trips, or personal and professional skills exchanges. Membership tiers range from $15 to $100 per month.

- **Voluntouring** (www.voluntouring.org): An online database and cultural exchange platform that connects travelers with hosts. In a placement, you work four to five hours daily in exchange for room and board. It's free to browse the site, but you may have to pay to access the opportunities.

- **Workaway** (www.workaway.info): Browse more than 50,000 cultural exchanges, house-sitting, and volunteer opportunities worldwide. This platform can work for solo or group travelers, families, and couples.

» **WWOOF** (www.wwoof.net): Worldwide Opportunities on Organic Farms connects you with hosts worldwide in exchange for room and board. Choose from ecological, cultural, and educational opportunities. You can choose to work on a family farm in Stockholm, Sweden, help save the Peruvian rainforest, or grow flowers in Italy.

Check the ratings and reviews of volunteer organizations and platforms before committing to a program.

Taking Your Career Networking to a New Level

By moving to a new country, you can grow your career options and professional network while coming up with new business ideas. Working across borders makes you more attractive in the job market because you can add communication, language, negotiation, leadership, and technical skills to your resume. In this section, I share ways to expand your career opportunities.

Attending conferences and events

Check websites such as Eventbrite (www.eventbrite.com), Meetup (www.meetup.com), and Facebook (www.facebook.com) to discover networking events. Follow professional organizations that host annual conferences or masterminds. As a content creator, I've attended a YouTube conference in California, a podcast festival in Florida, and a travel conference in London.

Mix things up by attending events outside your industry. These events can give you opportunities to meet diverse people and spark new ideas. Try SXSW (www.sxsw.com) in Austin, Texas, Web Summit (www.websummit.com) in Portugal or Brazil, or the Nomad Cruise (www.nomadcruise.com) — a floating conference for remote workers and travel enthusiasts.

Attend a virtual or in-person career fair if you're looking for a job offer abroad that can lead to a work permit.

Contacting chambers of commerce

A *chamber of commerce* is a group of business leaders and advocates in a community, region, or country. Members and volunteers can meet people, attend events, and enjoy discounts with local vendors. You can locate a chamber of commerce near your new (or future) home by searching online or in a national directory.

Getting active online

Find out which social networks are popular in your new country. LinkedIn (www.linkedin.com) has users worldwide. Complete a strong profile that highlights your work experience. Update your status to indicate what you're looking for on the platform — whether it's to find a job, clients, or business partner. Also consider X (www.x.com), Reddit (www.reddit.com), and websites and forums where people from your industry hang out. For example, entrepreneurs and startup founders might want to join AngelList (www.angellist.com) or Product Hunt (www.producthunt.com).

For remote workers, check out online hubs such as Remoters (www.remoters.net) and Nomads.com.

Create social media content about your experience working in a foreign country to hopefully attract like-minded people and prospective clients or employers. Choose a platform that you enjoy and start publishing! If you like to write, post articles on LinkedIn (www.linkedin.com) or start a blog. If you enjoy public speaking, apply to talk at events or start a podcast. If video is your thing, start a YouTube channel. Find out more about sharing your experience in Chapter 12.

Joining a coworking space

If you work remotely or from home, consider renting a desk or office at a coworking space. Prices can range from as low as $20 to $30 per month for a hot desk to a few hundred dollars monthly for a private office. Spaces typically hold regular events, happy hours, and lunches, and host guest speakers. Plus, you can access stable Wi-Fi, printing services, and copious amounts of coffee and tea.

On Coworker (www.coworker.com), choose from more than 25,000 coworking spaces in 172 countries. You can also use a map app to find a space nearby.

Staying in Touch with People at Home

Although you get to meet new people when you move abroad, it's also important to keep in contact with your friends and family from home. They can help keep you grounded when you feel adrift and provide support from afar.

CHAPTER 11 **Finding Your Community** 207

TIP Schedule regular check-ins, such as once per month or quarter, and add those check-ins to your calendar. Set reminders to reach out on birthdays, anniversaries, and holidays. Plan for time zone differences and choose a time to connect that works for all parties.

To stay connected with friends and family across borders, plan ahead. Before departing from your home country, discuss how your communication might change while you're abroad. Identify the best ways to keep in touch. Acknowledge each other's needs and listen to any concerns.

Once you're abroad, develop strong bonds with friends and family by asking questions other than "How are you?" Search online for apps, cards, blogs, or books of intimacy questions. You can also deepen your communication by searching "conversation starters" for couples, friends, families, or kids.

Communicating in multiple ways

You can use one or many methods of communication to stay in touch:

» **Snail mail:** Communicate the old-fashioned way by sending letters or postcards to your loved ones. Surprise them with a small care package of trinkets, snacks, and souvenirs that you think they might like.

» **Messaging apps:** Sending voice or text messages over Wi-Fi is free (compared with SMS texting). If you have an iPhone, use iMessage. If you have an Android phone, use a communication app such as Facebook Messenger (www.messenger.com), Signal (www.signal.org), Telegram (www.telegram.org), Viber (www.viber.com), or WhatsApp (www.whatsapp.com).

Create a messaging group for siblings, cousins, family, or friends.

» **E-mail:** For longer or more formal correspondence, send an e-mail or electronic newsletter instead of using a messaging app. If you send a group e-mail to family and friends, BCC respondents so that they can keep their privacy.

» **Voice and video calling:** Use FaceTime, WhatsApp, Skype, Google Voice, or Zoom to stay connected virtually. Most apps offer a free version with optional paid features.

For less direct communication, you can still keep your friends and family in the know with:

» **Photo sharing:** Create a shared photo album through Apple Photos, Google Photos, or a cloud storage site, such as Dropbox (www.dropbox.com) or Google Drive (http://drive.google.com). Aura (www.auraframes.com) makes a digital photo frame that lets you invite contributors to post pictures.

» **Music accounts:** Share your Spotify, Apple Music, or YouTube playlists with each other.

» **Social media:** Follow your friends and family on platforms such as Instagram, Facebook, Snapchat, TikTok, and X. Share posts and stories from your life, and like and comment on their posts.

TIP

» **Streaming parties:** You can watch streaming shows together by logging into Skype or Zoom and sharing your screen and audio. Alternatively, you can download Teleparty (www.teleparty.com) to host a watch party.

Visiting in person

Invite friends and family to visit you abroad or go see them. It's understandable if distance or financial constraints get in the way. Choose a cadence that works for you, whether it's monthly, yearly, or less often. If you don't have room for guests in your house, help them find a place that they can stay nearby and plan activities to do together while they're visiting.

REMEMBER

Some relationships naturally drift apart over time. You may have to put in more effort to keep bonds strong or let things go.

Don't take it personally if your friends or family members don't seem enthralled with hearing about your travels or new life overseas — it's a common reaction. They could be busy, disagree with your decision to move, or feel left out of your new life. Perhaps they don't have the time, resources, or interest to travel; or they could see it as bragging.

If you're feeling down about losing touch, remember your "why" for moving (which you can figure out in Chapter 1). Focus on the positives in your life and show genuine interest in their lives. Try to find common ground with your loved ones. Discuss topics that they can relate to, such as books that you both read, sports, movies, news, or show series.

Making the Most of Your Life Abroad

After you move abroad, embrace it! Use it as an opportunity to design your ideal lifestyle. Incorporate new, healthy habits into your daily routine. Wake up earlier, walk or bike instead of driving, and cook meals at home with local ingredients. Here are more ways to seize the day:

» **Explore your surroundings.** Use websites such as TripAdvisor (www.tripadvisor.com) and Airbnb Experiences (www.airbnb.com/experiences) to find things to do in your area. Visit your tourism board for in-person advice and find tours and activities. Add nearby destinations to your travel bucket list and plan how and when you'll go there. If you live in Rome, Italy, you can reach Lake Garda (Lago di Garda) in five hours by train. If you move to Manila, Philippines, you can relax on the beaches of Palawan after a two-and-a-half-hour flight. Let your imagination take the lead and see where it guides you! And invite new friends to travel with you.

TIP

Find a local tour guide on the website ToursByLocals (www.toursbylocals.com).

» **Reflect on your journey.** Keep a journal, diary, or log notes in your phone or tablet's Notes app. Celebrate accomplishments, acknowledge challenges, and plan for the future.

TIP

I recommend buying a five-year journal to track your transformation over time.

» **Carve out time for relaxation.** Many cultures have a term for the art of doing nothing. Consider practicing *niksen* (Dutch) or *wu wei* (Chinese); or look into Buddhist *zazen* (meditation). You can also embrace the cozy concept of *hygge*, popular in Norway, Sweden, and Denmark.

» **Stay curious.** As a guest in a foreign country, you have plenty of opportunities to expand your mind and worldview. Whether you learn a new word, try a new food, or accept a spontaneous invitation, remain open-minded to change and new experiences.

IN THIS CHAPTER

» Making plans and finding routine

» Connecting with the local culture

» Avoiding travel fatigue and managing homesickness

» Knowing when to slow down

» Inspiring others with your journey

Chapter 12
Living Your Best Life

Welcome to your new life! After you conquer the logistics of a move abroad (which I talk about in Part 2) and settle in (discussed in Part 3), you can begin fulfilling your vision. This chapter helps you embrace opportunities available in your surroundings, pursue new ventures, and overcome common challenges.

Planning Things to Do in Your New Country

One of the most enthralling aspects of moving abroad is the endless potential for new experiences before you. From appreciating life's simple pleasures to grand "pinch me" moments — such as coasting through Balian rice fields, swimming with Galapagos penguins, or meandering through the Palace of Versailles. I'm so excited for the memories that you're about to make!

How you spend your days is how you spend your life. Take full advantage of your new surroundings and be open to new challenges and adventures while creating a routine that works for you. You can't make a wrong decision here; just enjoy yourself and get creative. What type of moments do you want to create in your new home? What do you want your overseas routine to look like?

TIP For more on settling into a daily routine, see Chapter 8.

Regardless of where you're from, moving to a new place presents an opportunity to rethink your lifestyle, activities, and to-do list. The following sections can help you tune into your surroundings and expand the possibilities of life in your new home.

Celebrating local traditions

Embrace local culture by participating in your community's festivals, holidays, and gatherings. It can help you feel more connected and less isolated.

On my first day in Tokyo in 2018, I attended an elaborate tea ceremony, which taught me the importance of performing a ritual for its practice. We dressed up in kimonos (a feat of its own) and gathered around the tea master, or *chajin*. Then, we watched, mesmerized, while she meticulously prepared cups of matcha. The experience lasted several hours, after which I felt calm, happy, relaxed, and at ease with the others in the room. It quelled my anxiety about having traveled there alone and helped me feel at home at the very start of my two months staying there.

Here are a few ideas for ways to get involved in the local culture:

- » **Cooking classes:** Prepare traditional dishes under the guidance of a home cook or chef. When I took a cooking class in Bali, we first went to *Pasar Ubud*, a lively outdoor marketplace selling produce, spices, artisanal goods, and household items in Ubud, Bali, to shop for local ingredients. Perusing the market with local people helped me feel comfortable in my surroundings and get to know local ingredients.

- » **Language classes:** Consider staying with a family in a homestay scenario. Opt for in-person classes rather than online ones so that you can have opportunities to go on field trips with your teacher.

TIP Converse with staff at the language school, from the bus drivers to the administrators and janitors. The best way to learn about a culture is to talk to people. See Chapter 10 for more guidance on grasping a new language.

- » **Leisure and cultural activities:** Look for parks, cafes, theaters, and events. Join in olive oil or winemaking rituals in Provence. Attend a Maori *haka* dance in New Zealand or a symphony in Prague or Vienna. Enjoy cherry blossom season in Japan. And remember that you're doing it — you're living the life that you dreamed about.

212 PART 4 Living Your Life to the Fullest

- » **Outdoor group activities:** Even if you don't speak the language, you know the lingo of hiking, cycling, or swimming. It's often free and easy to join a walking tour or athletic meetup in your area.

- » **Seasonal activities:** Match what you do to the time of year. In the winter, visit Lapland, Finland, to see the *aurora borealis* (northern lights) and enjoy winter sports. From May to November, go whale watching in South Africa. During the summer, cruise on the Italian Riviera.

- » **Sports clubs:** Join a tennis, golf, or soccer game with community members. If you don't enjoy participating in athletics, consider going to watch and support local teams.

- » **Volunteering:** Be generous with your time, talent, or treasure. What goes around, comes around — so get out and support the people of your new community! Chapter 11 provides ways to get involved through volunteering.

TIP

For more ideas of things to do, check with tourism boards, social media, travel websites, and Google reviews. Seek out newspapers, magazines, community boards, and guidebooks at local restaurants and cafes, and ask neighbors for recommendations. They often know about hidden gems. While in Dublin, conversing with the gentleman sitting next to me at a coffee shop led me to visit the nearby Powerscourt Estate and Gardens, which is a sprawling mansion and hotel set on 47 acres of manicured grounds.

Picking up a new hobby

"When in Rome..." — 1500s, Unknown

While in your new destination, try your hand at some of the beloved activities of your host culture. Through participating, you make friends, build connections, and develop a stronger sense of meaning and accomplishment.

For ideas, you can find over 40,000 things to do through Airbnb Experiences (www.airbnb.com/experiences).

TIP

Sites such as Craftours (www.craftours.com) and Craft Abroad (www.craftabroad.com) organize creative tours and adventures. You can also find classes and gallery events available on Eventbrite (www.eventbrite.com).

If dancing is your thing, you can look up dancing programs at GoAbroad.com. Or, if you're musically inclined, try lessons in how to play exotic instruments such as the Indian sitar, Australian didgeridoo, the Swiss hang drum, or the Japanese shakuhachi.

CHAPTER 12 **Living Your Best Life** 213

Enjoy nature and stay active. Hike through England's Peak District National Park, zipline through a Costa Rican canopy, bike along sections of the Tour de France, or bathe in the clear waters of the Adriatic. Try soccer in Europe and South America, cricket in the U.K. and India, lawn bowling in Australia, or baseball and (American) football in the U.S.

TIP

Find adventure travel options on websites such as Overseas Adventure Travel (www.oattravel.com) or Wilderness Travel (www.wildernesstravel.com).

Adding fun things to your bucket list

You can wander this world for decades (like I have) only to discover that you always have more to see, no matter how far you go. That's why compiling a travel bucket list helps you prioritize what you want to do the most.

TIP

Write down places that you want to visit in your first year abroad. Sites such as Rome2Rio (www.rome2rio.com) can help you plan your travel. It shows you multiple ways to get between two places. Use flight aggregators such as Skyscanner (www.skyscanner.com) and Google Flights (www.google.com/travel/flights) to find low fares to destinations worldwide.

TIP

Embrace both solo and group travel opportunities. Solo travel increases independence and resilience, while group travel fosters connection. On my YouTube channel, *Traveling with Kristin* (www.youtube.com/@travelingwithkristin), find a video I published about traveling alone by typing into the Search text box "15 Things I Wish I Knew About Solo Travel" and pressing Enter; the video should pop up as a search result.

Reading books, watching videos, and researching online can help you know a lot about life. But experiencing it in person is something else. To explore a new destination more deeply, consider hiring local guides using platforms such as TripAdvisor (www.tripadvisor.com) or ToursByLocals (www.toursbylocals.com) for personalized experiences.

For specific travel inspiration, browse online forums such as Lonely Planet (www.lonelyplanet.com), Travel & Leisure (www.travelandleisure.com), and TimeOut.com. Also check tourism websites for local events and activities.

Although grand adventures are exciting, balance them with daily life. Set small goals, such as attending a local event, exploring a park, joining an exercise class, or trying new cuisines, to help you enjoy your new environment without feeling overwhelmed.

Timeleft (www.timeleft.com) coordinates weekly dinners with strangers in 300 cities and 65 countries. It's a great way to make new friends or expand your professional network. I attended a Timeleft dinner in Miami and met people from Mexico, Peru, Russia, and Uzbekistan.

TRAVELING SUSTAINABLY

Keep a green travel footprint by adopting these sustainable travel tips:

- **Be carbon aware.** If you fly, purchase carbon offsets at Cool Effect (www.cooleffect.org) or Sustainable Travel International (www.sustainabletravel.org).

- **Eat and shop compassionately.** Know about the farming practices and treatment of animals in the places that you visit, reduce your consumption of animal products, and avoid purchasing items made of or tested on animals.

- **Ethical travel.** Make mindful travel choices to minimize economic and environmental harm in the communities that you visit. Support local businesses, rather than global chains.

    Planeta.com offers free access to an eco-travel directory and more than 10,000 pages of news, articles, and research about sustainable travel.

- **Pack right.** Travel smart by being mindful of the products you buy. Take reusable water bottles and bags with you, instead of consuming plastic ones.

    You can find a list of eco-friendly travel products in my Amazon Store (www.amazon.com/shop/travelingwithkristin) by clicking the Eco-Savvy Traveler link.

- **Respect the environment.** When visiting nature, leave no trace. Always dispose of food and waste properly and abide by rules in protected parks and nature preserves. Abide by local recycling and compost norms. Avoid tourism attractions that exploit nature and wildlife. Visit animal sanctuaries and shelters instead.

- **Stay green.** Use the Travel Sustainable filter on aggregate websites such as Booking.com to find responsible hotels and accommodations. EcoHotels.com provides a range of options certified by the Global Sustainable Tourism Council (GSTC). Try camping or staying off-grid.

- **Travel sustainably.** Walk, bike, or use green transportation options when possible. Opt for train and bus travel over flying. Carpool and ride share.

Making Time for Rest and Relaxation

When you decide to move abroad voluntarily, you may want to pursue a freer lifestyle and a higher quality of life. While it can be difficult to shake culturally ingrained habits from your home country, such as participating in a "rat race" mentality, make rest and enjoyment priorities in your new destination.

Here are some tips for doing so:

>> **Explore wellness centers.** Let your surroundings support your health. Look online for spas, gyms, salons, and yoga retreats. Sauna culture is popular in many countries, including Canada, Estonia, Finland, and Sweden. While staying in Sofia, Bulgaria, I paid $20 monthly for a gym membership that included a sauna and steam room. Hanging out in community bathhouses and hot springs can also help you meet people. You can find these establishments in countries such as Hungary, Iceland, and Japan.

TIP

Apps or websites such as Outside (www.outsideonline.com) can help you uncover places to retreat, restore, and work out.

>> **Plan regular breaks.** Plan downtime during your workday or study schedule and keep weekends and holidays open. If you work on a project for two hours, set a timer on your phone to stand up and stretch your legs for 20 minutes. If you enjoy a relaxing retirement, take breaks from sedentary activities such as reading and watching TV. Go for a walk, meet friends for a golf or pickleball game, or go sightseeing.

>> **Prioritize self-care.** Make time for exercise, hobbies, and relaxation. The best thing you can give the world is a healthy you. What does self-care mean for you? Write down a few things that you like to do in your leisure time, including anything that you deem a guilty pleasure, such as sleeping late on Saturdays, indulging in a mani-pedi, or savoring a cup of coffee and a book.

>> **Set clear boundaries.** If you work or study abroad, set specific work hours. Let your colleagues, classmates, or clients know your availability and ensure that they respect your time.

TIP

To help set healthy boundaries, read *Boundaries*, by Dr. Henry Cloud and Dr. John Townsend (Zondervan).

UNWINDING THE LOCAL WAY

Don't resist joining in when your new community hits the Pause button! Here are some examples of how foreign countries relax:

- **French café culture:** The French (and Parisians, in particular) often spend hours in cafes, sipping coffee or wine and socializing.
- **Indian meditation:** The land of over 400 dialects practices yoga and meditation to achieve peace and well-being.
- **Israeli Shabbat:** Practicing Jews cease working and rest for 25 hours weekly — from sunset on Friday to sunset on Saturday.
- **Italian *aperitivo*:** Italians enjoy a leisurely pre-dinner drink or snack and take time to unwind from work so that they can socialize before dinner.
- **Japanese *onsen*:** The Japanese love to visit hot springs for communal bathing that relaxes and rejuvenates them.
- **Southern African sundowner:** Some sub-Saharan African cultures enjoy a beverage at sunset and spend time relaxing and reflecting.
- **Spanish *siesta*:** The Spaniards love their midday nap! It helps them recharge for the rest of the day.

Staying the Course During Tough Times

Living in a foreign country isn't ever perfect. You inevitably face challenges and low points, when you feel lonely or frustrated, and things don't go your way. Knowing this before you arrive helps set expectations and make your transition smoother. Start your journey abroad with a positive and realistic attitude. Two challenges you may face when living abroad are homesickness and feeling so much pressure to see and do everything that you burn out. This section helps you sense when issues arise and find solutions.

Addressing homesickness

Homesickness is a common experience, especially after moving to a new place or country, and it can feel similar to culture shock or loneliness. Symptoms include anxiety, sadness, lack of motivation, and trouble concentrating. It can affect anyone — whether kids at school, college students abroad, or adults adjusting to a new environment — and may appear suddenly or build gradually over time. Although not everyone feels homesick, know the signs so that if you do experience them, you can address them early.

To cope, try acknowledging your feelings and indulging in self-care — but avoid overdoing it. Stay connected with friends or family, and explore ways to meet new people, especially if you're new to the area. Physical activity, such as walking or attending a fitness class, can boost your mood and help combat homesickness. If needed, seek professional support from a counselor who specializes in helping expats. Personalizing your space by adding familiar items, or picking up a new hobby, can also make a big difference in feeling at home. If homesickness persists or worsens, it may indicate deeper issues, such as depression, so don't hesitate to reach out for help.

For detailed advice on overcoming culture shock and loneliness, which are both related to homesickness, flip to Chapter 10.

Long-term homesickness or discontent could also signal that it's time to move home or move on. For more on what to do in that case, refer to Chapter 13.

Avoiding travel burnout

Planning a relocation and traveling internationally require a lot of physical and mental energy. So gradually ease yourself into your new lifestyle, as Chapters 8 and 9 can help you do.

But you may not want to ease in if you plan a nomadic lifestyle where you move from place to place without a home base.

If you decide to become a roaming retiree or slow traveler, think deeply about the experience that you want to have abroad before you draft your itinerary. Excessive *country-hopping,* which involves changing your location daily, weekly, or monthly, can leave you exhausted. And this quick cadence prevents you from fully bonding with the people you meet and integrating into your destination.

There's nothing wrong with wanting to see the world as fast as you can. Heck, I've also done it! I've traveled to over 60 countries in 20 years. But most long-term travelers slow down or settle somewhere after a while. Find a pace that works for you.

REMEMBER

You could travel full-time for months, years, or more than a decade before you experience burnout. When and if it happens to you, know it's the typical arc of the modern-day nomad.

TIP

Read my book *Digital Nomads For Dummies* (Wiley) for tips on how to thrive in a nomadic lifestyle.

Here are some practices to help you stay present in your destination:

- » **Connect with like-minded people.** Long-term expats who have similar interests provide ideal companions for sharing experiences and enjoying downtime. You have things in common, and you face similar challenges together.

- » **Engage in mindfulness practices.** Meditate, do yoga, practice breathwork, and keep a journal of your travels.

TIP

Look up *Becoming A Happy Expat Journal*, by C.E. Flores (independently published), for 200 prompts to help you adjust to your life abroad.

- » **Establish a healthy routine.** Consistent time devoted to relaxation, exercise, and social activities helps balance the stress of adapting to a new environment.

TIP

Hal Elrod's book *The Miracle Morning* provides ideas and a structure for winning the day with your morning routine.

- » **Take a break.** Preserve some time to do absolutely nothing. Lie on the beach, gaze at the stars, or watch the snow fall besdie the warmth of a crackling fire. Ensure you have time to relax, breathe, and just be.

  Reserve space in your calendar for *niksen*, the Dutch art of doing nothing. *Niksen* can be anything you want: lazy Sundays in bed, leisurely walks, sitting outside and people-watching, listening to music, sketching, journaling — anything that you find relaxing.

- » **Limit screen time as much as possible.** Studies show that nothing good comes from swiping and scrolling your day away. (But you already knew that.)

CHAPTER 12 **Living Your Best Life** 219

DOCUMENTING YOUR EXPERIENCES — AND HOW THEY'VE CHANGED YOU

Reflecting on your journey abroad, whether talking with someone or writing about it in a journal, allows you to process the experience.

I recommend purchasing a five-year journal that encourages you to write a few lines daily about what you did and how you felt. Over time, you begin to glean patterns and opportunities for change. Perhaps you pick up a bit of an accent or a new skill through moving and traveling. Reviewing your journal can remind you of where your journey has taken you, and also guide decision-making if you consider moving to another country or back home.

Josh and Kalie, the hosts of the blog and YouTube channel, ExpatsEverywhere, have a motto that living abroad transforms lives. You can find interviews on their YouTube channel, www.youtube.com/expatseverwhere, where they ask guests how living abroad has transformed their lives.

For more on the transformative benefits — such as cultural awareness and empathy — that come from travel and living abroad, see Chapter 1.

Sharing Your Experience with Others

In Chapter 10, I joke that your family and friends might yawn at your travel stories. But that doesn't mean everyone feels the same way.

Technology has made it possible to share your journey with the world. With the click of a mouse button or the tap of a screen, you can distribute your writing, photos, and videos worldwide for free! In the following sections, I give you some tips for getting started in blogging, vlogging, podcasting, and public speaking. As a content creator who's dabbled in all areas, I can say that it's changed my life for the better.

When you share information online and add value, you help people and attract a like-minded community. Choose the style or platform that resonates with you and try it.

Blogging

Blogging, or publishing your writing online, allows you to document your experience living abroad and share your tips with the world. It's a good creative outlet for you if you love to write. After you pick a *niche* (what subject your blog focuses on), check out several websites that allow you to publish your blog, such as GoDaddy (www.godaddy.com) or WordPress (www.wordpress.com).

For more tips on blogging, check out *Blogging All-in-One For Dummies,* by Susan Gunelius (Wiley).

Podcasting

If you like talking more than writing, consider *podcasting*, which involves publishing audio content online or in apps that listeners can stream or download. The barriers to getting started in podcasting have never been lower. And it's a heck of a lot of fun! You get to talk about topics that you're passionate about, invite talented guests to your show, and correspond with listeners worldwide.

To get started, you need an audio recording device and a hosting platform where you can publish your podcast. You don't need to spend $300 on a new microphone — your cellphone and headphones can do the job. You can also record on your computer by using a free app such as QuickTime (http://quicktime.softonic.com). Podcasting platforms such as Buzzsprout (www.buzzsprout.com) and Libsyn (www.libsyn.com) make it easy to share your episodes. It's free to publish on Buzzsprout, but Libsyn offers plans from $7-20 per month.

To discover more about creating your own podcast, check out *Podcasting For Dummies,* by Tee Morris and Evo Terra (Wiley).

Public speaking

Talking about your experiences abroad can help you process them, learn from them, and add value to others' lives by sharing what you learn. You don't have to become a professional speaker to talk to people. You can apply to give a talk at a conference in your industry or join Toastmasters International (www.toastmasters.com), an organization that helps you develop communication skills.

And wherever you go, you can find networking parties, many of which host guest speakers. Browse what's on in your area by using Eventbrite (www.eventbrite.com), Facebook Events (www.facebook.com/events), or Meetup (www.meetup.com).

Sharing via social media

I probably don't have to tell you how to use social media, but it's a fun and free way to share your travels and overseas lifestyle. At the time of this writing, the most popular sites include Facebook, Instagram, Pinterest, Snapchat, Quora, TikTok, X (formerly Twitter), and YouTube.

Whether you share photos, videos, or written content, try to deliver value with each post for maximum impact. Or use it as a personal travel diary. Share the favorite places you visit, things you love doing, ways you save money, packing tips, or other advice.

Browse AnswerThePublic (www.answerthepublic.com) for a database of questions people ask online, which can inspire your posts.

Starting a YouTube channel

Video content provides a primary way to share information in our global society. Over 500 hours of content are uploaded to YouTube every minute, with 1 billion hours consumed daily.

Also, YouTube is the world's second-largest search engine, after Google. If you want to help people, answer questions, share your experiences, and find your tribe, YouTube is a good place to do it. Maybe watching YouTube videos inspired you to start traveling or living abroad in the first place!

To get started creating your own YouTube channel, check out *YouTube For Dummies*, by Doug Sahlin (Wiley), and visit my own channel (www.youtube.com/@travelingwithkristin) for inspiration.

IN THIS CHAPTER

» Paying the tax man and investing abroad

» Voting from another country

» Changing your citizenship status

» Avoiding international trouble

» Planning your legacy

Chapter 13
Long-Term Lifestyle Considerations

Living abroad is an evolving journey. With each passing month and year, your priorities change, and you change, which happens regardless of where you find yourself in the world. But living in a foreign country adds an extra layer of complexity.

What do you want your overseas legacy to be? Ultimately, you may decide to remain in a country permanently, even acquire citizenship, move on to other countries, or return to your home country. This chapter helps you handle recurring tasks such as paying taxes. It also presents how to approach sensitive matters, such as end-of-life planning and your expat exit strategy.

Paying Taxes at Home and Abroad

According to his tax preparer, Albert Einstein once said, "The hardest thing in the world to understand is income taxes," and you may agree. Whether you like it or not, paying taxes is a part of life. That is, unless you're a tax-savvy expert or a multinational corporation (which is way outside the scope of this book). However, you can find sources for paying low or no taxes in the section "Paying zero taxes," later in this chapter.

WARNING

I'm not a Certified Public Accountant, nor a tax or financial advisor. Please don't take any of the information in this chapter (or book) as individual consulting, tax, or financial advice. I recommend finding an international tax preparer in your home and destination countries. You can find them by searching online or downloading a list of providers included with the bonus materials for this book at www.travelingwithkristin.com/move-abroad.

Knowing your tax domicile

Where you need to pay taxes while living or traveling abroad long-term depends on various factors, including your:

» **Country of citizenship:** Where you're from and your home country's tax system.

» **Country of residence:** Where you live and your host country's tax system.

» **Duration of stay:** How long you stay in a country matters. After residing somewhere for 183 days per year, that country could consider you a tax resident, even if you don't have official residency status.

» **Income-generating activities:** How you make money, where you earn and receive it, your employment status, and your business structure can all affect where you pay taxes.

» **Visa or residency permit:** You may have certain tax obligations related to your residency category.

TIP

If your home country has a tax treaty with your host country, you might qualify for credits or exemptions.

REMEMBER

U.S. citizens may incur state (as well as federal) tax liabilities after moving abroad. If you live in a high-tax state such as California, you may opt to move to a lower or zero-tax state before relocating overseas. Consult with your tax advisor for more details.

Getting familiar with global tax systems

As a foreign resident or long-term traveler abroad, you may owe taxes in both your home and host countries. Or you may be able to change your tax domicile to one place. Either way, figure out which type of tax system applies in the countries where you live.

Countries around the world use one of four main types of tax systems:

- » **Citizenship-based taxation:** You're taxed based on where you're from, not where you live. You pay taxes to your home country, even if you move abroad. Examples include Eritrea and the United States.

- » **Residence-based taxation:** You're taxed based on where you live (typically for 183-plus days per year). Examples include Mexico, New Zealand, and most European countries. Some countries that have residence-based systems also charge taxes on worldwide income.

- » **Territorial taxation:** You're taxed on local income. If you live in one country but earn money in another, your foreign-earned income may be exempt. Examples include Costa Rica, Georgia, Hong Kong, Macau, Malaysia, and Singapore.

- » **Zero-tax countries:** Some countries don't have personal income tax, such as The Bahamas, Monaco, Saint Kitts and Nevis, Qatar, and Vanuatu.

Zero-tax countries often offer citizenship-by-investment programs, which you can read about in Chapter 4.

Here are a few examples of taxation around the globe:

- » **United States (citizenship-based taxation):** A Portuguese citizen who becomes a legal resident in the United States and works for a U.S. company may change their tax domicile from Portugal to the U.S. They must file a U.S. tax return but may not owe anything in their home country of Portugal.

- » **France (residency-based taxation):** A Canadian citizen who lives in France as a temporary resident for 183 days per year becomes a tax resident. Although they must report their Canadian or worldwide income earned abroad, they can avoid double taxation thanks to the Canada-France Income Tax Convention.

- » **Panama (territorial taxation):** A U.S. citizen living in Panama must file a U.S. tax return (because the U.S. has citizenship-based taxation). However, if they don't earn income within Panama, they don't have to pay taxes there.

- » **United Arab Emirates (zero tax):** The UAE doesn't tax personal income. A British citizen living in Dubai can change their tax domicile from the U.K. Whether they earn money in the UAE or abroad, they may not have to pay taxes in either country.

Some countries have a hybrid, progressive, or mixed tax system, with a combination of tax policies.

CHAPTER 13 **Long-Term Lifestyle Considerations** 225

TAX DOCUMENTS CHECKLIST

Collect documents related to the following categories for tax time, if applicable according to your personal situation:

- **Business income and expenses:** Generated as a company, freelancer, or sole proprietor, including income statements, balance sheets, cash flow, and asset information.

- **Individual income and expenses:** Income earned in your country of residence and your host country — such as wages, paystubs, bank statements, investment income, and rental income — as well as deductible expenses.

- **Charitable contributions:** Tax-deductible donations.

- **Childcare:** Information and expenses related to your dependents.

- **Cryptocurrency:** Records related to cryptocurrency purchases, sales, interest, and gains.

- **Foreign bank accounts:** Bank account names, numbers, and addresses, including investment accounts, which you hold outside of your home country.

- **Foreign corporations:** Information for any foreign companies that you own.

- **Foreign tax returns:** Tax returns that you file in other countries.

- **Health insurance:** Records related to your medical and insurance expenses.

- **Investment income:** Including dividends, interest, and capital gains.

- **Property records:** International real estate and property holdings and associated income, expenses, and depreciation.

- **Other income:** Alimony, retirement or pensions, gambling and lottery winnings, and other income.

Paying Uncle Sam

U.S. citizens worldwide must file an annual tax return while living abroad, and you may have to file additional paperwork. Get to know the IRS tax code well. You can also hire an accountant or CPA who specializes in U.S. expat taxes for help. A few companies include:

- **Greenback Tax Services** (www.greenbacktaxservices.com): Frustration and feelings of being overwhelmed with filing a U.S. tax return overseas led Carrie and David McKeegan to found Greenback — a tax preparation company for Americans abroad. Their team helps with Foreign Account Tax Compliance Act (FATCA) and Foreign Bank Account Report (FBAR) reporting, as well as state and federal tax filings.

- **H&R Block** (www.hrblock.com): H&R Block has developed a specialized tax service for U.S. citizens and green card holders abroad. They can help you file with an advisor or navigate the process online.

- **Taxes for Expats** (www.taxesforexpats.com): A top-rated, female-owned expat tax service for U.S. citizens abroad that has over 25 years of experience. The company offers tax planning, returns, and non-resident tax preparation for U.S. aliens and green card holders.

If you want to opt out of the U.S. tax system, you can consider renouncing your citizenship. In 2024, you have to pay $2,350 in administrative fees to renounce your citizenship, although you may incur legal, advisory, and other costs, such as an exit tax.

For more information about filing requirements for U.S. citizens abroad, visit the IRS International Taxpayers page U.S. Citizens and Resident Aliens Abroad (www.irs.gov/individuals/international-taxpayers/us-citizens-and-resident-aliens-abroad).

Paying zero taxes

Paying zero taxes sounds great, but is it realistic or ethical? That's for you, your accountant, and your country's tax laws to decide. You may legally reduce or eliminate your tax burden, depending on your country of citizenship, business structure, residence, and other factors.

If optimizing your tax strategy interests you, check out the following websites for ideas and guidance:

- **Expat Money** (www.expatmoney.com): Helps you establish second residency or citizenship, and offers international tax planning and investing advice.

- **Nomad Capitalist** (www.nomadcapitalist.com): Founder Andrew Henderson renounced his U.S. citizenship in part for tax freedom. Today, his company's flagship service helps high-net-worth individuals create an offshore tax plan and obtain multiple passports.

- **Tax Hackers** (www.taxhackers.io): Can help digital nomads legally pay zero percent tax globally. They help with company setups, tax filings, and paperwork so that you can focus on other things. The only catch is that you can't be a U.S. citizen or green card holder to qualify.

» **Wealthy Expat** (www.wealthyexpat.com): Aims to make second citizenship and tax optimization fast and easy. They work with only official government programs to create a bespoke plan for you.

Consult a licensed and qualified professional before following financial advice. Do due diligence on companies whose services you engage.

COMMON TAX PITFALLS

When adapting to a new country, old routines and deadlines can fall by the wayside. Don't make these common tax mistakes after you move abroad:

- **Discarding paperwork:** Although you might want to travel light, living abroad doesn't exempt you from sound record-keeping. Keep organized tax records for up to ten years. Scan and save digital files to a cloud storage provider for safekeeping.

- **Hiding money:** "Forgetting" to mention your offshore bank accounts is like trying to hide food from your dog — good luck. If your home country requires it, file it. U.S. citizens and residents who have a combined foreign bank balance of $10,000 or more must file a Foreign Bank Account Report (FBAR).

- **Missing deadlines:** Failure to file your taxes is a big no-no and can result in fines or imprisonment. Keep deadlines top-of-mind by setting monthly, quarterly, and annual reminders.

- **Making errors and omissions in reporting:** You may need to file additional paperwork when you move or live abroad, such as that darn FBAR for U.S. citizens. A good rule of thumb is never to assume anything — get professional guidance instead.

- **Thinking you can pay zero taxes:** Some people mistakenly assume that they don't have to pay taxes while living abroad. Or that moving to a zero-tax country automatically exempts them. Check with professionals in your home and host countries to understand your filing responsibilities. Don't listen to casual advice from expats, Facebook groups, Reddit, or the tax gurus at your hotel bar.

If you earn income abroad, you may want to send it back to your home country for savings, investments, expenses, or family support. Chapter 5 provides instructions for opening an online bank account and sending money between countries. Chapter 9 has requirements and tips for opening a foreign bank account upon arrival.

Investment Opportunities Abroad

You probably have similar investment options available to you both in your home country and abroad. Many offshore banking systems allow you to invest money as a foreigner with or without residency status. When you explore investment opportunities abroad, you may discover favorable deals and higher interest rates or returns. However, investments aren't guaranteed. And investing internationally can lead to a bigger tax burden or more complex tax reporting requirements.

Investment types abroad include:

- **Business investments:** Founding or investing in a business or startup.
- **Financial investments:** Stocks, bonds, mutual funds, currencies, certificates of deposit (CDs), and high-interest savings accounts.

WARNING

  Know the financial regulations in your host country before you invest or deposit funds in that country. Find out the limit for government-insured accounts, which might be lower than you're accustomed to.

- **Real estate investments:** Many countries allow foreign tourists and residents to invest in local property markets. If you're interested in buying real estate abroad, see Chapter 6.
- **Retirement accounts:** If you work abroad, you may be able to contribute to a retirement account in the host country where you're working and receive a pension in the future.

VOTING FROM OVERSEAS

Few people realize that you can vote from outside your country. For instance, U.S. citizens abroad have the lowest voter turnout in the country. Only about 3 to 8 percent of expats vote in presidential elections, compared with 66 percent of citizens living stateside.

Your vote matters, regardless of where you're from and where you live. To exercise your right to vote from abroad, first register to vote in your home country. Then, contact your local elections officials or embassy for available voting options. In many cases, you may be able to cast your vote by mail, online, or at an embassy or consulate abroad.

U.S. citizens abroad can register at Vote.gov or get help from the Federal Voting Assistance Program (FVAP; www.fvap.gov). You can vote even without a current U.S. address.

TIP

Investing in a business, stocks, government bonds, or real estate can be a path to a golden visa or citizenship by investment. See Chapter 4 for more about these types of residency and citizenship programs.

Extending Your Stay Abroad

After you live abroad for a while, you eventually have to renew or extend your visa or residency permit (unless you're country-hopping, which I talk about in Chapter 2). If you have a short-term visa that has a time limit of 30 to 180 days, think about renewal or extension options early on. But if you're on a long-term visa, valid for one or more years, you have more time before deciding what to do next.

In my experience as a relocation consultant, most people stay abroad longer than they expect. Fellow expats and I used to joke about various countries: "Come for a month and stay for a year" or "Come for a year and stay for ten."

Every visa or residency permit has a time limit. Before applying, figure out how long your permit stays valid so that you can plan for what to do when it expires. The following sections provide a summary of common visa types. See Chapter 4 for more about visas and residency options.

WARNING

Avoid overstaying your visa. Leave the country and return, if you need to, in order to remain on the right side of the law.

For short stays

If you entered a country on a short-stay or tourist visa, some countries (such as Canada, Costa Rica, and Mexico) may let you stay longer by applying for an extension or exiting and re-entering. In contrast, other countries require that you leave for 90 to 180 days before returning (including many European countries). In rare cases, countries such as Albania and Georgia allow tourists of certain nationalities to stay for up to one year on a passport, without a residency permit.

WARNING

Depending on various factors, you may receive fewer days than you anticipated when you arrive. I once received only 10 days to stay in Ireland while traveling on business, although the standard tourist visa allowance is 90 days.

Your purpose of travel and the immigration official at the port of entry play a role in how long you can enter a country for. Double check your passport stamp before assuming that you received the maximum number of days allowed.

While working (or studying) abroad

If you visit somewhere as a tourist and decide you want to live there, find out if getting a work or study permit is an option. Some countries allow you to apply for such a permit while already inside their borders, but you may need to return to your home country to submit your application.

Find out about digital nomad visas, freelancer visas, study visas, and work visas in Chapter 4.

Being a true resident

If you enter a country as a temporary resident, you may have authorization to stay in a country until you qualify for a different type of residence permit. Your initial, temporary stay could last one month to one year.

You can often apply for permanent residence status after you live in a country for at least two to five years. You must meet certain requirements for maintaining your residency status, such as spending a minimum number of days there per year. In some countries, permanent residency status is, well, *permanent*, while in others, you must renew your status periodically (typically every five or ten years).

Contact your residency advisor, consulate, or host country's immigration department to find out how to renew your visa or transfer to a different type of permit. Figure out the essential dates and requirements for your renewal or transfer, collect the necessary documents and forms, and submit them on time.

Going for citizenship

If you become a citizen, you can remain in a country indefinitely with full rights to live, work, vote, and receive social services. After five or ten years of permanent residency, you can often apply for citizenship by naturalization. However, a country may have other requirements, such as passing a language or cultural exam and taking a citizenship oath.

Renouncing Your Citizenship

People often ask me whether they must give up their home country citizenship to move abroad. The answer is no. You can travel to foreign countries as a perpetual tourist, and you can live abroad if you have a visa, or a work, study, or other residency permit, without renouncing your citizenship.

If you decide to become a full-fledged citizen of your host country someday, however, you may need to choose one passport over another.

Some countries allow dual citizenship, while others don't. For example, you can be born in Chile, naturalize as a citizen of Costa Rica, and acquire Spanish citizenship by descent from a parent. I am a U.S. citizen applying for citizenship from Hungary and Romania through my family's ancestry. However, some countries strictly prohibit holding dual nationality. China, Indonesia, Japan, and Singapore are a few examples in Asia. European countries such as Austria, Norway, and the Netherlands also restrict citizenships from holding two passports.

Don't make the decision to sever ties to your home country and culture lightly. It has significant pros and cons. Many people renounce for ideological reasons, such as political differences, or to avoid mandatory military service. Others want more freedom of choice in their travels or less paperwork to manage when applying for visas. Thousands of U.S. citizens renounce each year for tax reasons. But there are always trade-offs. Renouncing means that you lose:

- The right to come and go from your home country as you please. If you return, you enter as a foreigner based on the strength of your (new) passport. So you might have to apply for a visa to visit your former home country. Or your old country could even deny you entry altogether.

- Seeing your friends and family as often as you want — and in extreme cases, you might never see them again.

- The right to vote, access to social services, and the protections of your former government as an overseas citizen.

Some countries make it hard to leave. You may need to file paperwork, sit for an interview, and pay an exit tax to renounce. However, the process can be faster, simpler, or automatic for citizens of some countries, such as Germany, India, and South Korea.

Before renouncing your citizenship, get clear on why you're doing it. Take your time making such a permanent decision.

WARNING: Get a second citizenship before you renounce your first one. Few countries allow you to be a stateless resident.

Staying Out of Trouble

After seeing the 1999 film *Brokedown Palace* — about a U.S. tourist arrested in Thailand on bogus drug charges — I developed an irrational fear of getting in trouble while traveling, ending up on an episode of *Locked Up Abroad*. Although I had no reason to worry for my safety, I soon found out that reality can be stranger than fiction.

While in Costa Rica during 2006 and 2007, I heard news about a U.S. citizen named Eric Volz, who was wrongfully detained for murder in Nicaragua. He's since published a memoir, *Gringo Nightmare* (St. Martin's Press), about his experience. Soon after, the American study-abroad student Amanda Knox was arrested and imprisoned in Italy following a wrongful murder conviction. She's now an author, activist, and advocate for criminal justice reform.

I don't write this to scare you, but to remind you that *all countries have laws*. Whether you know about them or not, you're responsible for following them. If you don't, you pay the consequences. Your nationality and embassy can't necessarily help you.

REMEMBER

» **Alcohol:** Booze is legal in most of the world except some majority-Muslim countries. Some places, such as the UAE, may have restrictions or partial bans. In parts of the U.S. and Mexico, you can't buy alcohol during certain times or days of the week.

If you can drink legally, do so in moderation. As a relocation consultant, I've received phone calls in the middle of the night from clients who passed out drunk in the streets and were robbed or arrested for public intoxication. No judgment on my part, but take standard precautions. You can stay safe (and healthy) by practicing moderation or abstaining.

Open container laws, drunk driving laws, and the minimum age to consume alcohol vary by country.

» **Drugs:** It goes without saying, but drugs are either illegal or regulated everywhere. In some places, laws are changing (slowly), but err on the side of caution. For instance, recreational cannabis is legal in Canada, Thailand, and Uruguay, and decriminalized in Portugal, Switzerland, and Spain. However, it's banned in China, Indonesia, Malaysia, and many countries throughout Africa and the Middle East. Beyond drug consumption, many countries have severe punishments for selling or trafficking substances.

CHAPTER 13 **Long-Term Lifestyle Considerations** 233

- **Sex:** It's a good idea to practice safe sex anywhere in the world. Sexually transmitted infections (STIs) and sexually transmitted diseases (STDs) appear in all countries. Abstaining from sex is the best way to protect yourself. However, the CDC estimates that one in three people engage in sexual activities while abroad. If that's you, don't let your guard down in unfamiliar circumstances. Plan ahead — use protection and contraception, as needed. Depending on where you're traveling, condoms, birth control, and the morning-after pill may be harder to find than a Wi-Fi signal.

  Find STD and STI testing and treatment abroad by contacting your insurance company or healthcare provider. You can usually find testing offered at local hospitals, clinics, and labs.

- **Social contracts:** Wherever you travel, brush up on cultural norms. Activities that seem normal to you can be discouraged or illegal abroad. From holding hands to chewing gum, find out what's acceptable and what's not. For instance, criticizing the monarchy or government is a criminal offense in Thailand and Saudi Arabia. In China, kissing in public is frowned upon, but it's illegal in Qatar and the UAE. When out and about, follow local etiquette on roads and public transportation. Dress for your location and cover your head, shoulders, and legs to enter religious sites.

- **Scams:** Research the common tourist scams in your destination. Beware of pickpockets in Europe, taxis that overcharge, and anyone who greets you as "my friend!"

- **Visas and residency:** Overstaying your visa is a sure way to spoil your trip, leading to fines, deportation, or worse. Always keep your residency status and paperwork up to date.

REMEMBER

Don't work in a foreign country without permission. You can find news articles online about tourists and digital nomads who were deported for violating immigration laws.

For information about staying safe while living abroad and preparing for emergencies, see Chapter 7.

Designing Your Expat Exit Strategy

You can make living abroad a temporary or a permanent decision. You may migrate somewhere and live happily ever after. Or there may come a time when you feel ready for change. Perhaps you shift your focus to exploring a new country, or maybe you decide to move back home.

After you move abroad, formulate your expat exit plan. Ask yourself the following questions to look ahead towards the next chapter of your life:

- » Why did you move abroad? What do you hope to achieve?
- » How long do you foresee yourself living abroad and why?
- » How will you know when you've outgrown your current living situation?
- » Do you plan to change locations again in the future?
- » What may prompt you to return home?

On the contrary, if you love your new country and want to stay there forever, see Chapter 4 to find out about residency options and Chapter 9 for how to extend your status.

Don't think of moving home or moving on someday as failure — it simply reflects a change in your life and priorities.

Thinking about Going Home

The desire to move again or go home can hit you suddenly, like an epiphany, or it can percolate slowly. It's similar to the feeling that you may have experienced when you first thought of going abroad. Perhaps you made a quick decision after reading a blog article or watching a YouTube video. Or maybe you lived with a longing desire to go overseas for decades before you could make it happen.

One way to anticipate the winds of change is to keep tabs on your feelings. Journaling is a good practice for organizing your thoughts and developing a plan. Through the practice of writing morning pages each day (a strategy designed by author Julia Cameron), I decided to give up my loft in Coconut Grove, Florida, and live in Europe for a year.

If writing every day seems boring, set a recurring reminder in your calendar instead. Take yourself on a walk or a date with your dining room table to reflect on how things are going. *What do you enjoy about living in your host country? What are you struggling with? What would you like to be different?* Identify areas for change and note any possible solutions that arise.

CHAPTER 13 **Long-Term Lifestyle Considerations** 235

Changing gears (and countries)

Exchanging locations to pursue a new experience or returning home at the end of your time abroad can be a happy, exciting, and solemn experience rolled into one. You're grateful for the opportunity to live in another country, yet moving on is bittersweet. Whether you're leaving at the end of a study-abroad semester or a gap year, or out of your own volition, you need to coordinate some logistics before you go. You follow similar procedures to when you moved abroad initially, which you can reference in Parts 1 and 2 of this book. Here is list of essential tasks to handle when preparing to leave your host country:

- ❏ Arrange final medical checks and refill your prescriptions.
- ❏ Cancel monthly electricity, Internet, water, and phone services.
- ❏ Close bank accounts and transfer funds accordingly.
- ❏ Collect essential documents and items to pack with you.
- ❏ De-register with local government and tax authorities.
- ❏ Notify your employer, landlord, school, and other interested parties.
- ❏ Pay any outstanding bills and tax liabilities.
- ❏ Request copies of medical and other records.
- ❏ Return rented equipment, such as a cable box or router.
- ❏ Sell or rent out your home (if you own it).
- ❏ Ship necessary items to your next destination. Discard, donate, or sell everything else.
- ❏ Update or cancel your insurance policies as needed.

Saying your goodbyes

While planning your departure logistics, bid farewell to colleagues, family, friends, and neighbors in your host country. Consider sending thank-you notes to people you appreciate or hold a going-away party. Spend time with close contacts by going out for coffee, a walk, or a meal together. Plan how to remain in contact after you leave.

In planning what's next, refer to the beginning of this book. Check out the Table of Contents and note sections to re-read while you assess your next moves. If you don't know where to go next, flip back to Chapter 4 for help choosing a destination. For a refresher on drafting your overseas plan, see Chapter 5. Chapter 7 prepares you for departure. Are you looking for your next home away from home? Chapter 6 helps you find housing.

REMEMBER

Reflect on your time abroad, what it means to you, and how it's changed you. Journal about what you're grateful for, lessons learned, and what you'll take away from the experience.

Returning home and reverse culture shock

A plan to move abroad occasionally comes full circle. You return to where you started, albeit with a better palate for wine and a slightly mysterious accent. You may have countless reasons to move back to your home country — as diverse as your logic for leaving in the first place! Perhaps the excitement of a new place wore off, you miss your family, or you've had it with your neighbor's rooster. Or maybe you always intended to stay only temporarily. Either way, moving back is an adjustment.

Depending on how long you live abroad, you may feel more comfortable there than in your home country. Upon returning, you experience the surreal phenomenon of reverse culture shock. (I talk about regular culture shock in Chapter 10.)

You may find reverse culture shock confusing because your home — which used to be all you knew — now feels foreign (kind of like stepping into your childhood bedroom while home for the holidays). You might feel uncomfortable, disoriented, depressed, or just different.

How you experience reverse culture shock depends on:

>> **Where you went:** How different your host country's culture is from your home country.

>> **How long you were gone:** The longer you stay overseas before returning home, the more severe the symptoms can be.

>> **How much you enjoyed living abroad:** How homesick you become for your host country versus your home country.

Reverse culture shock may strike suddenly at the airport or intensify over the following days, weeks, and months. Conversations with friends or family feel different. Discussions that once seemed interesting now feel trivial. You may find yourself questioning things about your native culture that you never noticed before. If you're returning to the U.S., for instance, you may find yourself wondering: *Why are there only two political parties? Why don't we compost our trash? Why do our foods and drinks have corn syrup instead of sugar?*

Questions arise because travel exposes you to other ways of doing things. You may feel like an outsider in your culture or struggle to relate to old friends. You're not quite the same person who left months or years ago. You've traveled the world, met new people, gotten yourself out of some sticky situations, and potentially figured out how to read metro signs in other languages. Acknowledge that you're different and that life at home won't feel the same. Embrace this change as a sign of personal growth and start moving toward what's next for you in life.

COMMON REASONS EXPATS "FAIL"

If you follow your dream of living abroad, you can't fail. However, you may eventually decide to make a change. Regardless of your reasons, don't be afraid to follow your intuition and move on if you feel it's right. You always have the memories and experiences of living abroad to reflect on.

Common reasons to come home include:

- Because you want to; you miss your family, friends, and your favorite coffee shop.
- Burnout, especially among digital nomads and perpetual travelers.
- Changing goals; you have new priorities, received a job offer or transfer, or feel like it's time to keep on keeping on.
- Climate problems — it turns out you *don't* love monsoon season and hot weather.
- Emotional factors, such as culture shock and homesickness.
- Financial reasons, such as taxes or a rising cost of living.
- Legal reasons, especially in the case of a lack of residency options (hopefully nothing else!).
- Loneliness or lack of community and support systems abroad.
- Medical reasons, such as access to free or better healthcare.
- Nostalgic reasons, such as wanting to reconnect with your societal roots.
- Personal reasons, such as a new relationship, an impending wedding, or raising children.
- Political unrest, economic instability, or other risks in your location.
- To care for aging parents or a sick friend, family member, or pet.
- To finish a degree or go back to school.
- To retire in your home country.

Returning home isn't the end, it's another new beginning!

The good news is that — like regular culture shock — reverse culture shock doesn't last forever. The antidotes to reverse culture shock are the same as regular culture shock, which you can read up on in Chapter 10.

TIP

You can watch a video on my YouTube channel *Traveling with Kristin* (www.youtube.com/travelingwithkristin) about coping with reverse culture shock. Just search for "reverse culture shock" from my main page.

End-of-Life Planning for Expats

You probably find thinking about the end of your journey here on Earth uncomfortable — especially when you're busy living your best life. But a little planning now can save your family a lot of headaches and confusion later. When you move abroad, you experience the frustrations of navigating foreign bureaucracy, so plan ahead to help your next of kin.

Foreign laws can make it difficult for your loved ones to carry out tasks such as burial plans, repatriation of remains, and asset distribution. However, by taking a few not-so-fun steps now, you can get a lot of peace of mind in exchange. And your family will thank you for it.

Here are some things that you can do:

» **Designate beneficiaries.** Add beneficiaries to your bank and financial accounts, insurance policies, and retirement plans to ensure that your loved ones can transfer assets without questions or complications.

» **Create a will or trust.** A will specifies who gets what after you die. That goes for your bank accounts, properties, investments, life insurance policies, and your family heirlooms. It also names guardians for your offspring and an executor, who becomes responsible for managing your estate. Trusts differ from wills in that the trust owns the assets, allowing your family to skip probate court.

TIP

Update your will regularly. If possible, register it abroad or draft an extra one under your host country's laws. In Ecuador, that could be a notarized *constancia* (certificate) or *documentación juramentada* (sworn statement).

» **Establish medical directives.** A living will specifies the medical treatment that you want (or don't want) to receive if you can't speak for yourself. Ensure your document is legally enforceable — you may want one in both your home and host countries. If desired, consider including a do not resuscitate (DNR) or do not intubate (DNI) order.

CHAPTER 13 **Long-Term Lifestyle Considerations** 239

Set aside funds and arrange for end-of-life housing. You didn't come all this way to spend your final days somewhere you don't like!

- » **Plan your final journey.** Choose your favorite physician to call upon when you pass to the other side. Decide whether you want to be buried overseas, cremated, or flown home in a private jet. Designate a funeral service or transporter to pick you up. If you prefer to rest in peace on home soil, get repatriation coverage through international health and travel insurance companies such as Allianz (www.allianz.com), Travelex (www.travelexinsurance.com), or IMG (www.imglobal.com). Or use a specialized medical evacuation provider such as Global Rescue (www.globalrescue.com; see Chapter 7). Shipping companies may also provide repatriation services.

Family members have to cover the costs of moving you home if you don't have repatriation coverage. If you're without next of kin, your embassy or consulate can act as your legal representative.

- » **Assign a Power of Attorney.** Appoint someone to make decisions on your behalf if you're unable to (in addition to an executor of your will). You can designate a digital, financial, or medical POA.

- » **Write your obituary.** I'm no expert in this field, and if you're not up for this particular task, I don't blame you. Fortunately, you can find plenty of empathetic obituary and memorial writers online who can help.

- » **Store your documents safely.** Keep a physical and digital file of documents. If you don't have a list of your assets and beneficiaries in your will, include that list here. How else will your family members know how much Bitcoin you have? Or how to access the gold bars that you stored in Singapore?

Consider storing important passwords in a password manager such as Norton (http://my.norton.com/extspa/passwordmanager) or NordPass (www.nordpass.com).

Local laws and customs can impact your end-of-life plans. Contact your embassy or consulate for further details and reporting requirements concerning the death of a citizen abroad.

The Part of Tens

IN THIS PART . . .

Discover top living-abroad destinations.

Explore places to retire overseas.

Find out how to live abroad on a budget.

Avoid common moving-abroad mistakes.

> **IN THIS CHAPTER**
>
> » Exploring the top international retirement destinations
>
> » Comparing cost of living and healthcare options
>
> » Understanding visa and residency options for retirees

Chapter 14
Ten Places to Retire Abroad

After working hard and saving money all your life, you have an important decision in choosing where to retire. If you're like most folks, your concerns may include a country's climate, healthcare, cost of living, political stability, safety, and language. You might also wonder where you can find all these attributes in one place — somewhere that you can enjoy a high quality of life (that you can afford) while fitting in with the local culture. This chapter gives you ten attractive countries that offer retirement visas welcoming foreign retirees.

Costa Rica

In Central America, Costa Rica offers retirees a peaceful life amidst lush rainforests, scenic mountains, and beautiful beaches. The country's modern healthcare system, warm weather, reasonable cost of living, and retirement-friendly policies make it an excellent choice, especially if you're seeking a peaceful, nature-centric retirement.

Costa Rica offers three visas of interest to retirees:

- » ***Inversionista*** (investor): You can qualify for this visa if you make a minimum investment of $150,000 in real estate, the stock market, forestry, or other approved assets.

- » ***Pensionado*** (pensioner/retiree): Designed for retirees, you can qualify for this visa if you have a minimum income of at least $1,000 per month from a pension or retirement plan.

  The *pensionado* visa doesn't have a minimum age requirement.

- » ***Rentista*** (person of independent means): If you receive a fixed monthly income but aren't retired, you can apply for *rentista* status if you have at least $2,500 per month in income or $60,000 deposited in a Costa Rican bank account.

Each visa is renewable and can eventually become a path to permanent residency or citizenship.

Popular places to live in Costa Rica include the Central Valley towns of Atenas, Grecia, Heredia, and Escazu, the central coast beach towns of Jacó and Hermosa, and the northwest Guanacaste Province and the Nicoya Peninsula. The cost of living throughout the country varies greatly. Retirees can live a simple lifestyle on $2,000 per month, while couples may spend $3,000 or more. Owning a vehicle, eating out often, or living in an expensive area can increase your costs.

Costa Rica was ranked the best place to live in the world on *International Living's* 2024 Retirement Index.

Ecuador

Ecuador is located near the Equator in South America and offers breathtaking landscapes, affordable living, and a *jubilado* (retired) visa for retirees. Home to the Amazon rainforest, Andes Mountains, and Pacific Coast, many parts of Ecuador have a mild, spring-like climate.

The country's position on the Equator minimizes the threat of hurricanes, although flooding, landslides, and earthquakes do happen.

Ecuador's friendly and welcoming locals make it easy for expats to integrate into the community. Many retirees enjoy settling in the tranquil mountain town of Cuenca, where rent prices range from $300 to $700 monthly. The average cost of living for an expat in Ecuador is about $1,000 per month, making living on a small pension or Social Security income realistic. Property prices are also reasonable, with homes available for purchase from $50,000.

Ecuador adopted the U.S. dollar as its official currency in 2000.

One thing people like about retiring in Ecuador is being able to opt into the local healthcare system. The *Instituto Ecuatoriano de Securidad Social* (Ecuadorian Institute of Social Security; IESS) government system costs are calculated based on a percentage of your declared income (17.6 percent plus an additional 3.41 percent for a spouse).

If you're 65 and over, you can qualify for Ecuador's *jubilado*, or 9-I, visa if you have a monthly retirement income of at least $800. You can apply from within Ecuador or abroad.

WARNING

Always check travel advisories and research a country's political stability before moving there. An uptick in gang-related violence in Ecuador during 2023 and 2024 prompted a wave of migration out of the country and led the Ecuadorian president to declare a state of emergency.

France

If you dream of living *la belle vie* (the beautiful life) in the French countryside or Riviera, your wish can come true. France offers a long-stay visa equivalent to a residence permit (VLS-TS), valid for stays of 3 to 12 months. When you're actually living in France, you can apply to extend your visa for another year or get a long-term residence permit.

TIP

Apply for your VLS-TS visa before you depart for France. You can apply through the France-Visas website (http://france-visas.gouv.fr/en), through your local consulate, or with the help of a residency lawyer or advisor. Chapter 4 discusses visa and residency options and Chapter 5 provides tips on hiring professionals to help with your relocation.

Besides the incredible food, nature, culture, and history that you can experience in France, retirees appreciate the country's advanced healthcare system, which provides universal coverage to all legal residents and is ranked among the best in the world.

You can access the system if you're an EU citizen who has a European Health Insurance Card. If you're from outside the EU, you can join after living in France for at least three months. Residents pay from 0 to 25 percent of the cost of care, depending on your income level.

Although Paris has some of the most expensive hotels in the world, living in France can be pretty affordable. I recall eating a multi-course lunch at a chateau in St. Emilion for $12 to $15 per person. Our two-bedroom vacation rental in nearby Bordeaux cost less than $50 a night.

Everyday expenses in France are 10 to 25 percent lower than in the United States, and rent prices are 50 percent lower, although exact prices vary by city. So you can rent a quaint house in a French village for $700 to $1,000 a month. A one-bedroom apartment in Lyon's city center costs about $970 per month compared to $1,850 in downtown Atlanta. Generally, a foreigner can live in France for between $2,000 and $2,500 per month.

I probably don't need to tell you how good the food is in France — especially if you love wine, bread, and cheese (and dessert). But if you've never been in a French grocery store, it'll change your life.

Living in France isn't without challenges, however. Adapting to French culture and society can take time, especially if you don't know the language. Winters in France are long, dark, and gray, and buying or renting properties in popular cities can be expensive.

REMEMBER

Check whether a tax treaty exists between France and your home country. For example, U.S.-sourced pensions may be taxed in the U.S., but not both countries.

Malta

If you want to retire somewhere that has a mild to warm climate and sun year-round, look more closely at the island nation of Malta. Located in the Mediterranean, between Sicily, Tunisia, and Libya, it's one of Europe's smallest countries, with ancient historic sites that are older than the Egyptian pyramids.

The most popular places to live in Malta include the elegant capital of Valletta (Europe's first planned city), which was the European Capital of Culture in 2018. Founded in 1985, the European Capital of Culture initiative aims to strengthen bonds among European countries and highlight cultural diversity. One city per year receives the honor. About a ten-minute drive from Valletta, you can reach St. Julian's and Sliema, popular seaside towns filled with restaurants, bars, and nightlife.

Malta's healthcare system is top-notch, ranking among the top 20 countries in the world. Under the Malta Retirement Programme, which was designed for people outside the EU, EEA, and Switzerland, you need to have private health insurance. Companies that offer private insurance policies in Malta include Mapfre (www.mapfreinsurance.com), Laferla (www.laferla.com.mt), and Bupa Global (www.bupaglobal.com).

Malta's Retirement Programme offers a straightforward path to residency that you can get within six months. Besides having health insurance, you need to receive at least 75 percent of your income from a pension and own or rent a qualifying property of €220,000-275,000 if owned ($231,000-289,000) or an annual lease value of €8,750-9,600 ($9,200-10,000) if rented. The minimum property value requirement depends on your location within Malta.

WARNING

If your primary retirement income stream is from a pension, you may be able to qualify for Malta's Retirement Programme. But if you're living on income from cash flow properties or other investments, you might not.

Unlike some countries, Malta taxes foreign pensions remitted to the country at 15 percent (35 percent on other local income). The minimum tax is €7,500 annually ($7,872) plus €500 ($525) for each dependent or household staff member.

Malta has one of the largest expat populations in Europe for its size, so you can easily meet people there. But this isn't the best place to live if you're into a lot of nature. Because of the terrain, the island doesn't have any natural lakes, rivers, forests, or mountains. It also doesn't have a lot of agriculture compared to other countries, so you can't easily get fresh, local produce. Malta isn't food-sufficient and relies heavily on imports.

REMEMBER

Although English is one of Malta's official languages, learning Maltese can help you better adapt to the country's society and culture. You can learn Maltese on a language website, such as italki (https://www.italki.com/) or take a beginner course online through the Malta University Language School (https://www.universitylanguageschool.com/courses/maltese-for-beginners/).

Mexico

According to the annual Expat Insider Index, Mexico was voted the number one country for expats in 2023. It's a top choice for its low cost of living, abundant and affordable housing options, and ease of settling in. Foreign residents especially appreciate the friendliness of the local people and are happy with their social lives and ability to make friends.

CHAPTER 14 **Ten Places to Retire Abroad** 247

What I love about Mexico is the variety of climates and locations that you can choose from, from Mexico City — one of the largest cities in the world — to small towns and villages on the coast or in the interior.

Mexico boasts nearly 6,000 miles of beaches and a depth of history, culture, and development that can be lacking in some tropical beach and island destinations. The country has more UNESCO World Heritage Sites than anywhere else in the Americas (35 in 2024).

Do you love fishing and water sports? Check out the Baja Peninsula or Pacific Coast. Looking for a cosmopolitan experience? Consider Guadalajara, Oaxaca, or Mexico City. How about palm trees and white sand beaches? You can find that in the Yucatan Peninsula and Mayan Riviera.

Many retirees in Mexico settle in San Miguel de Allende, a colonial town that has a thriving art, culture, and food scene.

Mexico offers a temporary residency visa that retirees can obtain through proof of financial solvency. This visa is valid for up to four years, after which you can apply for permanent residency. One option to qualify is having investments or bank accounts showing a monthly ending balance of at least 5,000 days of the Mexico City minimum wage over the past 12 months. In 2024, this amount came to about $75,000 for the year. Retirees can qualify with an after-tax pension of 300 days of the minimum wage over the previous six months (about $4,400 in 2024). In both scenarios, applicants must provide certified bank or financial statements.

Apply for Mexican residency from a consulate in your home country at least a few months before departing.

Despite Mexico's popularity with tourists, retirees, and digital nomads, the U.S. State Department issued "Do Not Travel" advisories in relation to 6 of the 32 Mexican states in 2023: Colima, Guerrero, Mchoacan, Sinaloa, Tamaulipas, and Zacatecas. The reasons to avoid travel include the risk of crime and kidnapping.

Panama

Frequently a top contender on "best places to retire" lists, Panama is known for its modern infrastructure, tropical climate, low living costs, and the famous Panama Canal.

Sunny, safe, and warm, Panama attracts many U.S. and Canadian retirees seeking somewhere that has good healthcare, affordable real estate, and a retiree-friendly visa. Panama's dollarized economy (the Panamanian Balboa (PAB) is pegged to the U.S. Dollar), stable government, and tax incentives add to its allure.

With a cost of living ranging from $1,500 to $2,800 per month, retirees can live on a modest income throughout Panama. You need a minimum monthly pension of at least $1,000 to qualify for the country's *pensionado* (retirement) visa. This visa includes various perks, such as discounts on entertainment, medicine, and more.

If you're intrigued about Panama but don't know whether you want to live there, visit as a tourist first. Most foreign citizens can stay on a passport for up to 180 consecutive days.

If you buy property in Panama, you can receive a 20-year tax exemption and free healthcare for the first 30 days as a visitor.

Popular places for retirees include the mountain town of Boquete, the beach town of Coronado, and the capital, Panama City.

Philippines

If you want to live a simple lifestyle on a modest budget, consider the Philippines, where retirees report being able to live on less than $500 per month (although your quality of life is better on a budget of $1,000–$1,500).

Unlike many countries, English is widely spoken in the Philippines, making it possible to assimilate into the culture without learning Filipino (which includes Tagalog, Cebuano, and Ilocano dialects).

You can retire in the Philippines with the special resident retiree's visa (SRRV), a lifetime visa that allows recipients to work, study, invest, or retire there. The SRRV is a multiple-entry visa, which means you can come and go from the Philippines without additional paperwork.

The SRRV program has three categories, each of which requires a $10,000 to $20,000 bank deposit at an accredited bank:

>> **Classic:** The most common category; for those who receive at least $800 in monthly pension income ($1,000 per month for couples).

- **Smile:** If you're between the ages of 35 and 49, this visa allows you to live in the Philippines on an annual, renewable basis with a deposit of $20,000.

- **Human Touch:** Consider this category if you're a retiree over 50 who needs specialized medical care.

- **Courtesy:** This fourth category, for veterans and former diplomats, requires a reduced deposit of $1,500.

With approval from the Philippine Retirement Authority (PRA), you may apply your Classic SRRV bank deposit funds to a local property purchase or long-term lease. If you don't use your deposit toward housing, you can withdraw it if you leave the Philippines. For more information, visit the PRA website at https://pra.gov.ph/.

Portugal

Portugal is a top destination for retirees for its mild climate, beautiful beaches, and affordable cost of living (among the lowest in Western Europe).

Portugal offers something for everyone, from the buzzing capital of Lisbon to the relaxed beaches of the Algarve and the Silver Coast.

It's also safe. According to the Institute for Economics and Peace's 2024 Global Peace Index (which you can download from www.economicsandpeace.org/reports), Portugal is the fifth-most peaceful country in Europe and seventh-most peaceful worldwide. Expats also appreciate Portugal's healthcare system, which ranked 12th in the world in 2019, according to the World Health Organization. You can find English-speaking doctors at many private hospitals and clinics, such as Alegria Medical Centre in Lisbon, Hospital Lusíadas in Porto and Lisbon, and International Health Centres in the Algarve.

On the downside, property prices in Portugal increased by about 9 percent per year between 2017 and 2023, partly due to the real estate investment option of the Portugal golden visa. Although the program was discontinued in 2023, property prices remain high relative to the Portuguese minimum wage.

Portugal offers a D7 visa suitable for retirees who have an income of at least the national monthly wage, which was €870 in 2025 ($913). To qualify, you also need proof of accommodation, health insurance, and a clean criminal record, among other requirements. After residing in Portugal for five years and demonstrating basic language proficiency, you may become eligible for Portuguese citizenship and a passport.

Portugal repealed its Non-Habitual Resident (NHR) tax program on January 1, 2024, eliminating some tax benefits on global income.

Spain

If you enjoy drinking sangria in the sun and indulging in *tapas* (small plates of food) and *siestas*, consider retiring to Spain. Although it sounds cliché, it's true. Respondents of the annual Expat Insider Survey consistently rate Spain as one of the top five places to live in the world — especially for quality of life, leisure activities, and weather.

Coastal areas such as the Costa del Sol and Costa Blanca boast more than 300 days of sunshine annually. Spain is also one of the largest wine producers in the world, known for its famous sparkling cava, which originates in the Catalonia region.

 Climate change has made summers in Spain almost unbearable in some parts of the country. Heatwaves have been five times more likely since 2024, especially in interior and coastal cities such as Alicante, Granada, Malaga, Valencia, and Madrid. At Climate Central (www.climatecentral.org), staff labeled the heat as an "exceptional climate change event." Wildfires are also a risk.

If you're looking for a more temperate climate, consider the northern regions of Asturias, Galicia, and the Pyrenees mountains near France. Despite the potential downsides, expats love Spain, voting it their second-favorite country in the world (after Mexico) in the InterNations 2023 Expat Insider survey (www.internations.org/expat-insider/2023). People appreciate the country's high-quality healthcare, culture, and social scene. In 2024, Spain ranked first globally for recreation and leisure options. Opinions are mixed regarding the ease of settling in Spain, with growing public discourse about the impact of tourism, expats, and immigrants. Many foreigners find language barriers and bureaucracy challenging.

 Spain's non-lucrative visa offers retirees a straightforward path to residency. To qualify, you must show a monthly income of at least 400 percent of the IPREM, or Public Indicator of Multiple Effects Income, plus an additional 100 percent per family member. In 2025, the IPREM was €600 ($629) per month. Therefore, the minimum annual income to qualify for a single person to qualify for the non-lucrative visa would be €28,800 or $30,206.

Thailand

Retirees enjoy living in the Southeast Asian country of Thailand because of the warm climate, friendly people, and low cost of living — less than $1,000 per month. For a few dollars per meal, you can buy street food such as pad Thai or green papaya salad, and for $300 monthly, you can rent a fully furnished studio or one-bedroom apartment.

Thailand also ranks highly in healthcare and medical tourism. Well-developed areas such as the capital of Bangkok, the northern town of Chiang Mai, and the southern island of Phuket offer modern facilities and English-speaking staff.

For a quieter, less touristy experience, explore smaller towns such as Hua Hin, Pai, or Udon Thani.

You have multiple paths to becoming a resident of Thailand as a retiree. From age 50, you can apply for the O-A or O-X non-immigrant retirement visas, valid for one to ten years.

IN THIS CHAPTER

» Finding out what makes a good digital nomad destination

» Discovering the pros and cons of each country

» Exploring places to wander through with your laptop

Chapter 15
10 Places to Live as a Digital Nomad

The first book about being a digital nomad, titled (maybe a little obviously) *Digital Nomad* (Wiley), by Tsugio Makimoto and David Manners, was published in 1997. Since then, living a nomadic lifestyle has exploded — with millions of people trading their cubicles for beachside co-working spaces.

If you can travel full-time while working online from your laptop, you have the world at your fingertips. But where should you go first?

In this chapter, I share with you ten (or so) of the most popular destinations for digital nomads and what makes them so attractive. Whether you're seeking adventure, community, cost-savings, or an Instagram-worthy backdrop for photos, you can find it in this chapter.

TIP

Dive deep into becoming a digital nomad in my book *Digital Nomads For Dummies* (Wiley).

Bali, Indonesia

In the center of Indonesia's island chain, Bali is a tropical, colorful paradise that's become a digital nomad haven.

Before laptop warriors invaded the island, Bali was a popular destination for surfers, tourists, and wellness-seekers from around the globe. Now, nomads love its beautiful scenery, laid-back lifestyle, tropical climate, and affordable prices. You can live comfortably in Bali from $1,000 to $2,500 per month, depending on your accommodations. A studio might cost $400 to $500 per month, whereas a luxury villa goes for $1,000-$5,000 on a long-term basis. In response to the rising demand for housing, nomad-friendly cafes and coworking spaces such as Dojo Bali (www.dojobali.org) and Hubud (www.hubud.org) have cropped up.

The Indonesian government has acknowledged the island's rising global profile, launching a Second Home visa for foreigners in 2023.

Nowhere's perfect, however, and Bali has its problems. Although the island is generally peaceful, overtourism, and rising prices have strained the local people. The images of people riding off into the sunset on motorbikes are somewhat accurate, but they don't show the gridlock traffic nearby.

Nomad hubs in Bali include Canggu, Ubud, Sanur, and the Kuta-Seminyak area.

Bansko, Bulgaria

If you're looking for a peaceful environment where you can ski or hike in the morning, work in the afternoon, and attend game nights with friends, consider the town of Bansko in Bulgaria.

Located at the foot of the Pirin Mountains, Bansko is a tiny village that has a vibrant, tight-knit community of remote working residents.

Digital nomads enjoy living in Bansko because of its welcoming international community, thanks to spaces such as Coworking Bansko (www.coworkingbansko.com) and the annual Bansko Nomad Fest event (www.banskonomadfest.com).

Many nomads decide to settle into this place or return year after year. Spring and summer allow for hiking, horseback riding, taking a dip in the hot springs, and shopping at local markets. Many nomads enjoy road trips to nearby Greece, Turkey, Romania, Serbia, and North Macedonia. Come winter, Bansko transforms into a world-class ski and snowboard resort.

REMEMBER: Bulgaria officially joined the European Schengen area on January 1, 2025. Stay in Bulgaria on a non-EU passport now counts toward your total allowed days in the Schengen zone.

Buenos Aires, Argentina

Argentina's cosmopolitan capital, Buenos Aires, is known as the Paris of South America because of its European, multicultural vibe and attractions. The city is filled with museums, theaters, art galleries, markets, and restaurants, so you can find plenty to do and explore.

Buenos Aires may have a reputation for polo, wine, and churrasco, but it's also become a startup and nomad hub over the years. Nomads flock to the low price tag of living there — from $886 for an expat to $1,550 for a nomad, according to Nomads.com. They also appreciate the plethora of coworking spaces, with at least 87 to choose from at the time of this writing, according to the website Coworker (www.coworker.com).

If you want to explore beyond the city, the vineyards of Mendoza and the mountains of Patagonia are in your backyard. A ferry also goes between Buenos Aires and Montevideo, Uruguay. Popular neighborhoods for nomads include Belgrano, Colegiales, Palermo, and Recoleta.

TIP: Get more information about living in Buenos Aires at NomadsBA (www.nomadsba.com). NomadsBA also holds an annual conference for entrepreneurs and remote workers.

Cape Town, South Africa

For a mix of sun and fun with city and nature, Cape Town has it all. Located where the Atlantic and Indian Oceans meet, Cape Town will have you feeling like you're at the end of the world.

Digital nomads are drawn to Cape Town for the temperate climate, outdoor activities, and close-knit community. You can partake in surfing, hiking, kiteboarding, and lounging on the beach. The vineyards of Stellenbosch and options to go on safaris nearby are also a draw.

During your working hours, you can work from home or at one of Cape Town's eclectic coffee shops or coworking hubs, such as Workshop17 (www.workshop17.co.za) and Ideas Cartel (www.ideascartel.com).

Cape Town's affordable cost of living also makes it attractive. Long-term expats can budget about $1,500 per month, while short-term nomads might spend $2,500 monthly. On the downside, intermittent power and water outages can make nomad life challenging. If traveling there, ask your host or landlord about water tanks and backup power and Internet options.

WARNING

Safety can be an issue in Cape Town and Durban. The U.S. State Department ranks South Africa with a Level 2 Travel Advisory: Exercise Increased Caution because of the potential for crime, kidnapping, and civil unrest.

Chiang Mai, Thailand

Chiang Mai, Thailand might be the unofficial digital nomad capital of the world. The digital nomad community has loved it since at least the early 2010s, and the first-ever Nomad Summit (www.nomadsummit.com) was held here in 2015.

The city's affordable rental properties, delicious street food, and many coworking spaces provide a comfortable lifestyle that offers plenty of meetups and social engagements to attend.

Thailand launched its multiple-entry Destination Thailand Visa (DTV) for digital nomads in 2024. To qualify financially for this visa, you must show a recent bank statement with an ending balance of at least 500,000 Thai Baht (THB); about $15,000 U.S. dollars. The Thai government can process your application quickly, with some nomads reporting getting approved in a matter of days. The visa is valid for five years.

Madeira, Portugal

Located off the coast of Morocco and the Western Sahara, the Madeira Islands are home to the world's first-ever Digital Nomad Village (http://digitalnomads.startupmadeira.eu). Founded in 2021 by NomadX (www.nomadx.com), the village is set in the tiny town of Ponta do Sol, which translates to "Sunset Point," on the western side of Madeira. In the village, you can find coworking spaces, networking events, and a strong sense of community among nomads from around the

256 PART 5 **The Part of Tens**

globe. Madeira's capital, Funchal, is famous among nomads because of its vibrant nightlife, scenic ocean views, and well-developed infrastructure.

Since 2022, Portugal offers a two-year digital nomad visa (D8 visa) with an option to extend. The income requirement for this visa is four times the national minimum salary from a source outside of Portugal. At the time of this writing, the minimum salary was €870 ($900) per month, which works out to a minimum monthly income of about €3,480 ($3,600) for nomads.

TIP

If you visit Madeira, hike or walk along some of the island's 2,500 kilometers of nature trails, known as *levadas*. You can choose from more than 500 trails; find more about them on the Madeira tourism board website (www.visitmadeira.com). For information on digital nomad and expat meetups, visit the Madeira Friends website (www.madeirafriends.org) or Instagram page (@madeirafriends).

TIP

Other popular hotspots in Portugal include the Algarve (for beach lovers), Ericeira (for surfers), Lisbon (for city life), and Porto (for wine and culture).

Medellín, Colombia

Known as the "City of Eternal Spring" and "Valley of Software," Medellín is one of the top cities in the world for remote working. Digital nomads love its pristine weather, nightlife, and ultra-fast Wi-Fi. Medellín was once named the most "Innovative City of the Year" for its creative urban planning by Citi, the Urban Land Institute, and the Wall Street Journal. The Medellín of today boasts parks, libraries, schools, museums, community organization initiatives, and a metro cable car system.

While you can find a lower cost of living in other parts of Colombia, digital nomads live well in Medellín for $1,500 per month, or generously for $3,000 per month.

Colombia's Visa V for digital nomads launched in 2023, allows you to stay in the country for up to two years with an income at least three times the monthly minimum wage over the three months before your arrival. In 2025, that amount added up to an income of $1,030 in U.S. Dollars monthly.

While Medellín has much to offer, safety is a common concern, especially at night. Yet Medellín's crime rate has decreased since the 1990s. Many nomads choose to rent in El Poblado, Envigado, and Laureles neighborhoods.

CHAPTER 15 **10 Places to Live as a Digital Nomad** 257

Pipa, Brazil

Pipa, a small fishing town in northeastern Brazil, has become a paradise for digital nomads, surfers, and kitesurfers. Envision cliffs cascading into blue waters, with dolphins and sunsets aplenty.

The NomadX organization behind the Madeira Digital Nomad Village (see the section "Madeira, Portugal," earlier in this chapter) also hosts the Nomad Village Brazil (www.nomadvillagebrazil.com), a tropical retreat that opened in late 2022. The village offers a café, coworking space, yoga and dance classes, and one- and two-bedroom apartments for rent.

A downside to living in Brazil is security. Brazil scored 131st out of 163 countries on the 2024 Global Peace Index (GPI). The GPI ranks countries on how peaceful they are based on societal safety and security, ongoing conflict, and militarization.

TIP

Citizens from many countries can visit Brazil for up to 90 days with a valid passport. However, U.S. citizens need a visa (or e-visa) to enter Brazil as of April 2025. Brazil also offers a digital nomad visa (VITEM XIV) since 2024, which you can apply for from within Brazil or from a Brazilian consulate abroad. Go to the Brazilian government's website (www.gov.br) and enter "VITEM XIV" in the search text box, then press Enter. From the results that appear, click the link for "Visa - digital nomad (VITEM XIV)."

TIP

Find out about meetups and events in Pipa by following @digitalnomadsbrazil on Instagram.

Riviera Maya, Mexico

South of Cancún along the Yucatan Peninsula, the Mayan Riviera stretches through Playa del Carmen and Tulum — two beloved digital-nomad destinations.

Nomads choose this area for the warm, sunny weather, white sand beaches, and booming social scene. In Playa, you can work from coworking spaces such as Bunker (www.bunkercoworking.com) and Nest (www.nestcoworking.com.mx), as well as from Selina (http://selina.hoteles-playadelcarmen.com), a hotel for digital nomads.

In Tulum, you can enjoy tropical juice from Raw Love Café (www.rawlovetulum.com) while working from your laptop with your feet in the sand. Or, hang out at Holistika Hotel (www.holistikatulum.com) for the day, making use of its restaurant, coworking café, community center, art walk, and wellness services.

On the downside, restaurants, shops, and properties in the tourist zones of Tulum have become so expensive that some visitors compare them to prices in New York, Miami, and Los Angeles. I once overheard a doorman telling a group of girls at a beach bar that the cover charge was $81 per person. The cost of living for a nomad in Tulum in 2025 was estimated at $2,300 per month on Nomads.com, compared to $1,800 for a nomad in Mexico City.

WARNING

Although Playa del Carmen and Tulum are generally safe, the region has experienced a rise in crime and corruption. Be aware of scams targeting tourists at ATMs and foreigners at hospitals and medical centers. There have also been reports of police officers asking people for money and violent incidents at music festivals. Take proper precautions and avoid unnecessary risks.

Zagreb, Croatia

Croatia was among the first nations worldwide to launch a digital nomad visa in 2021. The country boasts a strong digital nomad community led by the Digital Nomad Association Croatia (https://dnacroatia.com/).

Although Croatia's coastal towns of Split, Dubrovnik, and Zadar get a lot of attention, many nomads flock to the capital of Zagreb for its modern infrastructure, speedy Wi-Fi (over 100 Mbps, on average), and vibrant city life. Getting around with Zagreb's public transportation is a breeze. A single bus, tram, or funicular ticket starts at around €1 ($1.03).

At an average living cost of around $2,000 per month for nomads, Croatia isn't the most affordable place to live in the world. But it's a great base to explore nearby European destinations. Budapest, Hungary and Ljubljana, Slovenia are two to five hours away by bus or train.

TIP

When in Croatia, seize the chance to sail the Dalmatian Coast and visit islands such as Brač, Hvar, Korčula, Pag, and Vis.

CHAPTER 15 **10 Places to Live as a Digital Nomad** 259

Traveling Nomadic Tribes

If you fancy going back to humanity's nomadic roots, consider living with a roaming group of digital nomads. By joining a digital nomad retreat or program, you can work and travel with like-minded individuals. It's a great way to meet fellow online professionals and be part of a community from day one. You get to explore new destinations with the guidance of experienced travelers, so you can avoid feeling overwhelmed or isolated.

Hacker Paradise (www.hackerparadise.org) and WiFi Tribe (www.wifitribe.co) are two of the longest-standing organizations in this space. Programs often include coworking spaces that have high-speed Internet, social activities, and housing, allowing you to focus more on work and play, and less on travel logistics.

WARNING

Some participants report that co-living and group travel can present more distractions than living alone. If you have a lot of work to do, make a plan to stay productive.

> **IN THIS CHAPTER**
> » Exploring affordable options in Europe
> » Living in South America without breaking the bank
> » Discovering the possibilities to live frugally in Southeast Asia

Chapter **16**

Ten Places to Live for Under $1,500 per Month

With living costs and inflation rising in many parts of the globe, you might be wondering: *Where can you live without breaking the bank?* But good news — there are places where your money stretches further.

In this chapter, I share with you ten places where you can live well for less than $1,500 per month. These destinations are suitable, whether you want to retire, work, or study abroad. For more ideas of places to retire or work remotely, see Chapters 14 and 15. For information about visas and residency and help choosing a destination, flip to Chapter 4.

Albania

If you want to experience a Mediterranean lifestyle for less than it costs to live in Italy or Greece, consider Albania. This hidden gem of Eastern Europea is known for its ancient historical sites, vineyards, national parks, and pebbled beaches.

Albania is a foreigner-friendly country that welcomes international tourists and residents. Passport holders from at least 80 countries can travel there visa-free, typically for 90 days. In addition, U.S. citizens can stay for up to one year with a passport. Albania offers various residency options if you decide to make the country your home, including the one-year digital nomad visa (Type D) or a temporary residence permit, both valid for one year and renewable. You can apply for a permit online at e-Albania (http://e-albania.al).

Many locals can live in Albania for less than $1,000 per month, as the monthly minimum wage in 2025 was 40,000 Albanian lek, or $416 U.S. dollars. However, expenses for expats can reach $1,300 per month or more, as they tend to spend more on housing, services, and eating out. The longer you stay in a country, the more you can lower your cost of living. It's the reason why digital nomads passing through on a short-term basis tend to spend more than long-term residents or local citizens. Depending on your location, studio and one-bedroom apartments rent from about $160 to $213 (€150–€200) per month.

Popular cities for foreign transplants include Durrës, Tirana, and Sarandë. To further lower your cost of living, consider lesser-known towns such as Bathorë, Kamëz, and Kashar.

The local currency is the Albanian lek (abbreviated LEK).

Colombia

For a warm climate and low cost of living in the Americas, look to Colombia. Due to its location near the equator, you can find a diverse landscape, from the Andean mountains to the Caribbean coast and islands. Bonus — it's a perfect climate for growing coffee! Popular destinations for expats to hang their hats include Medellín, with its year-round spring-like weather; Cartagena, with its historic coastal charm; and the capital city of Bogotá.

To save on your cost of living, consider moving to smaller cities and towns such as Manizales, Pereira, or Santa Marta. But you can save money in larger cities, as well. For instance, rent prices in the city of Cali (population 2.3 million in 2023) are nearly 40 percent less than in Bogotá. In similarly sized Barranquilla, you can live for less than $900 per month.

Although you may find the idea of eating out at restaurants tempting, preparing food at home helps you stay on a budget of less than $1,000 monthly.

Colombia offers multiple paths to short- and long-term residency. Its two-year digital nomad visa lets remote workers stay for up to two years, while retirees on the *rentista* (person of independent means) visa can qualify for permanent residency after five years.

Colombia's currency is the peso (COL or COP).

Cambodia

With a cost of living hovering between $600 and $1,200 per month for a single person, living in Cambodia is about 50 percent lower than in the United States. Although many expats find the affordable prices a draw, they flock to Cambodia for the warm climate, miles of beaches, and ancient temples to explore.

Renting an apartment in the capital of Phnom Penh costs around $300 per month, with rooms available from $150. Shopping at local markets is one way to keep your expenses down, although you can enjoy local street food dishes from $1 to $3 per meal. Southeast Asia is known for its motorbike culture as a way to get around. Scooters, mopeds, and motorcycles can rent for $60-100 monthly. You can also find dirt bike adventure tours on sites such as TripAdvisor.

Cambodia offers multiple visa options for foreigners wanting to stay long-term. Folks 55 years and older can apply for the retirement visa (Type ER), while the multiple-entry ordinary visa (Type E) suits digital nomads. Besides Phnom Penh, interesting places to live in Cambodia include:

- **Kampot:** A sleepy, scenic town in the southwest, bordering the Gulf of Thailand.
- **Siem Reap:** Home of the famous Angkor Wat temple. Due to the tourism industry, a fair number of local people may speak English.
- **Sihanoukville:** A coastal town known as the gateway to the Koh Rong Archipelago.

Cambodia's currency is the riel (KHR).

Georgia

The country of Georgia (not the U.S. state) sits where Eastern Europe meets West Asia — between Russia, Turkey, Armenia, and Azerbaijan. Georgia's flexible entry policy makes it popular for immigrants, nomads, and tourists. Citizens of 95 countries can visit Georgia visa-free for up to 90 days, and U.S. citizens can stay for one year.

Through the Remotely from Georgia program, digital nomads who have at least $2,000 per month in income or $24,000 in savings can also apply to stay for one year. That's more than enough to live in Georgia, where the cost of living ranges from $700 to $1,500 per month, on average.

The capital of Tbilisi, a UNESCO World Heritage Site, is the most popular place to live. There, you can find colorful buildings, medieval streets and fortresses, and fine Georgian wine and food. As the most populated city in the country, you can expect well-developed transport networks in addition to shopping malls, markets, and museums. To save even more on your cost of living, consider smaller cities and towns, such as Batumi, Gori, and Kutaisi.

As is the case in most countries, you become a tax resident in Georgia after living there for 183 days or more. See Chapters 5 and 13 for more information on paying taxes abroad.

The local currency is the Georgian lari (GEL).

Malaysia

If you're considering moving to Southeast Asia, add Malaysia to your wish list. Malaysia is a safe, affordable, multicultural destination with Chinese, Indian, and Malay influences. While Malay (or Bahasa Malaysia) is the official language, English is widely spoken.

It's a popular destination for investors, retirees, and remote workers. For investors and retirees, the Malaysia My Second Home (MM2H) visa allows you to live in Malaysia for 5 to 20 years, depending on the tier you qualify for. The minimum age to apply is 21 for the Silver and Special Economic Zone categories and 25 for the Platinum and Gold levels.

Digital nomads can live and work in Malaysia with the DE Rantau Nomad Pass, which is open to citizens of all nationalities. The initial term is 3 to 12 months, and you can renew it for up to 24 months.

Living in the capital of Kuala Lumpur (KL, as it's often called) costs between $900 and $1,300 per month. There, you can appreciate the city's varied food choices, developed transportation networks, and advanced healthcare facilities.

TIP

Malaysia's currency is the Malaysian riggit (MYR).

Peru

From the Amazon rainforest to the Pacific Coast and Andes Mountains, you can find a variety of climates and settings in Peru. The cost of living varies by location. As an expat in Peru, you can budget $593 per month in Arequipa and $794 in Lima, according to Nomads.com.

Ranked one of the most affordable countries in South America, the income requirements for Peru's visa options mirror the low cost of living. A monthly recurring income of at least $1,000 (among other requirements) qualifies you for the *rentista* (person of independent means) visa, designed for retirees and those who have passive incomes.

Beyond its expansive landscapes and famous historical sites (I'm looking at you, Machu Picchu), Peru is also known for its delicious cuisine consisting of corn, potatoes, quinoa, seafood, and meat dishes. A beer or coffee costs the equivalent of $2, a meal starts at $3 to $4, and a traditional pisco sour drink ranges from $4-8, or 15-30 nuevo soles (PEN).

WARNING

The high elevations in certain parts of Peru can take time to adapt to. Don't be surprised if you encounter oxygen masks in your hotel room, especially in the high-elevation towns of Cusco and Puno, and most particularly La Rinconada — the highest city on Earth.

CHAPTER 16 **Ten Places to Live for Under $1,500 per Month**   265

Paraguay

Paraguay is an off-the-beaten-path destination that's gaining attention for its stable economy, warm climate, and quick path to permanent residency. With a $5,500 bank deposit, you can qualify for the Paraguay permanent residency visa in three to six months.

Paraguay's cost of living is among the lowest in South America, after Bolivia and Peru. Property prices are also low, making it an attractive destination for expats on a budget. You can purchase a one-bedroom home or apartment in Asunción for $50,000 or rent one for $300 to $500 per month.

The average price per square meter for real estate ranges from $600 to $1,800. Comparatively, the median price per square meter of a home in Spain was $1,999 (€1,896) in 2024.

One of my relocation clients who moved to Paraguay from Canada marveled at the cost of a steak dinner, which cost him half the price compared to a steakhouse chain in his home country. An all-you-can-eat buffet at a mid- to high-end restaurant in Asunción can cost $12 (PYG 95,000 in Paraguayan Guarani). He lives comfortably in Asunción on his pension of $1,350 per month. He pays $500 monthly for a fully furnished one-bedroom apartment in a gated community with amenities. His monthly utilities, cell phone plan, and Internet add up to $100, with $700 left in his budget for transportation, eating out, healthcare expenses, gym membership, and pickleball and padel.

TIP

If you decide to move to Paraguay, learn some Spanish before arriving as English is not commonly spoken outside of major cities.

Early Bitcoin miners flocked to Paraguay for its low hydroelectric power costs. As a result, a close-knit cryptocurrency community has developed there, and you can find social meetups in locations across the country.

Romania

Romania was named the third-best country for digital nomads in 2024 by the website VisaGuide.World, ranking high for its low cost of living, safety, fast Internet speeds, and attractive tax policy. It also has a booming tech and start-up scene. Romania is home to Cluj-Napoca, the Silicon Valley of Eastern Europe. Under the Romanian digital nomad visa, remote workers can live there tax-free for their first year.

Rent prices for a one-bedroom property in Romania cost $500 to $600 per month in the capital of Bucharest, but you can find lower prices ($300-$400) in smaller cities, such as Brasov, Sibiu, and Timisoara. Overall, the cost of living in Romania for foreigners starts at $1,200 monthly.

If you enjoy outdoor activities and nature, Romania could be a destination for you. The country boasts stunning natural landscapes, including the Black Sea, Carpathian and Fagaras Mountains, Danube River Delta, and national parks and waterfalls. You can also visit castles, monasteries, fortresses, and historic old towns in Transylvania.

Romania joined the European Schengen Area in 2023, which means you can travel to member countries within the zone without border checks. Tourists from approved countries can remain in Schengen countries cumulatively for up to 90 per 180 days.

The national currency of Romania is the leu (RON).

Turkey

The bridge between Europe and Asia, Turkey offers a blend of cultures and experiences for an affordable price.

According to Nomads.com, living in Turkey as an expat costs $650 per month in the capital of Ankara, $700 per month in the beach town of Antalya, and $1,000 in the cosmopolitan city of Istanbul.

If you're considering settling in Turkey long-term, the Turkish digital nomad visa allows remote workers aged 21 to 55 to stay up to one year. For longer stays, consider a short-term residence permit or golden visa. With a minimum investment of $400,000, you can acquire Turkish citizenship and a passport.

Beyond the attractive food, climate, and history in Turkey, you can find a developed and affordable healthcare system. Medical tourists travel there to save money on hair transplants, fertility treatments, dentistry, and surgeries.

The Turkish lira currency (TRY) began declining in value against the U.S. dollar in 2013 and fell to a record low in 2025.

Learning Turkish can help you communicate in Turkey; not many residents speak English.

Although Turkey has been a secular country since 1924, some areas can be religiously conservative, especially in rural parts of the country. Make sure to respect the local culture wherever you travel.

Vietnam

Vietnam has long been a popular destination for foreigners because of its low cost of living, friendly people, and unique, multi-ethnic culture.

According to the annual Expat Insider Report by InterNations (www.internations.org), Vietnam is the world's cheapest country for expats. In 2024, the country ranked first out of 52 countries for personal finance, with 80 percent of expats happy with their cost of living. Find out more top countries from the report in Chapter 4.

As of 2022, more than 100,000 people from 100 countries lived in Vietnam. Some settle in the larger cities of Da Nang, Hanoi, and Ho Chi Minh City. Others choose medium-sized towns such as Nha Trang. Whether you live in North, Central, or South Vietnam or along the coast, you can live comfortably on a budget of $550 to $1,700 monthly.

In addition to saving money, you can more easily make friends in Vietnam than in other parts of the world. Vietnam ranks among the top ten countries for finding community, according to InterNations. Nowhere is perfect, of course. Expats commonly complain about Vietnam's slow bureaucracy, limited healthcare services, and limited public transport options. Language barriers can also present a challenge.

 Vietnam's currency is the dong (VND).

Chapter 17
Ten Moving-Overseas Mistakes to Avoid

IN THIS CHAPTER

» Knowing what not to do when planning a move abroad

» Understanding common mistakes expats make

» Avoiding inertia before and after your move

You're moving abroad. (What could go wrong?) Moving to a new country is an exciting concept. However, many folks romanticize the idea without fully assessing potential pitfalls and challenges. From financial missteps, to cultural faux pas, to rushing the process, large and small mistakes can become a source of stress and anxiety.

In this chapter, I examine people's most common mistakes when moving abroad and how to avoid them.

Skipping an Exploratory Trip

You wouldn't marry someone before meeting them (hopefully). Choosing a host country is similar. If possible, have a quick fling before committing to a job, residency permit, or long-term lease is the best choice.

You can read travel blogs, watch YouTube videos, and even take a virtual walking tour of a destination. But nothing compares to being there in person. With plenty of online content about various countries, planning your escape without going there first might seem tempting, but don't. If time and finances allow, take an *exploratory trip*, meaning a short stay in a country that you're considering moving to — anywhere from one week to one month, on average. During such a trip, you get a preview of what it's like to live there and sense if it's for you.

Exploratory trips allow you to get a feel for what your life will be like if you move to a country long-term. You can view rental properties in person, meet with residency lawyers, and visit places of interest such as grocery stores, banks, and schools. These trips also provide you with an opportunity to taste a country's culture and meet local people. Mohammed, a digital nomad who's lived in multiple countries, agrees. "My advice for anyone considering moving abroad but feeling unsure is to start small and take gradual steps. You don't need to uproot your entire life overnight. Consider taking a short trip to the country you're interested in and stay for a few weeks or months to get a feel for the environment. This will help you test the waters without a full commitment." For guidance on how to plan an exploratory trip, see Chapter 5.

REMEMBER

Having the time, freedom, and money to take an exploratory trip is ideal, but it's not a deal-breaker. Don't let not being able to take an exploratory trip hold you back from moving.

Investing in Real Estate (at First)

Buying real estate in a foreign country can be a wise investment. But taking your time making a decision pays off.

I once worked as a real estate broker in Costa Rica and often saw people buy a property the first day they arrived. Others invested in properties sight unseen. However, many new homeowners soon discovered that they couldn't handle the humidity, bugs, or the roosters next door. After a few months or years, they often wished they'd chosen a different location. In some cases, however, they couldn't re-sell their properties and so were stuck.

A friend, Dave, who moved from the U.S. to Portugal, purchased a house in a small urbanization in the Algarve. He cautioned about buying a home before you know the area well. "You need to be careful that the agent doesn't try to sell you on a place where they get special kickbacks," he said. "Or recommend an [overpriced] home in a touristy area versus a local neighborhood."

Making an exploratory trip or renting before you own allows you to check out various cities and neighborhoods before making a long-term investment decision. Claudia, who moved from Switzerland to Canada, told me: "[If I could do it again],

I wouldn't buy so quickly. I would rent for a year and then buy a house I could rent out partially to make extra income." See Chapter 6 for more about investing in real estate abroad.

Neglecting Visa and Residency Research

Traveling to a country you don't have permission to be in is like showing up at a party uninvited — you'll likely get turned away at the door. I'll never forget a panicked e-mail I received through my website from a man who was facing deportation from a London airport for saying that he was there to teach yoga. Sounds harmless, right? The only problem was, he didn't have a work permit. He reached out to see if I could help. (Spoiler Alert: I couldn't.) Let that be a lesson to us all — getting the proper permission to stay or work in a country is something to figure out *before* you board a plane.

Before going abroad, research ways to live in a country and contact a visa or residency attorney for help. Chapter 13 has more information on getting permission to live, work, or study in a different country, while Chapter 2 explores the various paths of moving abroad.

Failing to Integrate with the Culture

When you're in an unfamiliar place, it's natural to gravitate toward other expats or people who share the same language and culture. But spending too much time with fellow foreigners can keep you from getting to know a country's people, culture, and language.

For tips on adapting to your new surroundings and feeling less like an outsider, refer to the chapters in Parts 3 and 4 of this book:

>> Chapter 8 helps you navigate your first days and weeks in a new place.

>> Chapter 9 helps with local logistics, such as getting around, receiving mail abroad, and finding a doctor.

>> Chapter 10 helps you navigate culture shock, language differences, and mental health challenges.

>> Chapter 11 offers ways to meet people in your new community.

>> Chapter 12 discusses long-term ways to maximize your time abroad.

Patience is key when settling into a new country, yet many expats want to rush the process. Adds Mohammed, a digital nomad, "Instead of pushing for rapid results, focus on fostering genuine relationships, attending social gatherings, and respecting the slower, more deliberate process. Adapting [to a new place] requires patience, openness, and a willingness to learn from the people around you. Over time, these cultural differences become some of the most rewarding aspects of living abroad."

Isolating Yourself

Starting over in a new country where you don't have friends or know the language can feel awkward. Heck, no one would blame you for wanting to stay inside with a bowl of comfort food and your favorite streaming shows at times.

You know that your move abroad is going to get you out of your comfort zone. However, saying you want to get out of your comfort zone and actually doing it are two different things.

Don't isolate yourself for too long if you start feeling down, lonely, or overwhelmed. Getting outside and connecting with people serves you better than going it alone. Humans are social creatures (yes — even introverts).

Jeffrey, a slow traveler who's spent time in Costa Rica and Ireland, recommends communicating virtually with family often and getting lots of fresh air and exercise. Ujjwal, who moved from Nepal to the United States, suggests turning to friends, hobbies, and passions when loneliness strikes.

TIP

To connect with like-minded travelers and expats online, join my free Facebook Group, Traveling with Kristin (https://www.facebook.com/groups/digital nomadsuccess/).

Refer to Chapters 10, 11, and 12 for more ways to cope with culture shock, find community, and adapt to life in your new country.

Being Too Trusting

The world is full of good people. But not everyone you meet is your *amigo*. You can easily let your guard down when you're swept up in the excitement of moving abroad. So keep your wits about you. If you wouldn't invite a stranger into your house in your home country, don't do it overseas. I've heard stories of people who invited new "friends" over for dinner, only to find their laptops missing the next day. Be cautious, research common scams in your destination, and don't take unnecessary risks. Chapter 13 has tips on staying safe abroad. Contacts in your local expat community can also provide insights and advice.

Expecting a Place to Change for You

Marketing, online content, and social media can lead you to form a rose-colored picture of a place. But the reality is that nowhere is perfect. You might love the climate, food, and people you meet in your destination but have differing views on laws and cultural norms.

Perhaps you can't stand the slow internet and unstable infrastructure in your new country. Maybe you find it frustrating that dinner restaurants open later than you'd like in Argentina and Spain. Or maddening that your contractor never shows up on time (a seemingly universal complaint). Long bank lines, slow bureaucracy, discrimination, unpaved roads, and power outages are just a few differences you might experience compared to your home country.

However, starting with an open mind and knowing that a country won't change for you can help you cope with differences from the beginning.

TIP

The Culture Factor Group's Country Comparison Tool (www.theculturefactor.com/country-comparison-tool) lets you preview cultural differences between your home and destination countries.

Underestimating the Cost of Living

You can find a lot of chatter online about how to live dirt cheap in certain countries. In many cases, the claims are valid. But still, life costs money. Save a buffer and ensure that you have a reliable income stream before moving abroad.

The one thing all my relocation clients have had in common is a revenue stream. But sometimes, people don't save enough and don't have jobs yet, leading them to return home after a few weeks or months. Although experiencing life abroad for a short time is better than not going at all, you can give yourself more stability and peace of mind by going in financially prepared.

Have at least six months of living expenses saved up, or more, depending on your comfort level. Says Ujjwal, who emigrated to the U.S. from Nepal, "The immigration process costs thousands of dollars when considering documents and papers, airplane fares, and adapting to the local cost of living. [Moving abroad] can certainly be taxing in financial terms."

Over the long-term, living abroad can save you money. It's relative depending on where you're from and where you're going. Alex, a digital nomad from Boston, told me, "Moving abroad was a huge benefit. My cost of living dropped nearly 3x after moving to Latin America." For help drafting your living abroad budget, see Chapter 3.

Getting Too Many Opinions

When making a life decision like moving abroad, you naturally want to seek opinions from trusted contacts. However, giving too much weight to what friends, family, or strangers online say can dissuade you from moving or lead you in the wrong direction. Gather the necessary information, but always remain objective. Fact-check the sources of the information you receive and determine whether it's relevant to your situation. Keep your goals and objectives top of mind and don't let others' negativity hold you back.

REMEMBER

You are the master of your life. Moving abroad is a choice you can make on your own. You have the power and agency to do what's right for you — not everyone else.

See Chapter 4 for tips on choosing a destination and Chapter 5 to build your relocation plan.

Going It Alone

Planning an overseas move can be overwhelming, especially if you've never done it. While relocating, you inevitably discover things that you wish you knew before you started. This book can help you avoid many pitfalls, but if you feel uncertain or want help with the many tasks involved in moving abroad, look for professionals who can help you.

Said Joe, who moved from the U.S. to Costa Rica, "Don't try and do legal, residential, tax, immigration, importation, and real estate on your own. Find good professionals, listen to them, and pay them."

John, who lived in Italy, added, "When you travel, don't be an island unto yourself. Get out and talk with people, especially banking, legal, financial, medical, and other professionals. Every country has meetup groups to do this. All you have to do is ask around. Things will go wrong sooner or later. But if you're prepared, no sweat."

Chapter 5 gives tips and resources for hiring a relocation consultant, a moving company, a residency lawyer, and other professionals.

For support from me in planning your international move, contact me at https://travelingwithkristin.com/relocation.

Waiting Too Long to Move

Here's some tough love: Life is short, and nothing's guaranteed. Stop postponing your travel and living abroad dreams. If you've thought about leaving your home country for many years, start now. After moving abroad, many of my clients say they "wish they'd done it sooner" (their words, not mine).

Brenden, who lived in China and France, said, "The one thing I wish I knew before moving abroad is that I should've done it decades sooner." Karen, who moved from Canada to Albania and France for retirement, agreed, saying, "I wish I knew how much happier I would be [living abroad]. I would have done it a lot sooner!"

Erin, who moved from the U.S. to Mexico, told me she's "so grateful" for the changes she's gone through living abroad. "I don't believe I could have achieved so much personal growth or experienced true relaxation and a slower pace of life if I stayed in Texas. My only 'regret' is not doing it sooner."

By buying this book, you already took the first step toward achieving your goal. (Hooray!) If you have doubts, return to your reasons for moving, which you can uncover in Chapter 1. If you need additional support in your planning, find resources for doing so in Chapter 5.

There's no such thing as failure, only learning experiences. You don't have to live abroad "forever." If you change your mind someday, you can return to your home country while benefitting from the experience.

CHAPTER 17 Ten Moving-Overseas Mistakes to Avoid   275

Staying Stuck When Things Aren't Working

If, after moving abroad, you want to change countries or return home, you're not alone. You get to choose what to do next in your life.

Some people enjoy living abroad forever, while others prefer to do so temporarily. Acknowledge your feelings, and don't be afraid to move on or make changes when it's time. One of my YouTube subscribers said, of the country she moved to, "Living here met my expectations for a long time, and I have no regrets. I wouldn't be the person I am today [without having lived abroad], and I love who I became. However, the country has sadly lost its appeal in the last 3-5 years. The cost of living has become insane, and I don't like where the country is heading politically."

On the other hand, Richard, who moved to the UK, is staying there through the ups and downs. "[Living here] still meets my needs 25 years later!" He exclaimed, "I've had plenty of hard, but not entirely negative experiences. What doesn't kill you makes you stronger!"

As the Greek philosopher, Heraclitus wrote, "The only constant in life is change." When you're ready for change, flip to Chapter 13 for tips on crafting your expat exit strategy.

Index

A

accommodations. *See* housing
adventure travel, 214
after-the-move tasks, 87
airlines, 113–116
  apps for, 114
  baggage policies and fees, 114
  booking flights online, 115–116
  carry-on baggage, 118, 122–123
  excess baggage, 122
  navigating airport, 134–135
  roundtrip flights, 116
  staying organized, 114–115
  tips for air travel, 128
  value versus convenience, 113–114
Albania
  experience of moving to, 30
  living in for under $1,500 per month, 261–262
  taxes, 29, 58
  visas for, 60, 220
America. *See* United States
apps
  for airlines, 114
  for babysitters in Europe, 166
  for dating and friendship, 187, 200–201
  for finances, 71–73
  for getting around, 137
  for learning languages, 184–185
  for messaging, 208
  for organizing travel, 114
  for storing passwords, 240
  for translating languages, 186
  for transport systems, 157
  for travel expense tracking, 191
Argentina, digital nomads in, 255
arrival, 133–153
  first day, 133–140
  receiving paychecks or pension, 150–153
  settling in, 140–150
au pairs, 21, 166–167
Australia
  emergency numbers, 170
  exchange rates, 50
  pets, 83
  student visas for, 60
Austria, 62
automobiles. *See* cars

B

babysitters, 166–167
baggage. *See also* packing
  carry-on, 118, 122–123
  damaged, 135
  excess, 122
  policies and fees, 114
  shipping, 114
Bahrain, 170
Bali, Indonesia
  beaches, 189
  cooking classes, 212
  cost of living in, 254
  digital nomads, 254
  health and wellness, 57
  restaurant prices, 8
  safety, 57
banks
  home country accounts, 70–71
  online, 73
  opening local accounts, 73–75, 152–153
  receiving funds, 150–151
Bansko, Bulgaria, 254–255
Barbados, 28
before-the-move tasks, 86–87

Belize
  importing vehicles, 159
  retirement visas for, 60
benefits of moving abroad, 8–12
blackouts, 156
blogging, 221
body language, 202
Bosnia and Herzegovina, 56
Brazil
  conferences, 198
  digital nomads, 258
  real estate investment, 103
  residency status, 24
  safety, 258
  visas for, 258
bucket lists, 214–215
budgeting. *See also* finances
  assessing current income, 34
  calculating budgets, 18–19
  creating budgets, 32–34
  estimating moving fees, 37–39
  figuring out how much need to save, 39–41
  forecasting cost of living, 35–37
  for housing, 95–96
Buenos Aires, Argentina, 255
Bulgaria, 50, 58, 254–255
burial insurance, 112
business investments, 22
business liability insurance, 112
business visas, 59
buying property. *See* real estate

C

Cambodia, 263
Canada
  communication styles, 202
  dual citizenship, 66
  experiences of moving to, 11, 93
  LGBTQ+ couples, 55–56
  pets, 83
  religion, 56
  visas for, 220
  working in, 60

Cape Town, South Africa, 255–256
career networking, 206–207
  chambers of commerce, 206–207
  conferences and events, 206
  coworking spaces, 207
  online, 207
carry-on baggage, 118, 122–123
cars, 158–161
  bringing, 158–160
  buying, 160–161
  deciding what to do with, 80–81
  driving, 161–163
  insurance, 112
  payments, 8
cash. *See* finances
Cayman Islands, 58
cellphones, activating, 135–136
chambers of commerce, 206–207
Chiang Mai, Thailand, 256
children, moving with, 81–83
  adapting to life in different country, 82–83
  finding new schools, 81–82
  staying healthy and safe, 82
China
  communication styles, 202
  emergency numbers, 170
  experience of moving to, 30
cities, versus countryside, 53–54
citizenship
  applying for, 231
  from birth, 24
  by descent, 22–23, 62
  digital nomad visas and, 29
  dual, 66, 232
  by investing, 22
  renouncing, 56, 232–233
cleaning services, 147
climate, 49–50
clothes, packing, 119–121
college, attending abroad, 24–26
Colombia
  cost of living in, 9, 257, 262
  digital nomads, 257

living in for under $1,500 per month, 262–263
retirement in, 23, 60
safety in, 257
visas for, 262
community, 54–55, 193–210
career networking, 206–207
dating, 199–204
expanding, 10
making friends, 197–199
making the most of your life abroad, 210
meeting locals, 193–197
staying in touch with people at home, 207–209
volunteering, 204–206
cooking classes, 24–25
cooks, 147
corporate jobs, 20
cost of living
confirming, 50
determining current, 32
forecasting, 35–37
lowering, 8–9
Costa Rica, 52
experiences of moving to, 30, 66, 140, 188
friendliness of people in, 192
health and wellness, 169
popular places in, 244
real estate investment, 103
residency status in, 24
retirement in, 243–244
safety in, 57
Social Security benefits and, 35
visas for, 220, 244
countryside, versus cities, 53–54
couriers, 172–173
coworking spaces, 207
crafting, 213
crates, for pets, 84
credit cards, 136–137
credit card insurance, 113
rewards programs, 129–130
travel credit cards, 75–76, 129–130
Croatia, digital nomads in, 259

cruise line jobs, 21
cryptocurrency, 100, 130
cultural adaptation classes, 83
cultural biases, 201–202
culture shock, 12, 177–192
coping with change, 183–184
curve of cultural adjustment, 178–183
language, 184–187
loneliness, 187–188
managing expectations, 188–190
reverse, 236–237
solving problems, 191
understanding, 178
curve of cultural adjustment
finding your rhythm, 182
frustrations and adaptations, 182
initial shocks and honeymoon phase, 182
overview, 178–181
pre-departure, 181
transformation and integration, 183
customs, 135
Cyprus, 28, 56
Czech Republic, 29

D

dancing, 213
dating, 199–204
apps for, 187
communication styles, 201–202
dating apps, 200–201
gender roles, 202
matchmakers, 203
money and finances, 203
social norms, 202
strengthening relationships, 203–204
daycare, 166–167
Denmark, 57, 202
dentists, 169
descent, citizenship by, 22–23
destination, 43–66
identifying what you want in, 44–45
top living-abroad destinations, 47–48

Index 279

digital nomads, 51, 253–260
    Bali, Indonesia, 254
    Bansko, Bulgaria, 254–255
    Buenos Aires, Argentina, 255
    Cape Town, South Africa, 255–256
    Chiang Mai, Thailand, 256
    Madeira, Portugal, 256–257
    Medellín, Colombia, 257
    Pipa, Brazil, 258
    Riviera Maya, Mexico, 258–259
    traveling nomadic tribes, 260
    visas for, 20–21, 28–29, 59
    Zagreb, Croatia, 259
doctors
    finding, 168
    preparing for appointments, 168–169
    telehealth, 169
documents
    packing, 119
    storing, 71, 77–78
domestic help, hiring, 147
Dominica, 22
Dominican Republic, 103
downsizing, 126–127
drawbacks of moving abroad, 12–13
driving, 161–163
    driver's licenses, 162–163
    requirements, 161
dual citizenship, 66, 232
Dubai, UAE, 140
during-the-move tasks, 87
Dutch, countries where spoken, 53

E

Ecuador, 23, 60, 244–245
education and study, 24–25, 163–167
    arts and crafts, 213
    cultural adaptation, 83
    education visas, 59–60
    educational travel, 25
    enrollment, 164–165
    finding schools, 81–82
    homeschooling, 82, 165–166
    international schools, 164
    international students, 25–26
    languages, 185
    meeting locals through, 194
    music, 213
    private schools, 163
    public schools, 164
    renewing visas and residency permits while studying, 231
Egypt, 57
El Salvador, 100
electricity. See utilities
electronics insurance, 113
embassies, registering with, 148
emergencies
    assigning emergency contacts, 124–125
    contacting emergency services, 141–142, 170
    emergency evacuation and repatriation insurance, 107–108
    emergency travel medical insurance, 113
    registering with embassy, 148
emergency travel medical insurance, 109
employment. See work
end-of-life planning, 239–240
English, countries where spoken, 52
entrepreneurs
    digital nomad visas, 20–21, 28–29
    entrepreneur visas, 60
equality, 56–57
Estonia, 28–29, 58
European Union (EU)
    citizenship by descent, 62
    health insurance, 168
    pets, 83
exchange programs, 24–26
exchange rates, 50
executive education, 25–26
exit strategies, 234–235
expats, defined, 16
expectation management, 188–190
expedited entry, 134
exploratory trips, 63–64, 269–270

F

facial expressions, 202
failure, fear of, 15–16
family and friends
  effects of moving on, 183
  living far from, 13
  reuniting with, 24
  saying goodbyes, 127
  starting new, 24
  staying in touch with, 207–209
finances. *See also* investments; taxes; work
  accessing cash, 136–137
  assessing current income, 34
  bank accounts, 70–71, 73–75, 152–153
  buying property, 100
  calculating budgets, 18–19
  creating budgets, 32–34
  dating and, 202
  determining expenses, 32–34
  determining needed savings, 18, 39–41
  digital nomad visas and, 28–29
  estimating moving fees, 37–39
  exchange rates, 50
  finance apps, 71–73
  financial prep checklist, 70–71
  forecasting cost of living, 35–37
  housing, 95–96
  opening bank accounts, 73–75
  pensions, 18, 34–35, 70, 150–153
  receiving paychecks or pension, 150–153
  retirement and, 28–29
  tracking expenses, 191
  travel credit cards, 75–76, 129–130
  wiring money, 152–153
Finland, 57
flexpats, 16
flights, 113–116
  airline apps, 114
  baggage policies and fees, 114
  booking online, 115–116
  carry-on baggage, 118, 122–123
  excess baggage, 122
  navigating airport, 134–135
  roundtrip, 116
  staying organized, 114–115
  tips for, 128
  value versus convenience, 113–114
food, sourcing, 148–149
foreigner tax, 106
France
  cost of living in, 246
  experience of moving to, 30
  healthcare, 245–246
  retirement in, 245–246
  studying in, 26
  visas for, 245
freelancing, 20–21, 28–29
French, countries where spoken, 52
friends. *See also* community; family and friends
  frequent moves and, 65
  making, 197–199

G

gas service, 145. *See also* utilities
gender roles, 202
generators, 156
geography, 49–50
Georgia
  cost of living in, 264
  living in for under $1,500 per month, 264
  taxes, 58
  visas for, 60, 220
Germany
  childcare, 166
  renting in, 97
  work visas for, 29
gestures, 202
Ghana, 172
goals, setting, 14–16
government work, 26–27
Great Britain, 205. *See also* United Kingdom
Greece
  golden visas for, 62
  health and wellness, 52
  investment opportunities, 22

H

healthcare, 11, 167–171. *See also* culture shock
　blue zone countries, 52
　children, 82
　costs of, 9
　dentists, 169
　doctors, 168–169
　drinking water, 149
　emergency care, 169–170
　finding better, 51–52
　insurance, 108–111, 168, 170–171
　mental health, 183, 190
　researching healthcare standards, 58
　vaccinations, 82–83
high school, attending abroad, 24–26
high-context cultures, 202
hobbies, 213–214
home goods, finding, 146–147
homeschooling, 82, 165–166
homesickness, 83, 217–218
Hong Kong, 170
hotel jobs, 21
housing. *See* real estate; renting, 89–106
　budget and, 95–96
　choosing where to buy, 98–99
　clarifying property needs, 89–90
　costs of, 9
　damage to, 139
　investing in, 22, 98, 103–104, 270–271
　leasehold property, 100–101
　maintaining multiple properties, 65
　narrowing down location, 92
　negotiations, 101–104
　paying cash or financing, 100
　peculiarities, 97
　professional help, 99
　renters' insurance, 113
　renting short-term versus long-term, 65, 91–92
　scams, 96
　searching for property strategically, 92–95
　seasonality of, 96–97
　solving problems related to renting, 104–106
Hungary, 29, 58

I

Iceland, 55–56, 58, 189
immigrants, defined, 16
income. *See* finances
independent contractors, 20–21, 28–29
indirect communication, 202
Indonesia
　beaches, 189
　cooking classes, 212
　cost of living in, 254
　digital nomads, 254
　health and wellness, 57
　property, 98
　restaurant prices, 8
　retirement visas for, 60
　safety, 57
insurance, 107–113
　burial insurance, 112
　business liability insurance, 112
　car insurance, 112
　claims, 170–171
　credit card insurance, 113
　emergency evacuation and repatriation insurance, 110–111
　emergency travel medical insurance, 107–109
　local or international health insurance, 108–110
　personal liability insurance, 113
　property or renters' insurance, 113
　seniors, 111–112
　tech and electronics insurance, 113
international schools, 164
international students, 25–26
Internet. *See also* apps
　blogging, 221
　booking flights online, 115–116
　career networking, 207
　fast Wi-Fi, 157
　Internet services, 139, 157
　making friends through, 199
　podcasting, 221
　setting up, 144–146
　social media, 222
　YouTube channels, 222

investments
  business, 22
  citizenship or residency through, 22, 61–62
  opportunities for, 229–230
  real estate, 22, 98, 103–104, 270–271
Iran, 57
Ireland
  citizenship by descent, 62
  driver's license in, 162
  LGBTQ+ couples, 55–56
Italy
  citizenship by descent, 62
  climate of, 50
  experiences of moving to, 12, 93, 140
  gender roles, 202
  health and wellness, 52
  retirement in, 23
  Social Security benefits and, 35
  studying in, 25
  taxes, 58
  visas for, 29, 60

J

Japan
  communication styles, 202
  emergency numbers, 170
  health and wellness, 52
  pets, 83
  renting in, 97
jaywalking, 157
jobs. *See* work
journaling, 15, 210, 220

L

languages, 184–187
  immersion programs, 24–25
  learning, 52–53
  practicing with locals, 185, 195
  tips for learning, 186–187
leasehold properties, 98, 100–101
legal counsel, 99
lifestyle, 211–240
  avoiding legal trouble, 233–234
  career networking, 206–207
  culture shock, 177–192
  dating, 199–204
  defining, 18–19
  end-of-life planning, 239–240
  going home, 234–239
  ideal, visualizing, 45–47
  investment opportunities, 229–230
  living best lifestyle, 53
  making friends, 197–199
  making the most of your life abroad, 210
  meeting locals, 193–197
  planning things to do, 211–215
  renewing visas or residency permits, 230–231
  renouncing citizenship, 232–233
  rest and relaxation, 216–217
  sharing your experience, 220–222
  staying in touch with people at home, 207–209
  taxes, 223–228
  tough times, 217–220
  volunteering, 204–206
local health insurance, 113
local traditions, 212–213
loneliness, overcoming, 187–188
low-context cultures, 202
luggage. *See* baggage; packing

M

Madeira, Portugal, 256–257
maids, 147
mail, 171–173
  couriers, 172–173
  local address, 172
  virtual mailboxes, 173
Malaysia, 29, 264–265
Malta
  healthcare, 247
  investments, 22
  retirement in, 60, 246–247
map apps, 137

marriage
　effects of moving on, 183
　residency status from, 24
matchmakers, 203
Medellín, Colombia, 257
meeting people, 193–210
　career networking, 206–207
　dating, 199–204
　locals, 193–197
　making friends, 197–199
　neighbors, 148
mental health support, 183, 190
Mexico
　digital nomads, 258–259
　experiences of moving to, 30, 40, 140, 184
　pets, 83
　renting in, 97
　residency status in, 24
　retirement in, 247–248
　visas for, 60, 220
microchips, for pets, 83
mission statements, 14
mission work, 27
mistakes to avoid, 269–276
　being too trusting, 272–273
　expecting a place to change for you, 273
　failing to integrate, 271–272
　getting too many opinions, 274
　going it alone, 274–275
　isolating yourself, 272
　neglecting visa and residency research, 271
　real estate investment, 270–271
　skipping exploratory trips, 269–270
　staying stuck when things aren't working, 276
　underestimating the cost of living, 273–274
　waiting too long to move, 275
money. *See* finances; investments; work
Montenegro, 58
moving abroad, 7–16
　benefits of, 8–12
　drawbacks of, 12–13
　experiences of, 11–12, 30, 40–41, 66, 93, 140, 184, 188, 196, 198, 270
　most difficult things about, 192

motivations for, 8–12
　setting goal of, 14–16
　temporarily versus permanently, 7–8
moving companies, 125–126
moving costs, 33–34
multiple destinations, 64–66
music lessons, 213
Myanmar, 57

N

nannies, 166–167
natural disasters, 148
neighborhoods, choosing, 54, 92
Netherlands, 55–56, 202
New Zealand, 83
Nicaragua, 60, 170
non-lucrative visas, 60–61
Norway, 57

O

offices, renting, 207
Okinawa, Japan, 52
one-way tickets, 116
online banks, 73
onward travel, proof of, 116, 134

P

packing, 116–123
　carry-on baggage, 118, 122–123
　excess baggage, 122
　lists for, 117–122
Panama
　climate of, 50
　cost of living in, 248
　investments, 23, 103
　retirement in, 23, 60, 248–249
　Social Security benefits and, 35
　taxes, 58
paperwork, 123–125
　emergency contacts, 124–125
　organizing, 77–79

Paraguay, 266
passive income, 18, 23, 34–35
passports
  through citizenship by descent, 22–23
  through golden visas, 61–62
passwords, storing, 240
paychecks, 150–153. *See also* finances
  local bank accounts, 152–153
  wiring money, 152–153
pensions, 18, 34–35. *See also* retirement
  collecting abroad, 35, 150–153
  interruption in payments from, 70
  local bank accounts, 152–153
  wiring money, 152–153
permanent residency, 29, 231
permanently moving, 7–8
perpetual tourism, 64–65
personal liability insurance, 113
Peru, 23, 60, 265
pets, moving with, 83–85
Philippines
  cost of living in, 50
  retirement in, 23, 60, 249–250
  Social Security benefits and, 35
  visas for, 249–250
Pipa, Brazil, 258
podcasting, 221
Poland, 62, 202
political systems, 55–56
political unrest, 148
Portugal
  conferences in, 198, 206
  digital nomads, 256–257
  experiences of moving to, 12, 66, 93, 140, 198, 270
  healthcare, 250
  investments, 22, 103
  making friends in, 198
  purchasing property in, 100
  residency in, 61
  retirement in, 60, 250–251
  safety in, 250
  Social Security benefits and, 35
  taxes, 29
  visas for, 29, 250
Portuguese, countries where spoken, 52
possessions, deciding what to do with, 79–81
power outages, 156–157
private schools, 163
property. *See* real estate
public schools, 164
public speaking, 221
public transportation. *See also* airlines; cars
  apps for, 143, 157
  transport cards, 143
  unique options, 144

Q
quality of life, 9

R
racism, 56–57
real estate, 89–106. *See also* renting
  budget and, 95–96
  choosing where to buy, 98–99
  clarifying property needs, 89–90
  costs of, 9
  damage to, 139
  investing in, 22, 98, 103–104, 270–271
  leasehold property, 100–101
  maintaining multiple properties, 65
  narrowing down location, 92
  negotiations, 101–104
  paying cash or financing, 100
  professional help, 99
  scams, 96
  searching for property strategically, 92–95
  seasonality of, 96–97
real estate attorneys, 99
realtors, 99
relationships. *See* community; family and friends; marriage
religion, 56
religious work, 27
relocation assistance, from employers, 20

relocation experts and support, 85–88
    after-the-move tasks, 87
    evaluating need for, 85–86
    before-the-move tasks, 86–87
    during-the-move tasks, 87
    selecting experts, 87–88
remote work and income, 18, 28–29
    online hubs for, 207
    time zones and, 54
renting. *See also* real estate
    offices, 207
    peculiarities, 97
    renters' insurance, 113
    short-term versus long-term, 65, 91–92
    solving problems related to, 104–106
research projects, 24
residency
    digital nomad visas and, 29
    family categories for residency permits, 81
    by investing, 22
    permanent, 29, 231
    perpetual tourism and, 65
    residence permits, 61
    shipping credits and, 39
rest and relaxation
    in different cultures, 217
    making time for, 216–217
restaurant prices, 8
retirement, 23, 51, 229, 243–252
    Costa Rica, 243–244
    Ecuador, 244–245
    France, 245–246
    Malta, 246–247
    Mexico, 247–248
    Panama, 248–249
    Philippines, 249–250
    Portugal, 250–251
    retirement visas, 60–61
    Spain, 251
    Thailand, 252
returning home, 235–239
    changing countries, 236
    common reasons for, 238

exit strategy, 234–235
reverse culture shock, 237–239
saying goodbyes, 236–237
reuniting with family, 24
reverse culture shock, 236–237
rewards programs, 129–130
Riviera Maya, Mexico, 258–259
Romania, 29, 62, 266–267
roundtrip flights, 116
routines, developing, 149–150
Russia, 202

S

sabbaticals, 24
safety issues, 13, 57–58. *See also* emergencies
    keeping children safe, 82
    safety alerts, 148
Sardinia, 52
Saudi Arabia, 55
saunas, 216
saying goodbyes, 127, 236–237
scams, 104
school. *See* education and study
second passports, 61–62
seniors, insurance for, 111–112.
        See also retirement
Serbia, 58
Seychelles, 29
sharing your experience, 220–222
    blogging, 221
    podcasting, 221
    public speaking, 221
    social media, 222
    YouTube channels, 222
shipping, 37–39, 125–127
    baggage, 114
    coordinating international shipments, 126
    downsizing, 126–127
    international movers, 125–126
Singapore
    religion, 56
    student visas for, 60
    studying in, 26

skills, acquiring new, 10–11
Slovenia, 202
slow travel, 64–65
small business visas, 29
small towns, 194
social media
   as impediment to learning language, 187
   sharing your experience via, 222
Social Security benefits, 35
South Africa, digital nomads in, 255–256
South Korea, 60, 83
Spain
   driver's licenses, 162
   experiences of moving to, 30, 41
   investments, 22, 103–104
   LGBTQ+ couples, 55–56
   residency in, 61
   retirement in, 23, 251
   Social Security benefits and, 35
   taxes, 29, 58
   visas for, 251
Spanish, countries where spoken, 52
startup visas, 29, 60
storage, 80–81
student visas, 59–60
studying abroad, 24–26. *See also* education and study
suitcases. *See* luggage; packing
sustainable travel, 215
Sweden, 57
Switzerland
   emergency numbers, 170
   experiences of moving to, 30, 40, 196
   making friends in, 196

T

Taiwan, 29
taxes, 58–59, 76–77, 223–228
   common pitfalls, 228
   digital nomads and remote workers, 29
   documents checklist, 226
   domicile, 9, 224
   global tax systems, 224–226
   optimizing your tax strategy, 227–228
   reducing, 9
   U.S. taxes, 226–227
tech and electronics insurance, 113
technology. *See* Internet
telehealth, 169
temporarily moving abroad, 7–8
Thailand
   cost of living in, 50, 252
   digital nomads, 256
   emergency numbers, 170
   real estate, 98, 103–104
   retirement in, 252
   Social Security benefits and, 35
   visas for, 256
time zones, 54
timeline to move, setting, 41–42
toiletries, packing, 121
tour guides, 142
tourist visas, 60
travel burnout, 218–219
travel organization apps, 114
traveling nomadic tribes, 260
trusted traveler programs, 115
tuition fees, for international students, 26
Turkey
   additional passport from, 62
   cost of living in, 267
   experience of moving to, 41
   investments, 22
   living in for under $1,500 per month, 267–268
   religion, 56
   visas for, 267
Turks and Caicos Islands, 58

U

uncertainty, 15
United Arab Emirates (UAE)
   purchasing property in, 100
   real estate investment, 103
   residency in, 61
   taxes, 58

United Kingdom
  citizenship by descent, 62
  emergency numbers, 170
  experiences of moving to, 30, 93, 140
  property in, 98
United States
  communication styles, 202
  experiences of moving to, 12, 40
  gender roles, 202
  investments, 22
  purchasing property in, 100
  safety in, 57
  taxes, 226–227
university, attending abroad, 24–26
Uruguay, 60
utilities
  power and water outages, 156–157
  setting up, 144–146

V

vaccinations, 82–83
Vanuatu, 22
Vietnam, 268
virtual mailboxes, 173
visas, 59–61
  business visas, 59
  digital nomad visas, 20–21, 28–29, 59
  education or student visas, 59–60
  entrepreneur or startup visas, 29, 60
  family categories for, 81
  freelancer visas, 29
  golden visas, 61–62
  renewing, 230–231
  retirement or non-lucrative visas, 23, 60
  short stays, 230–231
  small business visas, 29
  tourist visas, 60
visualizing ideal lifestyle, 45–47

volunteering, 26–27
  meeting locals through, 197
  opportunities for, 204–206
voting, 229

W

walking tours, 142
water, 145
  outages, 156–157
  sourcing, 148–149
Wi-Fi, 157. *See also* Internet
wills, 70, 239–240
wiring money, 152–153
work, 18
  career networking, 206–207
  entrepreneurs, 20–21, 28–29, 60
  finding jobs overseas, 20–22
  government work, 26–27
  international placements, 20
  meeting locals through, 194
  moving through current job, 20
  new job opportunities, 11–12
  relocation assistance from employers, 20
  remote work and income, 18, 28–29, 54, 207
  renewing visas and residency permits while working, 231
  work permits, 61
working holidays, 27
worldview, broadening, 10
writer's retreats, 24

Y

YouTube channels, 222

Z

Zagreb, Croatia, 259

About the Author

Kristin Wilson, also known as *Traveling with Kristin* on YouTube, is a media entrepreneur, content creator, and thought leader specializing in living abroad and designing a global lifestyle. Through her books, podcast, YouTube channel, and consulting services, her mission is to help others craft their dream lives overseas.

She's the author of *Digital Nomads For Dummies* and host of the *Traveling with Kristin Podcast*, ranked among the top 1 percent of podcasts worldwide, with more than 600,000 downloads in 200 countries and territories. She has also served as the Go Overseas Mentor for *International Living*.

Kristin's work has generated more than 100 million views online. She's been a Top Writer on *Medium* and *Quora* and has been featured in mainstream publications such as *Atlas Obscura*, *BBC News*, *Bloomberg Businessweek*, *Business Insider*, *HuffPost*, HGTV's *House Hunters International*, *The Independent*, *The New York Times*, *The Today Show*, *USA Today*, *The Wall Street Journal*, and more.

For more than two decades, Kristin has lived abroad and traveled the world as an expat or digital nomad, having visited 63 countries along the way. She spends most of her time between Miami and Europe while assisting her relocation clients, producing electronic music, and working toward Delta Million Miler status. Find out more and apply for help with your international move at https://www.travelingwithkristin.com/relocation.

Dedication

For my niece and nephew, Koura and Austin — I can't wait to see where you travel someday.

For our sweet family dog, Chloe, my writing buddy whom I miss dearly.

To my loving family; and Great Aunt Livia and Grandma, who have always believed in me and encouraged my creative talents.

For everyone in the *Traveling with Kristin* community — you inspire me to keep creating every day.

Acknowledgements

Thank you to my agents, Grace and Val; my mentors, Liz D. and Liz G.; and the following fellow creators: Chase from the podcast *About Abroad*; blogger Ilana, who writes *Life Well Cruised*; Katrina McGhee, author of *Taking A Career Break For Dummies* (Wiley); Matt, who hosts the digital nomad podcast *The Maverick Show*; Megan from the YouTube channel *Portable Professional*; Mitch from the website *Project Untethered*; Nik, who (with Allie) make up *Away Together*; and Nora, who goes by *The Professional Hobo* (we'll meet in person someday!).

Publisher's Acknowledgments

Acquisitions Editor: Steve Hayes
Managing Editor: Ajith Kumar
Project Manager: Tracy Brown Hamilton
Copy Editor: Digital Quills, LLC
Technical Editor: Kalie from ExpatsEverywhere

Production Editor: Magesh Elangovan
Cover Image: © urbazon/Getty Images